Scale of Miles

0   50   100

Numbers in blue refer to chap[...] indicated

D1587622

E

Tha[...]

Samothrace

15

Lemnos

Imros
(Turkish)

T U R K E Y

A   E   G   E   A   N

S   E   A

Lesbos

16

Skiathos

Skopelos

14   Skyros

Psara

U
B
O
E
A

Chios

17   Samos

ATHENS

amis

Aegina

Zea   Andros

Tinos

Ikaria

6
Poros

Syros

8

Kythnos

Mykonos

Delos   9

Patmos

Hydra
ai 7

18

THE COMPANION GUIDE TO
The Greek Islands

THE COMPANION GUIDES

*It is the aim of these Guides to provide a
Companion, in the person of the author,
who knows intimately the places and
people of whom he writes, and is able to
communicate this knowledge and affection
to his readers. It is hoped that the text
and pictures will aid them in their prep-
arations and their travels, and will help
them to remember on their return.*

PARIS
THE SOUTH OF FRANCE
LONDON
VENICE
ROME
FLORENCE
JUGOSLAVIA
UMBRIA
THE WEST HIGHLANDS OF SCOTLAND
EAST ANGLIA
SOUTHERN ITALY

In preparation
TUSCANY
GREECE
TURKEY
SOUTH-WESTERN FRANCE
SOUTHERN SPAIN

THE COMPANION GUIDE TO
The Greek Islands

ERNLE BRADFORD

Collins

ST JAMES'S PLACE, LONDON

First Published *1963*
Reprinted *1964*
Second Edition *1970*

SBN 00 211127 6

Maps by James F. Trotter
© *Ernle Bradford,* 1963
Printed in Great Britain
Collins Clear-Type Press
London and Glasgow

Contents

	A note on the spelling of place names	*page* 13
1	The Sea and the Islands	15
2	Corfu, Paxos and Antipaxos	25
3	Levkas and Ithaca	44
4	Cephalonia and Zante	53
5	Salamis, Aegina and Euboea	64
6	Poros	77
7	Hydra and Spetsai	87
8	Andros, Tinos, Zea, Kythnos and Syra	98
9	Mykonos and Delos	114
10	Seriphos, Siphnos and Milos	129
11	Paros and Naxos	138
12	Ios, Amorgos and Sikinos	148
13	Santorin	160
14	Skiathos, Skopelos and Skyros	173
15	Lemnos, Thasos and Samothrace	186
16	Lesbos	197
17	Chios and Samos	206
18	Patmos, Leros, Calymnos and Cos	219
19	Rhodes	235
20	Symi and Carpathos	250
21	Crete. The End and the Beginning	258
	List of Hotels	270
	Index	279

Illustrations

The jetty at Poros [*Georges Viollon*] *facing page* 40
Pondikinisi Bay [*J. Allan Cash*] 41
The Arthilleion on Corfu [*Georges Viollon*] 56
Corfu Museum [*J. Allan Cash*] 56
Kalymnos [*Georges Viollon*] 57
Syra [*Georges Viollon*] 104
Views of Mykonos [*National Tourist Organization of
    Greece, John Baker*] 105
A Windmill on Mykonos [*John Baker*] 120
The Lions of Delos [*E. O. Hoppé*] 121
Mosaic floor on Delos [*John Baker*] 121
Volcanic island of Santorin [*John Baker*] 160
Mule-track on Santorin [*Peter Roderick and Bennett
    Associates Ltd.*] 160
Thera [*Georges Viollon*] 161
Olive grove on Lesbos [*Georges Viollon*] 192
Sigri [*E. O. Hoppé*] 193
A monk at Poros [*J. Allan Cash*] 224
Mykonos [*Georges Viollon*] 224
Samian shepherd [*E. O. Hoppé*] 224
Two-man band in Crete [*Georges Viollon*] 224
Rhodes [*Peter Roderick and Bennett Associates Ltd.*] 225
The Temple of Lindos [*Peter Roderick and Bennett
    Associates Ltd.*] 256
The Throne of Minos, Crete [*Georges Viollon*] 257
Amphoræ at Minos [*Georges Viollon*] 257

Caliban: Be not afeard: the isle is full of noises,
Sounds, and sweet airs, that give delight and hurt not.
Sometimes a thousand twangling instruments
Will hum about mine ears; and sometime voices,
That, if I then had wak'd after long sleep,
Will make me sleep again: and then, in dreaming,
The clouds methought would open, and show riches
Ready to drop upon me; that when I wak'd
I cried to dream again.

Stephano: This will prove a brave kingdom to me. . . .

THE TEMPEST

For Marie Blanche

A Note on the Spelling of Place Names

I can lay claim to little or no logic in my orthography. The spelling of Greek place names always has its problems. In the case of the islands, the subject is even further complicated by the fact that some of them have three or even more variants.

To take a simple and well-known instance, what is one to make of Corfu? If one adheres strictly to ancient or modern Greek, it might be written Kerkura or Korkura. If one takes the Latin form of the name, it would be Corcyra. Corfu itself is a corruption of the Byzantine Greek "Koruphai," but I have called the island Corfu because it seemed to me that this was familiar to most English-speaking readers.

Many of the islands have Venetian names—Thermia, for instance, which is also called Kythnos, but which a purist would probably write as Kithnos. Thermia, or Kythnos, lies a few miles north of Seriphos or Serifos, or Serpho or even Serfo. A little south again, one comes to Polykandro or Pholegandros or Folegandros. Even the Homeric Ithaca could be Thiaki, Ithaki or Ithakee—depending entirely upon which authority you care to follow.

Where I feel that an island has more Venetian than classical associations, I have tended to use the Italianate name. Zante is, I feel, Zante; and not Zacynthus, or Zakintos. In many cases, I have merely been guided by what looks easiest or most familiar to my eye. I am prepared to accept the dry comment: "De gustibus non est disputandum."

I could have been logical—or pedantic—and followed the English spelling nearest to the Modern Greek place names. But this would inevitably have involved me in the use of accents

A Note on the Spelling of Place Names

—a subject which I have found distasteful ever since schooldays. In any case, I prefer Hydra to Ídhra, and Crete to Kríti. It is, I know, an unsatisfactory defence, but I take refuge in the Philistine comment: "I know what I like."

E.B. 1963

CHAPTER I

The Sea and the Islands

It is the sea which determines the islands, and the thing which distinguishes one island, or group of islands from another, is the quality of the sea. The scientifically minded may find it difficult, if not impossible, to distinguish between one stretch of salt water and another. The traveller knows better, and so does the sailor. The North Sea has an entirely different character to the Caribbean. The Mediterranean, in temperament at any rate, is only a distant relation of the Red Sea or the English Channel.

Even scientifically, the Mediterranean has its points of difference, for it loses by evaporation two-thirds more than it receives from the rivers which drain into it. This loss is replaced by a steady inflow of water from the Atlantic, which enters through the Strait of Gibraltar. The effect of steady evaporation on this almost land-locked sea is that the Mediterranean has a higher salt content than most other seas in the world. The swimmer in the waters around the Greek islands soon appreciates this. The sea is buoyant. It lifts him up as confidently as did the dolphin which carried Arion on its back in safety to the port of Corinth.

There are two main points of departure for travellers visiting the Greek Islands (excluding those who come by private yacht or cruise ship). The first is by boat from Brindisi, or one of the other Adriatic ports. The second is by boat from Athens itself. In the first case, the traveller is welcomed by Corfu and the Seven Islands which lie in the Ionian Sea. In the second case, he embarks directly upon the Aegean Sea and is immediately in contact

15

with the Grecian archipelago. Between these two seas, the Ionian and the Aegean, there is a wealth of difference. The Mediterranean, small though it is, harbours areas whose characters vary as much as the Gulf of Lions does from the sultry, sun-smoked waters between Malta and Tripoli.

There are a few islands which it is possible to visit direct by air. Corfu is one and Rhodes another. Lesbos, or Mytilene, is also linked by air with Brindisi, Constantinople and Athens. Soon it is probable, with the extension of tourism and the consequent development of the Greek airlines, that more islands will be within reach in this way. But for the moment it is reasonable to assume that the visitor comes by sea. It is, after all, the proper way in which to reach an island, and though Corfu looks imposing—green here and silver there—when seen from an aircraft, it is nothing to the first sight of the island from the sea, when the summer mists begin to lift at dawn and the scent of the trees and flowers comes across the water.

The Ionian and the Aegean are very different seas. If the Ionian is female, then the Aegean is male. One is soft, enveloped often with that gauze-like haze which hangs so frequently over the Italian landscape. The other is clear and precise. The Aegean engenders an air in which sentimentality and woolly thinking are impossible. It is a carved and sculptural sea. The Greeks, with that curious accuracy of theirs which seems to have been as much the result of intuition as of deliberate thought, "sexed" these two seas by calling one of them after the goddess Io, and the other after King Aegeus of Athens. The names have stayed unchanged over the centuries, and so have the qualities which determined them.

Io was a priestess of the goddess Hera, the consort of Zeus. It was not surprising, then, that Hera was incensed when she found that Zeus had been deceiving her with Io, one of her own servants. Zeus, to protect his mistress from Hera's anger, promptly changed her into a snow-white cow. His queen, unwilling to forfeit her revenge, sent a gadfly which chased the unfortunate Io all round the world. Io, after leaving Dodona where she had been hidden, made first—pursued by the relentless gadfly—for the sea which still bears her name.

The **Ionian** is the central basin of the Mediterranean, and is bounded on the west by Sicily and on the east by Greece. In a few places it is as deep as two thousand fathoms. In classical times its importance lay in the fact that the trade routes between the mainland and the new colonies in Sicily and Southern Italy ran across this sea. The seamanship which the early Greek mariners had first learned "island-hopping" in the Aegean, was now applied to an altogether larger and more open stretch of water. Even so, in the manner of classical navigation, most of the trade routes followed the coast. From Corfu and Fano (northernmost of the Ionian islands) the vessels had an open sea-crossing of little more than sixty miles to the southern heel of Italy. Following round the Gulf of Taranto they came to the rich colonies of Sybaris and Croton, and then—along the instep of the mainland—to the Straits of Messina. The colonies of Taormina and Syracuse lay only a little southward down the coast of Sicily.

The character of a sea is determined by its winds and weather, just as these again determine the character of its islands and islanders. In the Ionian two winds predominate, the Sirocco and the Gregalé, or the Bora as it is known in Corfu. The Sirocco which blows from the south is a warm, even hot wind, originating in North Africa. Often, by the time that it reaches the islands, it has also picked up a high humidity which places a restraint on all physical action, deadens thought, and exacerbates the nerves. Fortunately, it is not as virulent on this western coast of Greece as in Malta or Sicily to the west. (In Sicily, indeed, it is said that at one time, if the Sirocco had blown for over ten days, all inexplicable crimes of violence and passion were dismissed. They were considered not to lie within the doer's rational cognizance but to owe their origin solely to the south wind.)

The Sirocco blows mostly in spring and autumn, but its counterpart, the Gregalé, on the other hand, is a winter wind. Springing off the mainland mountains, the cold air rushes down to take the place of the warmer air rising off the Ionian. The Gregalé is the most dangerous wind in this part of the Mediterranean. Its full effects are fortunately not felt in the islands. It is on the far side of the sea, on the eastern coasts of Sicily, Gozo and Malta, that the full fetch and thunder of these winter gales is felt. (This was St. Paul's tempestuous wind, called Euroclydon, which drove his ship helplessly from Crete across the Ionian to ground in the Maltese bay that bears his name.)

In the winter the small-boat sailors and fishermen of the Ionian islands do not venture far afield for, apart from the principal winds, heavy squalls often descend off their mountainous islands. When they hurl down the narrow valleys and off the mountain peaks, the local sea is truly Homeric, a fitting reminder that one of the Seven Islands is the hero's Ithaca. But in the spring and summer, the sea around this western coast of Greece is often calm and practically windless for days on end. It is now that, under oars or with the ubiquitous diesel engine, the offshore fishermen bring in the excellent fish which make eating a pleasure in these islands. Apart from the magnificent lobsters of Corfu (usually the clawless Mediterranean *langouste*, but sometimes the northern heavy-clawed, true lobster) the Ionian is rich in dolphin, mullet, ray, squid and tunny. All night long it is starred by the many lamps of the night-fishermen. Their carbide or acetylene flares, pooled in the clear water, hang like necklaces around the islands.

The **Aegean,** the island-studded sea of the Greek archipelago, is entered either round Cape Matapan, the ancient Taenarus which houses the entrance to the Underworld, or more often nowadays, through the rocky slit of the Corinth Canal. Since most cruise boats and island steamers come first to Athens through the canal, and since it provides most travellers' first introduction to the Aegean world, a few words about it will not be out of place.

Four miles long, by 70 feet wide and about 26 feet deep, the canal was begun in 1881 and took twelve years to complete. It is cut through almost solid rock and is an impressive example of

18

nineteenth-century engineering. During the Second World War it was rendered almost useless by the number of ships sunk in or just outside the canal. The Emperor Nero, when he visited Greece in 66 BC, had seen what an advantage to commerce such a canal would be, and had ordered work to begin on it. His death two years later, combined with the technical and material difficulties encountered, prevented any further attempts to unite the Aegean Sea with the Gulf of Corinth and the Ionian Sea. In classical times, ships wishing to cross the Isthmus of Corinth, thus avoiding the long and stormy route round Cape Matapan, were hauled over the narrow neck of land on rollers. It was the command of this overland shipping route which gave the city of Corinth its maritime importance, leading to a prosperity which ultimately rivalled that of Athens. The canal is mainly used today by Adriatic shipping bound for Piraeus or Constantinople, and by Aegean shipping westward bound. The strangest assortment of craft follow one another through its narrow, moat-like waters—cruise ships and cargo vessels, fishing boats and coastal schooners. Behind an old steam yacht (now converted to interisland trade) may come a modern diesel coaster with, hard on her heels, a graceful caique towed by a motor boat.

At the far end one emerges into the Aegean. The tragic death of Aegeus, father of Theseus, is permanently recorded by the name of this sea. Theseus, triumphant after his conquest of the Minotaur, had left Ariadne behind him on Naxos and was hastening for the shores of Attica and his father's kingdom of Athens. "Ariadne was soon revenged on Theseus," writes Robert Graves in *The Greek Myths*. "Whether in grief for her loss, or in joy at the sight of the Attica coast, from which he had been kept by prolonged winds, he forgot his promise to hoist the white sail . . ." This was an arrangement that had been previously made with Aegeus, who would know by the sight of a white sail that all was well, but if a dark sail was hoisted, that his son Theseus had perished in the labyrinth of Crete. Seeing the dark-tanned sail (such as the fishing boats still carry) approaching from the south, Aegeus was overwhelmed by grief. He hurled himself into the sea

19

from the Acropolis rock, near the point where the Temple of the
Wingless Victory was later to stand.

The sea to which he gave his name is, strictly speaking, not
a sea at all, but an arm of the Mediterranean thrust between Asia
Minor and Greece. On the other hand, if the Ionian, the
Adriatic and the Tyrrhenian are to be allowed their separate
definition of "seas," this cannot be withheld from the most famous
of all—the sea which cradled western civilisation, and which
cradled also the arts of navigation. For it must never be forgotten that the Aegean was the birthplace of Greek seamanship
and hence, directly and indirectly, of almost all western seamanship and exploration that has followed during the past 2,000 years.
Out of the Aegean has also come a word that is now part of the
English language, "archipelago." It means to-day any group of
islands, but it derives from the Greek for " The Sea of the Kingdom."

The character of this island-studded sea is formed principally
by two factors: its geographic position and its climate. Geographically, it is the sea which divides Europe from Asia, and yet
at the same time—because the islands lie like stepping-stones
across it—it is not so much a moat between one world and
another, as a bridge. The closeness of island to island meant that
in the infancy of shipbuilding and navigation, man was able,
during the clement seasons of the year, to maintain communications across a watery world. Scudding between the rocky islets,
merchants and traders were able to exchange the goods of one
civilisation with those of another. Because a small ship is hardly
ever out of sight of land for more than a few hours, it was possible
for these early navigators to bring their ships and cargoes safe to
port without compass, chart, or sextant.

The climate has played an equally important part in the development of Aegean civilisation, and of the islands and their
inhabitants. Quite apart from the proximity of island to island,
the weather conditions were favourable for primitive navigation.
"The Etesian winds," as the Admiralty Pilot calls them, blow
from a northerly direction over this sea from the end of spring

right through to the autumn. Indeed, from March until November, the wind over the Aegean is predominantly in the north. It is hardly stretching a point too far to say that, without this prevailing wind, Greek civilisation and Greek culture might never have arisen. Certainly it would never have spread so that it embraced not only all Greece and the Peloponnese, but also the coast of Asia Minor.

Whether one travels through the Aegean by ship, or caique, or private sailing yacht, it is impossible to ignore this summer wind. Even the most unobservant landsman cannot help but remark the extraordinary clarity of the Greek and Aegean sky, which is quite unlike any other sky in the world. It is here that one sees at once the difference between the Ionian and the Aegean seas—a difference that is reflected also in their respective islands.

Even in midsummer there is a briskness in the Aegean air. The blue of the sky is sharp, and broomed by the wind. The softness, the hint of trailing mist over the sea or in the upper reaches of sky which is to be found in the Ionian, is absent in the Aegean. The northerly wind, flowing down from Bulgaria, Turkey, and beyond them from Russia, is prompted by the hot air rising over the Aegean and the Mediterranean, southwards to Alexandria and Egypt. "Metme" or "Meltemi" the modern Greek calls these winds that back and veer between north-west and north-east over the summer months. The word probably derives from the Venetian—for many centuries masters of these narrow seas—"Bel Tempo," " The season of good weather." Certainly, it was upon these regular seasonal winds that the Greeks of antiquity based their sailings and navigation. Their ships were hauled ashore in the autumn, and were not launched again until the "prodroms" or forerunners, the light winds of spring which heralded the return of the Etesians.

It is the **Meltemi** which give the Aegean its unique quality. Every day they begin to blow at dawn, reaching their maximum round about noon, and dropping off at sunset. It is their cool invigorating rush which dissipates that bugbear of so many Mediterranean lands—the noonday lassitude and the high

humidity which curb thought and action alike. At midday in an
Aegean island, one can stand on a rocky peak or sit in a quayside
taverna and feel, in a shade-heat of 90 degrees, the stimulating
wind that helped to make Aegean civilisation. On the northern
coasts of the islands, the short seas pile up and break in splinters
of foam; in the channels the south-going current rushes past;
but in the open sea between the islands one can see the small
boats taking the wind on their beam, and carrying the wine and
oil of one island to exchange it for the sponges and citrus fruit of
another.

The wind not only gives the sailor an easy point of sailing for
crossing between Greece and the coast of Turkey. It was with the
Etesians astern of them that the Mycenaean merchants could sail
from Argos on the Peloponnesian mainland to their parent state
of Crete. From Crete, the sailors whose trading had enriched
Knossos and Phaistos, could run down to Egypt and the Nile.
Usually on these long north-to-south voyages, a cargo would be
taken down during the height of the summer season (when the
northerly winds were strongest), and a cargo brought back again
during the following spring before the Etesians had set in.

Unlike the Ionian, the Aegean generally speaking is not a deep
sea. Only in a few places, notably just north of Crete, does it
attain a depth of one thousand fathoms or more. The islands
which raise their craggy shoulders out of this sea are remnants of
what was once a landblock connecting Europe with Asia Minor.
They are the peaks of old hills, the summits of mountain ranges,
and a glance at a chart or map shows how they splay out from
Greece and Turkey to follow the lines of the main ranges on
either side of the dividing sea. Because it is predominantly
shallow, the Aegean can be a very treacherous area, and a
dangerous breaking sea can soon be kicked up on the rocks and
shallows around the islands. It is not difficult to understand why
the ancient Greeks called a halt to maritime activity for six
months of the year. During the winter the islands reverted to
their native loneliness. They looked inwards towards their own
small lives, and not outwards—as in summer—towards the

extrovert activities of trading and sailing. This natural dualism was in itself, perhaps, conducive towards that healthy balance in Greek thought, which paid respect equally to the active social life of man and to his inner spiritual needs.

To-day the islands are rarely cut off from the outside world as long as they were in the past. Yet I have met islanders who told me that during the Second World War they sometimes heard nothing from the mainland for months on end. (Quite recently, anchoring in Port Ios, I found that mine was the first boat the islanders had seen for three weeks.)

The sea is Greece. Where the first images of other countries that come to mind may be rural or urban—Hyde Park Corner or counterpane landscape for England, the Rivoli or the châteaux of the Loire for France—the image of Greece is the sea. Even the inland shepherd knows the sea-world. From mountain cliffs and thyme-scented crags he watches its shining march into the land. The "uncountable laughter" of the waves as they turn on the northern beaches is matched by the listless swell in the unvisited coves of Thermia, or the pumice-laden sea that seems to quiver beneath the weight of Santorin.

In these seas the red mullet is the best fish, while tunny, caught during the season when it closes the coast to spawn, is good as it is everywhere in the Mediterranean. Properly cooked, the octopus should never be despised, while the squid, either in its own ink, or just its tentacles chopped and fried, is a taste that needs little acquiring. There are innumerable smaller fish, whose names one forgets as soon as one learns them, which go well in fish soup. The thin jade-boned garfish is—like the northern whiting— delicate in flavour if eaten within a few hours of being caught. Almost everywhere, the weed-wigged rocks on the sandy bottom produce firm-fleshed *langoustes*, as well as small crabs that should not be despised just because they look like toys compared with those of our colder seas. I have eaten shark, porpoise and even seal, but they are not for sensitive palates. Yet I have known them so disguised that a friend, who would have recoiled from shark, was happily unaware of the origin of those large, rich flakes

23

that he was eating. But I feel that to eat a porpoise is to eat a brother, for they too are mammals and their intelligence must be undisputed.

The porpoise or the dolphin play constantly around the bow waves of ships. Sailing in small boats, one can often garner a school that will stand along with one for hours on end. They rise close alongside to breathe—that half-snorting sigh—and then dive and tumble in the disturbed water. Squeezed along by the water pressure in front of the bows, the porpoises will stay there effortlessly, just as long as it suits them. Then, with a quick flurry, they will all be gone. Soon, if you watch closely, you will see the sea somewhere near your ship break into a wild splatter of foam as a school of small fish leap for their lives. Riding two to six feet below the surface, the porpoises use the large waves pushed up by the midday Meltemi as a form of sea-toboggan. Often, journeying between one island and another, I have seen them with their bird-like snouts protruding through the steep-faced crests of water as they surf-ride down the Aegean.

Keats in his sonnet to Homer wrote:

> *Standing aloof in giant ignorance,*
> *Of thee I hear and of the Cyclades,*
> *As one who sits ashore and longs perchance*
> *To visit dolphin-coral in deep seas.*

The romantic view of Greece and her islands is one that is not substantiated by facts. Too often our nineteenth-century writers seem to have combined their classical reading with memories of English Palladian architecture, or bosky gardens laid out by "Capability" Brown. The reality is different. It is a harsher, stronger, and altogether more brilliant world. Even in the "romantic" islands like Corfu and Rhodes, which approximate most nearly to the Keatsian conception of Greece, there is a classical clarity in the air, and in the thoughts which the air engenders. The islands are not sugared but astringent.

CHAPTER 2

Corfu, Paxos, Antipaxos

Seven principal islands form the Ionian group, hence their Greek name Heptanesoi. The most important are Corfu, Levkas, Cephalonia, Zante, Ithaca, and Paxos. Cerigo is the seventh island. Apart from these there are numerous islets, some attractive and fertile like Antipaxos, and others like Cerigotto no more than minute sea-washed rocks. Although the islands are reckoned as one geographical group, historically they were quite independent of one another until the fifteenth century. It was in 1386 that **Corfu,** to secure Venetian protection against the Mohammedan pirates from North Africa (as well as the corsairs of Albania and Dalmatia), asked for the protection of the Venetian fleet. Only too willing to secure their lifeline of trade with the East, the Venetians obligingly occupied Corfu and, in the subsequent century, the rest of the Ionian islands.

From the fifteenth until the late eighteenth century the islands formed part of the Venetian Empire. It is this which has welded them into a distinct group, and given them an Italian quality which sets them apart from the islands of the Aegean—even from those islands which at one time or another also came under the rule of Venice. Venetian architecture, Venetian names, and even an aristocracy dating back to the Great Republic, are the legacy of those three centuries. There is a marked Italianate quality to be found in the Ionian islands, most of all in Corfu which for so long formed a major port for Venetian commerce.

Four boat-services weekly, from either Brindisi or Piraeus link Corfu with Italy and Greece. There are also two ships every week from Venice and intermittent sailings from other Adriatic ports. By air it is only an hour's flight from Brindisi, or one and three-quarter hours from Athens. Visitors touring Greece in

their own cars can also cross from the Peloponnese by the car ferry at Corinth, and then take the coast road. From Navpaktos (better known as Lepanto) the main road runs north via Arta and Yannina, ending on the coast opposite the Corfu channel in the sheltered harbour of Igoumenitsa. From Igoumenitsa a car-ferry crosses to Corfu three times a day in summer, but this may sometimes be held up if there have been strong northerly winds blowing down from the Adriatic. In summer the boat services linking Corfu with Athens and Brindisi are being increased, and it is likely that in the near future the same will happen with air services. Of all the Greek islands Corfu is by far the easiest of access.

Corfu is green and fertile. It announces its presence to the visiting ship by the scent of pines, herbs, orange and lemon groves. In the mountainous north of the island, small chapels and monasteries cling to almost inaccessible peaks, while in the centre of the island the land folds away in rich plains. It is the contrast of fertility with sharply-defined outcrops of limestone that gives Corfu within a length of forty miles and a breadth of ten, its special character. In places where the soil is too sparse for cultivation a scented maquis, composed of myrtle, ilex and bay, straggles around the rocks and tenacious olives. Lawrence

26

Durrell has suggested, not without a certain poetic justification, that Corfu was Prospero's Island. Certainly it "is full of noises, sounds and sweet airs that give delight and hurt not." Traditionally, it is the island home of the sea-going Phaeacians, those master mariners of the ancient world who loaned Ulysses the ship and the crew that restored him to Ithaca. Angered by this assistance afforded his enemy, Poseidon (who until then had been the patron of the Phaeacians) turned their boat to stone as it was returning from its errand of mercy. Just south of Corfu town, off the Bay of Khalikiopoulo, lies a small islet, **Pondikonisi,** or Mouse Island. Local legend has it that Mouse Island is the petrified boat of the Phaeacians. If one looks out towards it in the evening, just as the sun is sliding behind the hills of Corfu, the illusion that it is a ship making for the safety of the bay is very strong.

The town of Corfu itself, despite damage from air raids during the Second World War, still retains a golden cosmopolitan charm. My first impression is of its Latin quality: it is certainly more Italian than Greek.

Since so many islands in the Aegean bear the signs of their Venetian occupation, it is worth recording, however briefly, the history of the Venetian Empire in the Aegean and the Levant. It began in the early thirteenth century, a period when Venetian commerce and shipbuilding were flourishing. With the proclamation of the Fourth Crusade in 1202, it was natural for the leaders to apply to Venice, the principal maritime power, to furnish their transport. The crusaders' army numbered 9,000 knights, 20,000 foot-soldiers, and 4,500 horses. The Doge Dandolo agreed to provide the warships and merchantmen for the crusade, for a sum of 85,000 silver marks, and half of all the conquests. He also agreed, in return, to keep the army supplied and victualled for the period of one year. When—as so often happened with the crusaders' finances—the money failed to arrive on time, the Doge saw an opportunity to benefit the republic. The maritime states of Zara and Dalmatia had revolted from Venice in 1166, and Dandolo agreed to postpone the receipt of the money on the condition that the crusaders should reduce

27

these two dissident subjects before proceeding to the Holy Land.

Zara was quickly recovered, and it was while the crusaders were preparing the conquest of Dalmatia that an even more ambitious scheme suggested itself to their leaders and to the Doge. They decided to attack Constantinople. This attack on the eastern bastion of Christendom (by the army of Christian knights supposedly on their way to harass the infidel) was an act which has made the Fourth Crusade deservedly infamous. Aided largely by the fleets of Venice, the attack was successful. Constantinople fell and was sacked by the crusaders. In the partition of the spoils of the Eastern Empire, Venice demanded—and received—in her own grandiloquent phrase: "A half and a quarter of the Roman Empire." To her went the Cyclades, the Sporades, all the islands and the eastern shores of the Adriatic, the shores of the Propontis and the Euxine, and the coastline of Thessaly. At the same time the republic bought the island of Crete from the Marquis of Montferrat.

Venice was now firmly established in the Aegean and the Levant, commanding the trade route between Constantinople and Western Europe, and between Europe and Asia Minor. The islands of the Aegean became for Venice, as they had once been for Athens, the stepping-stones that led from Europe to Asia. In the many island harbours like Corfu, the Venetians built their trading depots and mustered the seamen for their merchant ships and war galleys. For over three hundred years, despite the growing power of Turkey, Venice maintained her supremacy in the Ionian and Aegean. It was during this long period of Venetian rule that the tradition of seamanship and ship-building was fostered.

As well as the Venetian atmosphere about Corfu, there is something that reminds me of Bath, Brighton, or Bristol. There seem to be Regency associations. The dilemma is soon resolved. For nearly fifty years Corfu was the capital of " The United States of the Ionian Islands" which was administered by the British. The Royal Palace, to the north of the town just off George I Square, becomes immediately explicable. Built in

1816, in white sandstone imported from Malta, the palace was formerly the residence of the British governors, who brought to this remote Ionian island their conception of how a gentleman's residence should look. Nearby, in a small square that seems deserted during the day (but not once twilight has released the siesta-bound inhabitants), the statue of Sir Frederick Adam serves as a reminder that the British brought more permanent things than their temporary rule to the Ionian. Sir Frederick Adam was responsible for the great aqueduct which brought a permanent water-supply into the city from Benitsa some twelve miles away. Elsewhere in the Ionian islands, one finds other evidence of this British desire to ensure a clean and efficient water-supply. In Paxos I have seen the iron pipe, stamped V.R., through which the water flows into the capital of Port Gayo.

Controversy still exists about the derivation of the island's name, but the most acceptable explanation seems to be that the Byzantine town was known as *Stous Korfous*, the Two Breasts, from the shape of the two hills near the old citadel. Earlier still, it had been known as Scheriae, and then Drepanon, from the word for a sickle. The latter is certainly accurate for the island is shaped exactly like a sickle—or a half-moon hanging off the stark mountains of the mainland.

It is with some justice that Corfu has been called "The Garden of the Ionian." But visitors, for whom Corfu is their first sight of a Greek island, should not take it as in any way representative. Its lush vegetation and fine fruitbearing trees and orchards are, if anything, untypical. Because of its geographical position off the mountains of northern Greece and Albania, Corfu is fortunate enough to trap a larger rainfall than most of the islands. Corfu was also lucky in coming for so long under the protection of Venice, and not suffering the fate of Greece and the Aegean islands in becoming part of the Ottoman Empire. Where the Turks neglected their lands, failed to encourage afforestation or agriculture, and contributed no more than the ubiquitous goat (that murderer of saplings), the Venetians went so far as to award prizes for those who planted trees. Many of the giant olives which now form part of Corfu's wealth were planted during the Venetian occupation. To those accustomed to the gnarled limbs of the olives which, like deformed wrestlers, cling to most Greek hillsides, the sight of Corfu's olives is unforgettable. Unpruned, some of these giants reach heights of nearly fifty feet. The oil pressed in Corfu is about the best in the Mediterranean, a wonderful green in colour and smooth in texture and taste. (Like everywhere else in the Mediterranean, visitors unaccustomed to true olive oil are advised at first to use it sparingly. Once he or she has grown used to it—and to the wine which off-sets it, and the food which it complements—they will find it difficult ever again to reckon the tasteless oil which passes for "olive" in the north as suitable for anything except sewing-machines.) The oranges of the island are among the best in the Mediterranean. The wild strawberries are exquisite. There are some very drinkable local wines, particularly the red. Roses, clematis and marguerites grow wild everywhere, and some of the cottages in the small inland villages have an almost fairy-tale atmosphere in their surrounds of flowering shrubs.

The British can claim credit for some of this prosperity and fertility. The improvements made to the water-supply between 1815 and 1864 meant that irrigation was practicable in areas where before there had been no more than a village well. New roads, on which several of the modern ones are based, also enabled the peasant-farmers from outlying districts to bring their produce more easily into the city. But the British administration was not popular. Accustomed for centuries to the genial Mediterranean and Levantine methods of doing business (and of ensuring that justice might be delicately weighted) the Corfiotes, and indeed the inhabitants of the islands generally, failed to appreciate rigid Victorian standards of justice and honesty. Besides, the British failed—as always—to appreciate national differences of temperament. Writing in 1864, Viscount Kirkwall describes how a certain Colonel Napier, then stationed in Corfu, reacted to the problems of an administrator. ". . . On one occasion, hearing screams, and learning that a titled Ionian was beating his wife, he rushed into the house, and inflicted on the spot, with his riding-whip, a severe personal chastisement on the astonished husband. To be sure, he immediately afterwards sent to offer to the sufferer complete personal satisfaction. But the Ionian, ignorant of Western refinements in such matters, and unused to the pistol, refused to understand how the being shot at could fully atone for the disgrace of being flogged."

A further comment by Viscount Kirkwall, recommending a friend to rent his own house when visiting the island, leads us to the modern problems of hotels and where to stay. ". . . . In this way," the Viscount wrote, "you escape the oil and garlic flavour which usually permeates all native cookery. The garlic grown in the island is insufficient for home consumption; and I was assured that, to supply the deficiency, 2,500 lb. worth of the unsavoury comestible is annually imported. The constant use of garlic, and the rare use of soap, impress an Englishman very disagreeably." The traveller to-day need not worry, although he will gain more from his visit if he can appreciate both the oil, and the intelligent use of "that sovereign herb"—to quote in opposition to Viscount Kirkwall a seventeenth-century English physician, who advocated the garlic for all stomach complaints and even as a remedy against the plague.

Corfu is particularly well served by its hotels and they present a wide range of choice. For those who want luxury, and all that goes with a first-class hotel, there is the Corfu Palace. Recently taken over by a Swiss hotelier, it is even having a swimming pool built in the grounds. Greek hotels, incidentally, are classified by the Tourist Board as either Hotels De luxe, or A, B, C, and D. The C and D hotels are quite often scrupulously clean family establishments, but they may be a little primitive as regards washing and sanitary arrangements. On the other hand, like the small inn at Hypso (two miles north of Corfu on the bay), the simplicity matches the sand and the sea which lie just under the windows. Another good hotel in the town itself, though smaller than the Corfu Palace, is the Astir. There are also a number of B and C hotels, some of which may be good but—like everything else in the catering business—this kind of information can fluctuate from year to year, or be completely altered by a change of management. A really comfortable and pleasantly old-fashioned place is the *Pension Suisse*, clean and, with its slightly faded air like an old sepia print, perhaps more in keeping with the mood of the island than many more modern establishments. South of the town at **Benitsa** there is the Avra, another small and pleasant inn, with orange and lemon groves at the back, and looking on to the sea. Six miles north of the town there is a first-class hotel, the Castello Mimbelli, at Dhassia. This is in a wonderful position on a hill above the sea, the hotel running its own private bus to take swimmers down to the beach a little over a mile away.

Cafés, restaurants and bars most people prefer to find for themselves, but even here Corfu has a variety—from simple, cave-like Greek tavernas with plates of mezé (snacks), *ouzo* and cheap wine, to the greater sophistication of the continental cafés on the Esplanade. In some of these one notices the refining hand of the French. Although the Esplanade was built by the British, recalling in its design the fact that Governor Sir Thomas Maitland (1816-24) was a friend of Nash, the terraced houses with their arcades were built by the French who occupied Corfu during the Napoleonic Wars. They remember the Rue de Rivoli. A tragic loss in the Second World War was the Public Library, one of the finest in the Mediterranean, which formerly stood in the square at the south of the Esplanade, and housed over 40,000 volumes, many of them a legacy from that great philhellene Lord Guildford.

Going southwards from the Esplanade one reaches the broad street running along the harbour front and called after the Empress Elizabeth of Austria. There is an old fortress, just back from the waterfront, which was built by the Venetians in the mid-sixteenth century. It stands on a breasted promontory at the northern end of the harbour, with a 50-foot moat securing it from the mainland. It is now a military college, but it is possible for students of fortress architecture (and this is a very fine example) to get permission to visit it. At the far end of the peninsula, Cape

Sidero, Corfu's lighthouse fronts the bay. From here the view of the island's northern mountains—dominated by Mount Pand-crator or, to give it its Venetian name, Monte San Salvatore—is unforgettable. In the fertile land just north of Corfu town, all is green and edged with golden sand, then the mountains rise up crowned with their white chapels and monasteries. To the right lies the blue arm of the strait, and beyond that again are the severe heights of the Albanian ranges.

When the British handed Corfu back to Greece they blew up many of the old Venetian fortifications that had for centuries baffled the Turks. Fortunately they left the Old Fortress and some of the grass-lined ramps. In the mid-Victorian era explosions were rare enough for them to be considered romantic and spectacular. As one of the Governor's party who witnessed the destruction of the old fortifications wrote, "Torrents of the densest smoke accompanied, and too often partially concealed the picturesque effects of the explosions." Unfortunately this was not the last that Corfu was to see of man-made violence. The old town suffered heavily during the last war and, although it has been rebuilt, many of its narrow cobbled streets have gone for ever. Enough still remains—shadowed in summer by their tall white houses and protected in winter against the cold north winds—to preserve that Italianate feeling which serves to throw into sharper contrast the chaffering, Levantine quality of the market and the open-air fruit and vegetable stalls. The sellers of cucumbers, grapes and innumerable varieties of dried beans proclaim their wares, while lemonade and anis-flavoured water is dispensed from polished glass-and-brass cylinders that are like a memory of Victorian geysers.

"Tsintsinbeera" is a word that may puzzle for a few minutes. It is no more than yet another English legacy:—ginger beer, and more like the true ginger beer that our grandfathers may have drunk here, than anything to be found in modern England. "Kek" is a further word that has entered the language—the Corfiotes' Greek is enriched with many foreign importations. "Kek" usually refers to a particularly heavy and excellent type of plum and fruit cake. One wonders whether the Earl of Elgin ever sampled it. He landed in Corfu in March, 1861, on his way to take up the position of Governor-General of India. "He wore a complete suit of white plain clothes, with a wideawake transformed into a white turban, in early preparation for the hot latitudes he was bound for. With us the weather was quite cool. The decidedly plethoric aspect of the Viceroy of India was not promising as regarded his future health, considering that he was proceeding to India, for the first time, at an advanced period of life."

It was men like Elgin and "King Tom," Sir Thomas Maitland, who imposed on the island, through their officers and through their refusal to accept any norm save that of England, the game which is still played in Corfu—and indeed known as "To Gamé," The Game. Cricket, as far as I know, flourishes in only two places in the Mediterranean: Malta and Corfu. In Corfu there are two principal clubs, Corfu Gymnastikos and—appropriately enough—the Byron Cricket Club. Cricket week is held in September, and the British Mediterranean fleet usually sends over one or two sides to compete. Since the rules have become slightly altered in Corfu, the bewilderment of the visitors is often acute. Boundary hits, for instance, are worth three or five runs, rather than four or six. Waiters carrying salvers laden with ice-cream, lemonade and ginger beer, are liable to invade the outfield. Passions akin to those engendered by bull-fighting flare up around the proficiency of batsmen and bowlers. Invariably, even if the match has already been won, a game is carried on until nightfall, thus ensuring that as many as possible get their chance to have a knock at the ball. It is cricket with a difference. But, sitting in the evening sun with a plate of wild strawberries and a glass of semi-sparkling local wine, one may well say "Vive la différence!" Cricket had also introduced two further words into the Corfiote vocabulary:—"Howzat?" and "Oaut!"

Just off Nikiphorus Street at the northern end of the Esplanade lies the church of **St. Spiridion,** patron of Corfu. No visitor to Corfu can escape hearing the saint's name invoked on as many suitable, as unsuitable occasions. A member of the Council of Nicaea, (AD 325) he was the Bishop of Cyprus, and his embalmed remains were kept in his native island until the Turkish occupation determined the faithful to remove what relics they could to Greece. The mummified body of the saint finally reached safety, so it is said, strapped to the side of a mule, and disguised as a bale of fodder. It was not until St. Spiridion reached Corfu in 1489 that his career as a wonder-worker seems to have started. The exposure of his relics in a procession through the town saved the island from plague in 1630. Again, in the great siege of 1716 when the island was besieged by the Ottoman fleet, the canonised Cypriot Bishop lent his power and strength to the troops fighting under Count von der Schulenberg and preserved the island from the infidel. In the darkness of the fine old church he now reposes in well-earned peace, his casket a magnificent example of Renaissance gold-work. Only four times a year is the saint asked to leave the cool incense-laden church: on Palm Sunday, Holy Saturday, August the 11th, and the first Sunday in November. Preceded by the Bishop of Corfu, and flanked by priests and acolytes, the saint then makes the circuit of his city, returning in a climax of colour and devotion along the Esplanade.

One should go to the **Kanoni** or Cannon Promenade if only to see Mouse Island. There are many valid reasons, both archaeological and aesthetic. It is easily reached by bus from the centre of the town, and is little more than two miles' walk—a walk worth taking for those who like wandering through unfamiliar streets and being absorbed into the clashing, noisy life of Corfu's poor. On the way, one passes through **Palaeopolis** where extensive excavations have revealed the ground plan of the ancient capital. Unfortunately, wars and steady occupation over centuries have left little outstanding intact, while nearly all the more interesting smaller works of art are to be found in the Corfu museum. Apart from the remains of the temple of Artemis, the main interest of the old site lies in the fact that one can see here— as in so many other parts of the Mediterranean—how the ancients whenever possible chose a peninsula for their cities.

35

This peninsula was closed by a wall from the mainland of Corfu and had to its north the harbour of Alcinous (the modern Kastrades) and to the south the Hyllaic port, the modern Kalikiopoulo. Although the ancient Hyllaic port has silted and aqualung divers have carried out some investigations, it seems likely that a well-equipped expedition might make some valuable finds in this area.

The Kanoni itself is no more than a semicircular platform on which a large cannon was once mounted. From here one gazes down on the monastery of Vlachernes at the head of its narrow breakwater, with Mouse Island accessible by rowing boat less than half a mile away. Now that one is in this area it is well worth-while, whatever one's tastes, paying a visit to the **Achilleion** for its site is one of the finest in the island. It has been called "the only ugly building in Corfu," but for those with a taste for Sur-realism, its extraordinary gim-crackery makes an appeal. The Italian architect Carito built it for Elizabeth of Austria in 1890-91, but it is the ghost of the Kaiser that haunts this pseudo-Greek palace. The enormous statue of " Achilles Wounded," the work of the German sculptor Herter, was not as is sometimes supposed commissioned by the Kaiser, but by his predecessor the Empress, who had something of a cult for the Greek hero. It was the Kaiser, however, who caused the inscription to be made on its base "To the greatest of the Greeks, from the greatest of the Germans." There is something over-lush and sentimental about the gardens, fine though they are. They, and indeed the Achilleion itself, represent one side of the German character; nostalgia, and a romantic longing for the south. The other side, a self-conscious insistence on the Spartan virtues, is well enough revealed by the Kaiser's simple iron bedstead, and by the saddle which served him as a chair.

Many of the properties are divided by hedges of flowering aloe, but this does no more than add to the landscape's richness. The olives which predominate in the southern half of the island are saved from monotony by the dark green spears of the cypresses. When the wind passes over the olives, so that their leaves turn in a rustle of silver, the cypresses look like pinnacle rocks rising out of a sea. The innumerable small bays and headlands give one the illusion of passing from one island to another. This, combined with the variety of the Corfiote landscape, prevents that feeling of ennui and *taedium vitae* which can soon creep upon one in islands less diversified than this.

Palaio Castrizza, the Old Castle, is a promontory on the west coast of Corfu easily reached by taxi from the town. The drive takes one right across the island through some of its most attractive country, and the monastery is worth visiting for its magnificent site, as well as for a good twelfth- or thirteenth-century Ikon of the Virgin. Bérard and others have managed to identify Scheriae, the land of the Homeric Phaeacians, with this north-western corner of Corfu. As a Corfiote friend re-marked: "Never mind what you think—you must admit that the town of Alcinous *ought* to have been here."

There were twelve monks in the monastery when I visited it, and the oldest, who from his appearance must have been nearly a hundred, insisted on picking a posy of flowers from the garden for my wife. I was happy to be able to leave him with a packet of cigarettes, tobacco being one weakness from which even the ascetic hardly ever escape.

The cigarette in Greece, incidentally, is often the passport to friendship and, in many places where I would not have been able to give a tip for fear of offending, I have found that cigarettes are always acceptable. Time, too, in out of the way places is sometimes measured by tobacco. It is not unusual to be told that such-and-such a place is "two or three cigarettes away." This is a very elastic measurement, and the nervous chain-smoker should always double the figure.

Above the monastery the castle of St. Angelo on its romantic peak may tempt the climber, but as I was there on a hot June day I was content to admire from a distance. In the fertile lowland to the south the road zigzags through old olives to the marshy Roppa plain where the River Ermones leaves the land and plunges into the bay. This without doubt is one of the loveliest places in

37

the island, the river glancing down from one rocky basin to another until it reaches the sea in the tranquil sandy bay of Ermones. At this point I am prepared to agree with my Corfiote friend. Here, if anywhere, is the beach where Nausicaa should have surprised Ulysses.

Corfu is big enough and varied enough to keep a traveller busy for weeks in exploration. It would be ideal to make a base in one of the small hotels like the Avra at Benizza and explore the island on foot. Spring or autumn would be the seasons for such an investigation "in depth," for the midsummer heats and the long cicada-laden afternoons of July and August are no time to be active afoot. One pleasant way, however, in which even in the height of summer one can explore the island's coastline is to hire a boat—something that can usually be arranged through a hotel or through the Tourist Bureau. A small *benzina*, the generic term for a motor boat whether in fact petrol- or diesel-engined, can take one to many places on the coast that are otherwise almost inaccessible. Some of the little-known bays and coves of Corfu are ideal for those who like to swim or laze in the sun, alone or with a companion. A *benzina* cannot take one very far in a day, but now that tourism is being developed in Greece, charter yachts are becoming available in Corfu. A week or fortnight's charter, to explore the island and some of the others in the Ionian group, would be the perfect antidote to the stress of the modern world.

Corfu has seen wars, revolutions, sieges, naval battles, treacheries and power politics enough in its time. If the island and the islanders—like an Ireland of the Ionian—prefer now to contemplate history in an amber dispassion, their attitude is comprehensible enough. Sailing south down the eastern coast of Corfu one passes Cape Bianco, the ancient Leucimna, southernmost point of Corfu. It was between here and the Sivota islets that the battle took place between the Corfiotes and the Corinthian fleet which precipitated the Peloponnesian War. I was sailing off here one day, in company with a local fisherman, when he pointed out a small hillock near the cape. "Castro Nereido!" he said. The Castle of the Nereids! It seemed appropriate enough that the daughters of Nereus, that Old Man of the Sea, should still be remembered in the island of the Phaeacians.

"Pan," writes Robert Graves in *The Greek Myths*, "is the only God who has died in our time." Certainly, he is the only god whose death has been historically reported. The event is related by Plutarch in *Why Oracles are Silent*. It happened during the reign of Tiberius, and the news was first heard by an Egyptian pilot, Thamus (or Tammuz), who was bound for Italy via the island of Paxos. (Paxos lies about ten miles south of Cape Bianco.) Christian commentators in later centuries were not slow to make the point that the event occurred during the reign of the emperor under whose jurisdiction Christ was put to death, and must have been the moment of the Crucifixion—that moment in time when the false gods died, and man was reborn to a new life.

The story is best told by an anonymous annotator on Spencer's *Pastoral in May*. "Here, about the time that Our Lord suffered his most bitter Passion, certayne persons sailing from Italie to Cypruse at night heard a voyce calling aloud, Thamus, Thamus! who giving eare to the cry, was bidden (for he was pilot of the ship,) when he came near to Palodas, to tell that the great god Pan was dead; which he doubting to do, yet for that when he came near to Palodas there was such a calme of wind that the ship stood still in the sea unmoored, he was forced to cry aloud that Pan was dead; wherewithal there was such piteous outcries and dreadful shrieking as hath not been the like. By which Pan of some is understood to have been the great Sathanas, whose kingdom was at that time by Christ conquered, and the gates of hell broken up; for at that time all Oracles surceased, and enchanted Spirits that were wont to delude the people henceforth held their peace."

Pausanias, however, describing his visit to Greece a century later found that the shrines and places sacred to Pan were still active. On this score alone I incline to the modern theory that what the pilot Thamus heard were the ritual words used in the lament for Tammuz (Adonis):—"Thamus Pan-Megas Tethneeke" ("The Almighty Tammuz is dead" rather than "Thamus, Great Pan is dead!"). But no one familiar with this story can sail past

Paxos in the still, dark hours without wondering whether it was indeed here that the message was first heard:

'Tis mute the word they went to hear in high Dodona's mountains,
When winds were in the oakenshaws and all the cauldrons tolled.
And mute's the midland naval stone beside the singing fountains
And echoes list to silence now where gods told lies of old . . .

(A. E. HOUSMAN)

One point at least I can resolve—for some have challenged the tale on the grounds that Thamus could never have heard the message if he were busy on a sailing ship at sea. I have sailed past **Paxos** in a ten-ton boat at night and have heard the clatter of goats' hooves as a herd, disturbed no doubt by my passage, bounded up the rocky slopes. A voice crying out the ceremonial lament for Tammuz would have been easily audible on a still night.

Those who can spare the time to visit Paxos, either by yacht, fishing boat or in the weekly steamer from Corfu, will not find their day wasted. After the Italianate opulence of parts of Corfu, Paxos presents a picture of a more or less typical Greek island. Corfu was described by the traveller Antony Shirley in the seventeenth century as "A Greekish Island" and—whether he meant the interpretation or not—"Greekish" I find it, but not true "Greek." Paxos, with its sunbaked soil, silver rocks and stunted olives leaning before the wind, is more Greek. If the first taste of this harshness which is inseparable from Aegean beauty daunts the visitor then he must either try to acquire a palate for dry wines, as it were, or return to the sweeter vintage of Corfu and, thence, logically, to Capri or Ischia.

There is only one village proper on Paxos. This is the small port of **Gayo,** which is entered from the north through a narrow channel. A whitewashed convent shines on the emerald islet of the Virgin and once, entering here at sunset, I surprised the nuns doing their washing by the water's edge. Boccaccio, incidentally, in his novel *Landolfo Buffolo* mentions the scarcity of fresh water in the Ionian islands and describes a Corfiote woman engaged in cleaning "her kitchen utensils with sand and *salt*

40

The jetty at Poros

Pondikonisi Island, off Corfu

water." There is nothing wrong, in fact, with sand and salt water for the heavy iron or copper kitchen utensils which can still be found in many an Ionian kitchen.

Port Gayo consists of a small square fronting on to the quayside, one excellent country taverna, The Black Cat, and about two streets. The total population of the island is only a few hundred. The main building in the village is the small whitewashed church, outside which the village priest is usually to be found, sitting in a wicker chair and gossiping with friends. Port Gayo is the place to sail into at the close of a warm summer day. In certain terms it has little or nothing, in others practically everything. A ruined Venetian fort guards the southern entrance of Madonna islet and in almost all weathers a small boat can lie in safety alongside Port Gayo's quay. The lobsters caught off the island are excellent, the olive oil is of the best, and the taverna serves a very drinkable wine. There is no hotel in Paxos although the visitor prepared to rough it would easily be able to find a bed. There is nothing to do, and very little to see—except olives and goats and sudden vistas of the Ionian bursting on the western coast. The island is just under ten miles long and about a mile and a half wide.

Curiously enough, for one brief moment, Paxos featured in British history when Mr. Gladstone, who was High Commissioner Extraordinary to the Ionian Islands, came here in 1858. .... "At Paxo, as everywhere else," wrote Viscount Kirkwall, who clearly disapproved of the great man, "he showed the most unbounded veneration for the dignitaries of the Greek Church. In Corfu, he had excited the, perhaps illiberal, disgust of the English by publicly kissing the hand of the Archbishop and dutifully receiving his blessing. .... The simple Bishop of Paxo appears, also, to have been ignorant of the etiquette which the High Commissioner Extraordinary practised with ecclesiastical dignitaries. Mr. Gladstone, having taken and respectfully kissed the Bishop's hand, leaned forward to receive the orthodox blessing. The Bishop hesitated, not knowing what was expected of him; and not imagining, perhaps, that a member of the Anglican Church

41

could require his benediction. At last, however, he perceived the truth, and, bending forward, he hastened to comply with the flattering desire of the representative of the British Crown. But at this moment, unfortunately, Mr. Gladstone, imagining that the deferred blessing was not forthcoming, suddenly raised his head, and struck the episcopal chin. The Resident and other spectators of the scene had considerable difficulty in maintaining the gravity befitting so solemn an occasion. . . ."

About a mile south of Paxos lies its minute dependent, **Antipaxos.** It is about two miles long and half a mile wide, and produces some of the best wine in the Ionian. Unfortunately, although almost the whole island is given over to the vine, it is difficult to obtain outside of the island itself, Paxos, or certain discriminating private houses and tavern-keepers in Corfu. It is naturally semi-sparkling, and the colour of a fine claret. The goat cheese, as almost everywhere in Greece, is good and so are the *barbouni,* or red mullet. There is no way of reaching Antipaxos save by yacht or fishing boat, but those who have managed to reach Paxos should not miss the opportunity of visiting its small sister. Antipaxos has other attractions than wine, for in spring, round about mid-May, the rock doves flighting up from North Africa and the shores of Egypt make it a port of call. Those who may be reluctant to shoot doves are unlikely to have any qualms about eating them, either roasted, or in a casserole, and washed down with the island wine. There is a small anchorage on the east coast where yachts and fishing boats can lie, but village or port there is none. When I visited Antipaxos, the Prefect of Corfu told me that the island had only forty inhabitants, all of whom were engaged in tending the vines. In spring the air is scented with many flowering shrubs. Madonna lilies and sun-flowers were growing wild around the ruins of a cottage near the anchorage, and the pale green of mastic shrubs spread all over the eastern coastline. It is the west side of the island that is heavy with vines, and here—to act as wind-breakers—the in-habitants have built high walls, through which one wanders as if down small deserted lanes. A priest and a field-guard (a cross between a game warden and a country policeman) complete the island's population. Their town, their market, and their only source of entertainment is Port Gayo in Paxos, and on rare occasions they pay a visit to Corfu. In the winter Antipaxos is often cut off from the outside world for weeks on end.

CHAPTER 3

Levkas and Ithaca

Levkas, Cephalonia, Ithaca and Zante are all easily reached from
Corfu, either by island steamer, or coaster. Levkas, or Santa
Maura as it was known to the Venetians, lies just off the coastline of Acharnania. A mountain ridge forms its backbone, its
sides and flanks are low-lying lagoons and marshes where the
sea-salt whitens in sour-smelling pans under the midsummer sun.
Ravaged by earthquakes, the most recent occurring only a few
years ago, Levkas has a semi-abandoned air, and the capital in
the north-east of the island was completely ruined in 1948. The
rebuilding that has taken place suggests that the inhabitants
have little confidence in the future. There is something sad and
impermanent about the houses that straggle down to the quayside. The taverna where I went seemed on the verge of dis-
integration. The wine of Levkas on the other hand is as good as
any to be found in Greece, a rich dark red—called more accurately "black" in Greek—which has a rare potency.

As one sails down the coast towards the narrow channel that
separates Levkas from the mainland, the town of **Preveza**
signals the opening to the Gulf of Arta. Akri point on the southern
side of the entrance, rising above the shore of Actium and the
shallow waters of the small bay where the world was once won
and lost, is marked by a whitewashed chapel dedicated to the
Apostles. Here Anthony watched the destruction of his fleet
while, only half a mile away, Octavian stood on the isthmus of
Epirus to view his light, easily-manoeuvred ships tear Anthony's

to pieces. The rout was completed when the ships of Cleopatra's Egyptian navy fled. They were followed by Anthony himself, whose army promptly went over to the victorious standards of the future Augustus.

This is an area heavy with ancient tragedy. Nearby are the cliffs of Zalonga under which I once anchored—cliffs from which the heroine Elena, wife of the Greek patriot Marco Botzaris, followed by the other women of Suli, threw themselves and their children into the sea, rather than be captured by the Turks. It is an oppressive stretch of sea, commemorated best in a haunting folk song:

> *Fish cannot live without water,*
> *Flowers cannot bloom in the sand—*
> *And we cannot live without freedom!*

At first sight Levkas appears to be a peninsula leaning out from Acharnania, and such it was in early times. Homer refers to it in the *Odyssey* as a promontory of Epirus. It was in the mid-seventh century BC that the Corinthians, who were busy establishing colonies along this coastline to safeguard their shipping routes, founded the city of Levkas and separated the promontory from the mainland by dredging a canal. The prevailing north wind, seismic disturbances, and the steady drift of mud and sand, had silted up this canal by the time of Augustus. Augustus, at the same time as founding Nicopolis on the Gulf of Arta to commemorate his victory at Actium, had the ancient canal re-opened. The modern channel, through which the coastal steamers and caiques pass, has a depth of about fifteen feet and follows the ancient route due south from the Bay of Demata into the Bay of Drepano. Entering from the north one sees the fort of Santa Maura dominating the channel on the port side, while the town of Levkas faces it across the mud-flats and the wind-whipped gulf of the lagoon. Windmills spin along the sandy mainland strip known as the Plaka.

There is no hotel in Levkas, although it would be comparatively easy for the hardened traveller to find himself a bed for the night. The poorer a man or a place, so much the more does he seem to reverence the duty owed to strangers—in Greece at any rate. It was here in Levkas that a fisherman insisted on helping me with a repair to the water pump of the engine in my small boat. We worked for two hours in a hot and humid afternoon and, at the end, my offer of money was turned down with aristocratic dignity. My helper even insisted that our drinks in the nearby taverna must not be paid for by a stranger. I found then—something which stood me in good stead at other times—that cigarettes for himself and tinned coffee for his wife could be accepted without a loss of self-respect.

But there is little to detain a visitor in Levkas, unless by any chance he should happen to be a disciple of the German scholar Dörpfeld. As long as the world lasts there will always be scholars who will devote immense labour and ingenuity in attempting to overthrow all previously accepted conclusions. Dörpfeld, in his *Alt Ithaka*, published in 1927, determined to prove that Levkas, and not the modern Ithaca, was the home of Ulysses. Ignoring the fact that Thucydides states that Levkas was a peninsula, Dörpfeld set about establishing Levkas as the Homeric island. He found the main port of Ithaca in the great eastern bay of Vlikho. (It is true that this could well have been the hero's home port, but what is wrong with the noble bay of Vathi in Ithaca itself?)

On my first visit to Levkas some years ago I met a Dörpfeldian in the shape of the local harbour-master, who naturally had good reason to stimulate interest in his island. Shortly afterwards, re-

reading the *Odyssey*, I found what seems to me conclusive proof that in no sense could Levkas have been the Homeric Ithaca. Telemachus when he is describing his father's kingdom in King Menelaus' court says of it: "There is no room for horses to exercise in Ithaca, nor are there any meadows. It is a pasture land for goats and more pleasant than those lands where horses roam." This is an apt and admirable description of Ithaca, but not of Levkas with its wide, flat plains.

The spinal ridge of hills terminates to the south in the long white cliff from which the island derives its name. The White Rock, Leucas Petra, to which Homer refers in the *Odyssey*, now bears the Venetian name Cape Ducato (the Ducat). It was from this point that the fabulous *Catapontismus*, Sea Dive, was performed. A temple of Apollo, some remains of which can still be seen, once stood on the headland 230 feet above the sea, and it was from here that the priests of Apollo would hurl themselves into space, buoyed up—so it is said—by live birds and feathered wings. The relationship between this ritual and the god seems obscure, although there was an early connection between Apollo and various birds. One authority tells us that a cock, the Bird of Dawning, was present at Apollo's birth, and Callimachus in his Delphic hymn mentions the swans that circled seven times round Delos while Leto was in labour with Apollo.

There seems no doubt that the Levkadian Leap was used as a form of Trial by Ordeal. Sappho is reputed, on dubious authority, to have hurled herself to death from the rock. There is no record of any of the priests having been harmed in this strange ritual, although what assistance they might have derived from their feathered pinions is doubtful. Boatmen with nets waited below to rescue the divers after their initiation. From what exact point on the cliff the priests and others hurled themselves is difficult to determine, although it is deep water all round, except at the far end where the peninsula runs down in rocks into the sea. It was as a cure for unrequited love (Apollo acting in his capacity as God of Medicine) that Sappho is supposed to have leaped into the Ionian. At a later date, Ovid confirms that the virtues of the flight and the healing waters below the cliff had been known since the time of Deucalion, the Greek Noah.

Only ten miles due south of Levkas lies **Ithaca**, small and rocky, a hard land. Yet it has sufficient grandeur to deserve its claim to be the most famous island in the world.

"Be sure you are quite old when you drop anchor in Ithaca," wrote Cavafy. "Rich with the experience you have gained on your voyage, do not expect the island to give you riches. Ithaca has given you your wonderful voyage. Without Ithaca you would never have started. It has no more to give you now." Fortunately, the true and geographical Ithaca still has plenty to give the traveller.

I find in an old log-book of mine from the first time I visited Ithaca in May, 1952, these brief notes: "To have come to it over a gentle summer sea would have seemed inadequate or trivial. But we had thunder to the north, wind scouring the sea, and rain in our faces. Over the southern half of the island hung a ragged curtain of violet dark cloud, out of which the lightning flickered. A few seconds later, the island was lost to view. Occupied by the storm, it was already serving as a base from which the thunder clouds were spreading out over the sea towards us. Fortunately, just before the storm obliterated the island, I had taken a bearing of the entrance to the Gulf of Molo and we steered a compass course through the low-flying scud and spindrift. . . ." The Gulf of Molo is a deep thrust of sea that practically divides Ithaca into two islands. Composed of two mountainous masses, the northern and larger half is capped by Mount Anoi, and the southern by Mount Perachoron beneath which lies the Grotto of the Nymphs. Connecting the two main masses lies the narrow, half-mile peninsula whose core is Mount Aetos, over one thousand feet high.

Ithaca is served by a number of cruise and steamship lines from Piraeus and Patras, as well as from most of the Acharnanian ports and the other Ionian islands. The harbour and capital is **Port Vathi,** a deep narrow inlet running off the Gulf of Molo, and safe from almost all winds except from the north-west. Until recently the town was clearly sixteenth-century Venetian. Tragically, the earthquake of 1953, which devastated all this region, destroyed almost all of Vathi—even the Actaeon, formerly the only place in Ithaca in which one could stay. It was in the Actaeon that I first tasted the roast hare of Ithaca, one of the island specialties. A small bar nowadays has a room or rooms above it, and a new tourist hotel is being built.

The town of Vathi, which spreads in a crescent shape along all the southern shore of the bay, is—despite the recent earthquake—a pleasant place in which to find oneself. The cleanliness of its narrow alleys would put many a modern city to shame, and the whitewashed houses shine as clean and brilliant as the wakes of the fishing boats. Olive oil and wine are about the only exports of the island, but most of the men are fishermen and every small bar can produce a little fresh fish to complement the wine and the *ouzo*.

Some scholars may have disputed the island's claim to be the Homeric Ithaca, but I think most who view it without prejudice and with only the *Odyssey* in their hands will never doubt. "Ithakee," The Precipitous Island, was not questioned by antiquity. Perhaps more scholars, if they left their book-lined rooms or ever visited it by small boat and explored the coast, would accept it, even if the location of actual sites remains difficult or almost impossible.

Dr. Schliemann and Sir William Gell both elected to find the site of the hero's town on the isthmus of Aetos. More recent scholars have opted for the enchanting small port of **Polis** on the north-western coast, facing towards Cephalonia. There is good reason for thinking that this northern end of the island held the Homeric capital, not only on account of the archaeological finds that have been made there. Polis, incidentally, is an easy taxi drive from Vathi, through magnificent scenery that compensates for the somewhat hazardous road. At **Stavros,** the village in the north of the island where the two-pronged peninsula develops, it is easy to see why this part of Ithaca should have attracted sailors at any period of history—but especially in the days prior to man-made, artificial harbours. Classical and pre-classical ships were very similar to the viking ships of the north. In winter or bad weather, such ships could be hauled ashore by simple windlasses operated by men or animals. Ideal for the ancient navigator was a section of land where two or more bays offered him safe shelter against the prevailing winds, so that if the westerlies blew he had only to move round to another harbour and vice-versa. The northern quarter of Ithaca has at least four natural harbours— Polis to the west, Aphalais Bay to the north, Port Phrikes to the north-east, and Kioni to the east. Since all these anchorages are sheltered by the island, and by Cephalonia from any southerly winds, it is clear that they provide ideal shelter for all seasons of the year.

From **Pelikata,** the village on the plateau overlooking Phrikes, all four main harbours are easily visible. In the small museum here, among other pieces of pottery found locally, there is a sherd inscribed "To Odysseus." There is no doubt that it comes from a votive offering (it has been dated as second century BC) to the Homeric hero who, like so many of his companions, suffered a sea-change into a demi-god in later years. Nearby is the Black Fountain, supposed by some to be the Melanidros Spring of the Odyssey. Nearby, too, is the cool whitewashed chapel of St. Athanasios, which stands on the square masonry base of an ancient building sometimes called The School of Homer. But there is no good reason for thinking that the Homeridae, the Guild of Homeric poets, ever had any such institution on the island.

From Port Vathi a walk of little more than an hour brings one to the Nymphs' Grotto where Ulysses hid his treasures. **Marmarospaelia** is the modern name for this cave which lies in the hill to the south-west of Vathi. Below it to the west is a bay with a shelving beach, which is just what the narrative demands. So cool a place must surely have been sacred to the nymphs. Even on a blinding hot day the limestone interior, flanked by damp stalactites, has a feeling of remoteness from the world outside. Whether this was truly the Cave of the Nymphs seems unimportant. That some spirits who haunted rocks and caves received their offerings here is almost certainly proved by the primitive altar. One objection that has been made to the identification of Marmarospaelia with the Cave of the Nymphs can be easily dismissed: Homer describes the cave as "near" the sandy beach, whereas it is a good half-hour's walk—and a hard walk up-hill. But there is no reason to suppose that the ancient poet, even allowing for the fact that poets are notoriously vague about time, should have been any more accurate than a modern Greek. When I went ashore in Vathi and inquired of my guide how long it would take us to reach the cave I was assured that a half-hour would do it—yet it took us a good hour walking at a fair pace!

The best way to get to Raven's Rock and the fountain which is generally accepted as being the Fountain of Arethusa is to take a *benzina* or fishing boat from Vathi. It can be reached by road, but Ithaca is an island that should be seen from the sea for the rugged eastern coast below Vathi is inspiring. One lands in the **Bay of Perapigadi,** perfect for swimming, and Arethusa's Fountain is about an hour's climb up a stony goat-track. (Midday is no time for this excursion.) Of all the places mentioned in the *Odyssey*, only Korax, the Raven's Rock, and the Fountain of Arethusa seem to be perfectly met by their existent geographical counterparts. One look at the beetling purple rock—over which I saw hawks, but not ravens, wind-hovering in the lifting air— and it is difficult not to believe that this is the Homeric site. Hard by is the fountain, with the green of ferns a welcome sight after the dusty path. There is the sound of trickling water, best of all sounds in hot southern lands, to confirm that here is one fountain which does not die even with the heats of summer. Here, perhaps, Eumaeus came to fill his goat-skin.

A short walk to the crest of the hill reveals the plateau of Marathia which again fits logically with the place where Eumaeus had his home, and where the fifty sows and their litters were housed. From here another path leads down to **Port Andreas** in the south. This again is best seen from the sea, for it is one of the most lovely bays and inlets of Ithaca. Open only to the south, the bay winds inland for nearly a mile between cliffs scented with thyme, and there are oleanders in bright splashes along the slopes. It may well be that it was here Telemachus landed, after his escape from the suitors who had lain in ambush for him on Asteris island. The latter has been identified with the small "star-like" rock, Daskalio, in the channel between Cephalonia and Ithaca.

It is a pity to pursue identifications too far when in Ithaca. I have seen scholars and savants with their foreheads creased in frowns as they disputed at Mount Aetos, or grew indignant over the rival claims of fountains. Ithaca, despite the tragic dilapidations and losses caused by the earthquake, is an island to be enjoyed. Every way one looks the interlacing arms of the sea are a reminder that the *Odyssey* is the epic of a seaman. It, too, was written to be enjoyed, and not to be a dustbowl of acrimony.

CHAPTER 4

Cephalonia and Zante

Astraddle the entrance to the Gulf of Patras and screening Ithaca from the west, lies Cephalonia, largest of the Ionian Islands. Ships from Piraeus and Patras call here several times a week, and the island is also linked by regular services with Zante, Ithaca and Corfu.

Rich and fertile, Cephalonia like Corfu is an island where olive and citrus fruits flourish. It has some of the finest mountain and forest scenery to be found anywhere in the Greek islands, and the dense wooded slopes covered with the Cephalonian Fir scent the whole air with their resinous tang. Unfortunately, Cephalonia has suffered even more than Ithaca from earthquakes, with the result that few buildings of historical interest survive in either of its two ports, Argostolion or Lixourion. Like nearly all the Ionian islands, Cephalonia stands on that deep fault in the earth's crust which has made this whole area notorious for seismic disturbances since classical times. Again like Ithaca, Cephalonia is mountainous, its spinal ridge running from north-west to south-east. Unlike its sister island, however, Cephalonia has deep valleys and fertile plains, where cotton and currants provide the principal crop and the island's main source of income.

Tetrapolis, the Four Cities, was Cephalonia's ancient name, and the remains of the four—Cranioi, Palaeis, Pronnaioi and Sami—have been discovered. Cranioi, the ancient Cranaea, by far the best preserved, is easily reached by car from **Argostolion,** the capital and principal port. Both Argostolion and Lixourion lie on the fine natural harbour formed by the deep gulf of Livadi

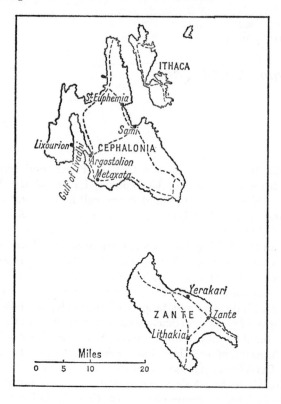

which penetrates the island from the south for a distance of seven miles. Argostolion had only one hotel, the Pharao, when I visited the island but I was told that a Tourist Board hotel was about to be built. The city is a Venetian foundation but little of interest has been left from its two major disasters, the great earthquakes of 1867 and 1953. Like Corfu, the town still retains traces of both Venetian and British influences. Among the latter, there is a bust of Admiral Napier, Cephalonia's first British Governor, in the square that bears his name. The Admiral was a great philhellene in the Byronic tradition and his name is still

remembered. A Cephalonian lawyer, with whom I was diffidently discussing the politics of Greece over a bottle of wine, remarked: "Ah, what Greece needs is a man like Napier—above
corruption!"

It was here in Cephalonia that the greatest philhellene of them
all came on the last stages of his journey. It was in the village of
Metaxata, about seven miles by road from Argostolion that
Byron wrote:

> *The dead have been awakened—shall I sleep ?*
> *The world's at war with tyrants—shall I crouch ?*
> *The harvest's ripe—and shall I pause to reap ?*
> *I slumber not; the thorn is in my couch;*
> *Each day a trumpet soundeth in my ear,*
> *Its echo in my heart——*

It was here, in the house which can still be seen in Metaxata,
that he wrote in his journal: ". . . Standing at the window of my
apartment in this beautiful village, the calm though cool serenity
of a beautiful and transparent Moonlight, showing the Islands, the
Mountains, the Sea, with a distant outline of the Morea traced
between the double Azure of the waves and skies, has quieted me
enough to be able to write." Yet if Byron found some pleasure in
the scenery of Cephalonia and of his beloved Ithaca (which on
one occasion he had even thought of buying), it was soon to be
dissipated in the never-ending disputes about money and prestige
which bedevilled the Greek revolution. It would be sentimentality not to record that it was in Metaxata also that Byron
wrote: "The worst of them [the Greeks] is that (to use a coarse
but the only expression that will not fall short of the truth) they
are such damned liars; there never was such an incapacity for
veracity since Eve lived in Paradise."

Apart from Argostolion and Lixourion there are two other
ports, both on the eastern coast, **Santa Euphemia** and **Sami.**
Steamers call at both of them and one can find a fishing boat or a
benzina to take one over the narrow strait to Ithaca. Looking
across the channel from wooded Cephalonia towards the craggy
outline of Ithaca it is not difficult to see why, in Homeric times, the

larger island was the more important in the confederacy that was led by Ulysses. It seems proof in itself of the hero's ability, that the laird of an island as small and poor as Ithaca should have been in command of the contingent furnished by these islands.

Cephalonia's principal source of interest to visitors and archaeologists alike lies in its magnificent Mycenaean remains. At Metaxata and Mazarata, both of which can be reached by car from Argostolion, there are caves containing hundreds of tombs. They were enriched with sarcophagi, vases, gold jewellery and copper weapons and utensils. Nearly all the important pieces can now be seen in the Argostolion museum. The drive to Mazarata takes one right across the plain where ancient Cranaea lies.

It would now appear that in Mycenaean times, Cephalonia was one of the most important islands in that thalassocracy. Only in Mycenae itself have greater treasures been found, or a greater evidence of the Mycenaean culture. It is not surprising, then, that the evidence of Cephalonia's ancient importance should have provoked Homeric geographers into yet further arguments and disputes. It has been suggested that the western arm of Cephalonia, the peninsula where Lixourion now stands, was really the Homeric Ithaca. As evidence for this some have quoted the famous passage in the *Odyssey*, where the hero describes his island home: "Steadfast it stands, highest above the waves, and westward; the rest lie apart towards the eastern sun." No one can deny that Cephalonia itself is to the west of Ithaca, and the Lixourion peninsula again is the westernmost part of all the Ionian islands. However, there are yet other arguments which seem to dispose of this theory. Arguments about Homeric geography will not cease "till a' the seas gang dry. ...."

Like the other islands of the Ionian, Cephalonia in classical times became involved in the struggle for sea hegemony between Athens and Corinth. Prompted by their own trade rivalry with Corfu, Cephalonia started as an ally of Corinth but was ultimately forced by Athenian sea-power to join the Athenian confederacy. In 189 BC the eastward expansion of Rome brought the

Corfu. *Above*, a view from the Achilleion; *below*, the Museum, once the residence of the British Governors

Kalymnos

Consul Marcus Fulvius into these waters. Finding that the important channel between Cephalonia and Ithaca was dominated by pirates operating out of Sami, he proceeded to invest the harbour. The siege was long and violent, lasting four months, and is described by Livy. In the end, the city fell to the Romans. The sites of the two ancient citadels which protected the town can still be seen, as well as the remains of parts of the Roman city, which was erected to further the conquerors' eastward move into the Gulf of Patras. Sami to-day is no more than a quiet fishing port.

It is impossible to visit Argostolion without being asked to take a taxi to the two famous water-mills. They are only about quarter of an hour to the north of the port and, although it is only the scientifically-minded whom they can stir to great enthusiasm, it would be a pity to miss them. Their uniqueness lies in the fact that they are unlike any other water-mills in the world and, as far as I know, no one quite understands how they operate. The mills turn like any other water-mills, but it is an inrush of the sea, down a tunnel more than 100 feet long, which causes them to spin. The mills are five feet below sea level, and the great problem is—what happens to the sea-water after it has disappeared into the ground beyond the mills? Scientists and savants have been bothered by the water-mills of Argostolion for many centuries, and two British scientists during the nineteenth century got into a very heated argument on the subject. Perhaps there is somewhere a learned paper which has satisfactorily disposed of the mystery, but if so I have not seen it. The guide who showed me the most northerly of the two mills denied that there was any natural explanation. The whole thing, he maintained, was a miraculous act of God, and served to prove that Cephalonia was not only more important but more blessed than Corfu or any of the other islands.

During the British occupation of the Ionian, Cephalonia was consistently the most fractious island. Almost from the very beginning, while the other islands seemed to be quite happy under the new dispensation, the Cephalonians agitated for union with

Greece. In 1848 they revolted unsuccessfully against the British, the revolt being marked by considerable brutality. One of the incidents reported by Viscount Kirkwall describes the murder of a certain Captain Parker of the local garrison who was married to a Greek lady. ". . . Concealed behind the rocks, a small party of men discharged their guns at the captain. He fell wounded at the foot of a tree, the trunk of which is still marked by a cross, constantly renewed by the care of the residents of Cephalonia. His leg had been shot through. His terrified wife fled, and rushed down the hill to save her life; but the murderers took no notice of her, for she was a native of the middle class. They now left their hiding places, and butchered the wounded Englishman as he lay bleeding on the ground. They then escaped and left the corpse. When help came, the captain's little dog was found seated by its master's body, moaning sadly; nor till the latter was carried away could it be moved from the spot. The fidelity of the dog made it famous, and it is said that it did not long survive its master. In the English burial ground at Cephalonia (where a tomb has been raised to the memory of Captain Parker) the dog is represented as faithfully sitting on, and guarding, its master's final resting place."

As in Levkas, the earthquakes which have afflicted Cephalonia over the centuries have left behind an atmosphere of sadness. It is not only the sight of ruined buildings that produces this feeling of melancholy—for nearly all of the Ionian islands have suffered both in the past and recently—but the atmosphere of Cephalonia is quite different from that of Ithaca.

Such judgments, of course, are subject to a purely personal bias, my only visits to Cephalonia having been accompanied by high humidity and heavy thunderstorms. Standing up fronting the Ionian, the island is probably more subject to eastward-moving depressions than the others. Certainly the high peak of Mount Elato or Ainos, some 5,000 feet above the sea, catches whatever rain clouds are in the area. This fact will also account for the flowers, fruit and shrubs of the island, which are among its greatest beauties. Not oleander alone—to be found almost everywhere

58

in Greece—but in Cephalonia, scented shrubs and flowers riot
in the gardens, arbutus, thyme and lentisk cling round the pathways, and few other islands can match its almonds, carob trees
and vines.

There was "no winter," wrote Edward Lear who was touring
the Ionian Islands in 1863, "but *en revanche* 43 small earthquakes."
It was in the same year that another English visitor wrote: "A
slight earthquake on the 25th of March was the last I was destined
to experience in Cephalonia. . . . During the fourteen months I
had been on the island, I had recorded twenty-six days on which
earthquakes took place. But as on some occasions two and even
three shocks occurred in the same twenty-four hours, there is
little doubt that I may reckon at nearly fifty the total amount of
the earthquakes which I experienced." Edward Lear, despite
what he called "his natural timidity," returned again and again
to the Ionian islands. His water-colours and lithographs are perhaps the best portrayals of them that have ever been made. Lear
caught—as no photographer ever can—the bones and structure
of the islands. The camera emphasises the surface, so that the
rich valleys of Cephalonia look lush, and the orange groves of
Corfu, overripe. Lear's work, on the other hand, comes far
nearer to the truth of the islands. His *Views in the Seven Ionian
Islands* was published in 1863. The modern traveller who pro-
poses to visit them can gain a good foretaste of the pleasure in
store from the work of this Victorian artist. Lear's fame as a
humorist has unfortunately eclipsed his very real achievements
as a draughtsman and water-colourist.

Levkas in the north, Cephalonia and Ithaca in the centre, and
Zante to the south, form a crescent moon of islands sheltering the
entrance to the Gulf of Patras. Zante has now readopted its
ancient name Zakintos (Zacynthus). This probably derived from
an ancient Greek word for "a hill." Cynthia was the goddess of
hills, and a number of mountains in Greece bear the suffix
-cynthus or -kintos. The capital which bears the island's name
lies on the south-east facing towards the Peloponnese. It is easy to
reach, either by boat from Katakolo on the mainland opposite or

from Patras. Zante is also linked with the other Ionian islands by regular steamer services.

Twenty-five miles long by twelve wide, Zante is as fertile as Corfu and has a scenic beauty without rival. Tragically, a great deal of its architectural attractions have gone. The earthquake of 1953 affected Zante more than anywhere else in the Ionian, causing great loss of life and laying waste many of the old houses which formerly lent a Venetian air to the city and the port. Only one small hotel was available for visitors who like some semblance of comfort when I visited the island, although at least two tavernas had rooms adequate for those with Spartan tastes. The Tourist Board, I was told, intended to build a comfortable new hotel here within the next year.

The town is in a lovely situation, lying around the gentle crescent of the bay, with Mount Skopos (The Viewpoint) just to the south, capped by the convent of Panayia Skopotissa. A smaller hill to the north protects the other end of the town and harbour, and on top of it the Venetians built their citadel, remains of which can still be seen. Despite the changes wrought by the earthquakes of 1893 and 1953, the town and, indeed, in a way all Zante, still has a Venetian aura. The English seem to have left little here during their occupation, except an interest in the currant trade, and even this has declined in recent years. But the arcades, the names above shops, and many of the words in the local dialect recall the great days of Venice, when Zante was known as "The Flower of the Levant."

The island in many ways still deserves this sobriquet. Stand on Mount Skopos—easily reached from the town—and see how the island falls away from the silver limestone crags into long fat folds of vines, with the gold of cornfields breaking the overwhelming pattern of green—olives, figs, vines and orange and lemon groves. Here, as in so many places where volcanoes or earthquakes threaten man's life, it is easy to understand why—far from fleeing the dangers—the inhabitants return again and again to the same houses and valleys. Here, as on the slopes of

Vesuvius and Aetna, the volcanic soil is so rich that "drop but a seed, tread it under foot, and it will grow."

Zante's history follows much the same pattern as its neighbours. In Homeric times "wooded Zacynthus" formed part of the kingdom of Ulysses, and Mount Skopos was almost certainly the ancient Elatus, "the mountain of silver firs." But the firs have gone, most probably used for shipbuilding, many centuries since. Commanding the strait between the mainland and the island as well as the strait south of Cephalonia that leads to Patras, it is not surprising that Zante was of foremost importance to whatever power sought maritime supremacy in these waters. In 455 BC, Athens brought the island into her confederacy, and 25 years later the Spartans unsuccessfully attempted to capture it. Philip of Macedon, before marching through Acharnania into Aetolia, made sure of his left, and seaward, flank by annexing Zante. Its subsequent history was similar to the other islands, becoming first a port and part of the Roman empire, and then falling prey to whatever invaders were moving southwards into the Peloponnese. Vandals, Saracens, Normans, Venetians, French, Russians and, finally, the British have at one time or another hoisted their standards over the island.

Zante's achievements in the world of art and letters came in the late eighteenth century, when the island became for a time "a nest of singing birds." It was in Corfu, on the 8th May, 1798, that the first publication was issued from the first printing office ever established in Greece, but it was in Zante that the poet Ugo Foscolo (1778-1827) was born. Another Zantiote poet was Andreas Kalvos, a friend of Ugo Foscolo. In Zante, too, was born the greatest of all modern Greek poets, Dionysios Solomos (1798-1857). Solomos almost certainly took his Christian name from the local Zantiote Saint, Dionysios, whose church in the town is decorated with paintings by another Zantiote artist, the painter, Kutusi, who was a pupil of Tiepolo.

The son of one of the Hellenised Venetian aristocratic families, Solomos went to Italy for his education, returning to Zante when he was twenty. His early poems were written in Italian and

61

apart from an ear for metre, showed little indication of his future genius. It was only after his return to Zante that Solomos, at first diffidently and then with growing confidence, began to write in demotic Greek. It was an immense and courageous step to take, for demotic Greek was then considered in the polite circles of Zante rather as English was in the court of our Norman kings. Greek was the working-class language, and no one had thought before of using it to convey the finer shades of emotion or sentiment. Solomos, like his friends and relations, had been brought up on Italian poetry and the influence of Dante remained strong with him all his life. A later influence was Lord Byron, to whom Solomos addressed a fine ode, but it was the legends and the spirit of his native Greece that gave him his real strength. By trial and error he evolved the first great poems in the Greek demotic language, a feat which in its way curiously paralleled Dante's own achievement. "He found a dialect and left a language." In one way or another everything in Greece's subsequent literature stems from this Zantiote poet. His *Ode to Liberty* was subsequently adopted as the Greek National Anthem. His greatest poem, though incomplete, was probably his *The Free Besieged*, an epic dedicated to the defenders of Missolonghi. Like Shelley, whom in some respects he resembles more nearly than Byron, Solomos was a philosopher as well as a poet. If sometimes the philosophy tends to over-ballast the poetry, his work is always redeemed by his tender feeling for the predicament of human beings, and by the passages of natural description in which the Ionian and her islands suddenly flower out of the printed page. In one poem, a mother weeps in the graveyard beside the tomb of her dead children: "But then, all of a sudden, a cool breeze stirs. It comes whispering to her, and it is heavy with the scents of the dawn." Or, again, he describes the "Cretan nightingale beside his nest, high on the desolate rocks, showering over the distant plain and sea his music all night long. The stars fade and the breaking dawn, in wonder, lets fall the roses from her hand. . . ."

However much has been destroyed in terms of architecture, the countryside of Zante remains as it has always been—lanes dominated by cypresses, narrow lanes whose hedges are formed by pomegranates, smilax and quince. One of the loveliest views is from **Yerakari,** about six miles north of the town, where a white-washed church shines like icing-sugar against the violet hills to the north and the deep blue Ionian along the fertile eastern coast. The western side of the island, on the other hand, is mostly precipitous cliffs. These shelter the island's central plains against the winter surge of the Ionian.

Like Cephalonia, Zante has its natural wonder, the famous pitch wells which were first recorded by Herodotus. They lie in **Keri** at the southern end of the island and are approached through a shady wood. Unlike the famous pitch lake of Trinidad —a somewhat frightening spectacle—the pitch wells of Zante are in accord with the island's elegiac mood. The pitch rises to the surface through small pools of water, being skimmed off when the tarry concentration is thick enough. It is curious to reflect that the pitch still serves the same purpose as it did when Herodotus came here:—it is used for caulking and anti-fouling the local fishing boats and trading vessels.

Zante has the best fruit in the Ionian after Corfu, or—not to exacerbate local rivalries—every bit as good, while the local red (unresinated) wine is very drinkable. It was while I was drinking a glass of it that a Zantiote introduced me to another minor wonder of the islands. Being no philatelist, I cared little for the serrated blobs of paper he showed me, but others who see beauty in stamps may like to pursue their quest while in this part of the world. The stamp I was shown was one of a set of three, issued by the British during their occupation of the islands. It showed the head of Queen Victoria framed inside the Order of the Garter, on which was printed IONIKON KRATOS. My acquaintance was very excited about it, since the stamp had been used— rarer, therefore, and more valuable than the unused, of which he assured me he had several. At any rate, here in Zante was one proof that the British had once owned "The Flower of the Levant."

CHAPTER 5

Salamis, Aegina, Euboea

In the last week of September, 480 BC, there occurred one of those momentous battles by which the history of the world is changed. To the men who fought in it, it did indeed seem that their world was at stake. But they could have had no inkling that the result of it would determine the course of European civilisation. Salamis, like the destruction of the Spanish Armada or the Battle of Trafalgar, was a sea battle which determined for centuries the pattern of life to be lived upon the land.

If one has time to visit the bare island of **Salamis**, so much the better, but it is the Bay of Salamis which one must see. From **Piraeus**, either by bus or car, it is only about two miles to the Devil's Tower, an old Venetian watch-tower on the headland overlooking the Bay between the mainland of Attica and Salamis. Here, so legend has it, is the place where Xerxes sat on his throne of gold, to watch the battle that was to make him master of Greece. A little east of Salamis lies the islet of Psittalia which completes the circlet of water in which the battle was fought. It was here, in this narrow strip of water, that the complacency of Xerxes was destroyed, and the last despairing effort of the Greeks was justified. To show how apparently hopeless was the Greek position at this moment I quote from Professor H. D. F. Kitto in *The Greeks:* "The northern Greeks had all submitted and were fighting now with Persia: Attica was lost, no one was left but the Peloponnesians, a few islands, and Athens. The Peloponnesian land forces were at the Isthmus, busy fortifying it, and, of their sea-captains, most were in favour of moving the allied fleet back

64

there from Salamis. .... Themistocles saw that the narrow waters inside Salamis would give the Greek fleet a chance of victory, while at the Isthmus they would certainly be defeated—even if the fleet held together, which was unlikely."

The story of the battle is told by Herodotus, and by Aeschylus in *The Persians*. The exact details of the day's manoeuvres still

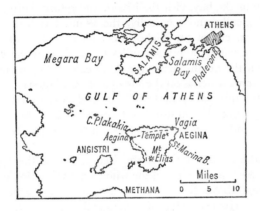

provide a debating ground for scholars and historians. But, basically, everything revolved around the inability of the vastly superior Persian fleet to manoeuvre in such constricted waters, waters which were known to the Greeks as only seamen and fishermen can know a stretch of sea on which they have been born and bred. The fleet of Xerxes numbered over a thousand vessels, and that of the Athenians and their allies less than four hundred. The heavier but slower Greek ships used the coast of Salamis like an anchor on which they slowly turned, presenting an impregnable front to their enemies. They shattered the Persians and drove them in their hundreds on to the rocky and inhospitable cliffs at the feet of Xerxes. "And when the sun set where were they?"—Only 300 Persian ships, it has been estimated, managed to reach **Phaleron Bay** in safety. With the winter coming on, and with the fleet that guarded his supply lines destroyed, there was nothing left for Xerxes but flight. Even the throne upon

65

which he had sat to watch his certain victory—surrounded by secretaries ready to note down the names of courageous Persians for future honours and rewards—was abandoned. It was later dedicated by the victors in the Acropolis.

Salamis is easily reached by boat either from Megara or Piraeus, and there are a number of excursions which start from Piraeus, tour the bay, visit the island, and return within the day. Archaeologically and scenically, the island has little to show. The old convent of St. Nicholas occupies a pleasant site in a small fertile valley, about six miles by road from the village of Salamis on the north, facing the Attic coast. The monastery of **Faneromeni,** which is on the site of a classical quarry, is situated in an attractive valley and has a lavishly decorated church— something somewhat unusual in Greece. It has also a fresco of "The Last Judgment" by the eighteenth-century painter, Mark of Argos.

From the southern tip of the island, where the lighthouse stands, there is a fine view of the whole bay, with Mount Hymettus shining above the smoke of Athens, and Aegina brilliant across the narrow stretch of water some five miles to the south.

It is only fifteen miles from Piraeus to **Aegina** and there are a number of boat services every day in summer. The ships for Aegina, Poros and the other islands adjacent to the Gulf of Athens, leave from the clock-tower on the waterfront. There is usually one departure between 7.30 and 8 a.m. for Aegina which enables one to return in the same day. If it were only for the view of Attica, Salamis and its bay, Aegina and the blue Saronic gulf, it would be worth making the crossing. Unfortunately, boats bound for Aegina town and harbour go round the western side, the least attractive sea-approach to the island. Those who intend to stay in the island and have time to spare, should try and hire a boat out of Aegina to make a circumnavigation, for the eastern side of the island is romantically beautiful. Santa Marina bay in the north-east corner is ideal for swimming and underwater fishing, with a view of the great temple of Aphaia standing in its crown of pine trees.

Approaching Aegina from Piraeus, one rounds the long sandy spit of Cape Plakakia and sees over the boat's bows, a little to the south, all that remains of the temple of Aphrodite:

> *A marble shaft that stands alone*
> *Above a wreck of sculptured stone*
> *With grey-green aloes overgrown.*

> (RENNELL RODD)

Now the town stands up and shines white against the land, with the blue cupola of St. Nicholas's church looking like a bubble of sea that has strayed on to the shore. South, and a little to the right, is Methana, humped against the land like a huge stranded whale. The straits between Aegina, Angistri, Methana, and Poros are usually flickering with the white sails of yachts and fishing boats.

Like their ancestors, the modern Aeginetans are hardy sailors, sponge-divers, fishermen, and coastal traders. It is nothing to see a small open boat shrugging her way to windward under patched sails made of American flour-bags, while an asthmatic small diesel engine bangs away under the feet of a dozen or more passengers. If the visitor has not realised it before, it will soon become clear how true it is that the Greeks are a race of seamen. In the rest of the Mediterranean it is rare to see women or children anywhere in a boat—the Latin races deeming the sea a strictly masculine world. In Greece, on the other hand, one sees women and children far out between the islands, in boats with perilously little freeboard, sitting in a muddle of crates, pottery jars and chickens in cages. Often a bearded priest is with them, making his way from one island to another and completing, as it were, the picture of a whole human community afloat.

The Aeginetans are also, as in the past, fine potters and modellers. Among the first things that will be offered the visitor —even before he has stepped ashore—will be wine and water jugs. Small boats circle the steamer the moment it appears, and out of them sprout hands waving the local wares. Only too many of these pots and jugs are crudely and unattractively painted—in theory, to make them more acceptable to tourists. Ask when

67

ashore in the first café or taverna for a plain simple jug like the one they themselves have on the bar. . . . These, like the water jugs to be found all over the eastern Mediterranean, are of porous, unfired clay. The water sweats through the sides to form a barrier of coolness against the heat of summer. I have used one myself for over a year and always had cool water to drink.

The small town of Aegina is on the same site as the classical city, its position determined by the fact that this flat and fertile land on the west coast is sheltered from the northerly winds. The moles forming the harbour are built on a bank of shoal, at the end of one of them a small whitewashed chapel seeming almost to stand in the sea. The most imposing building is the cathedral of St. Nicholas, appropriately enough in this seamen's island, since Nicholas is the sailor's patron saint. Whereas St. Nicholas seems to have taken over the mantle of Poseidon in the Aegean sea, in the Ionian—possibly due to Latin influence—it is the Madonna who looks after sailors. (Throughout Sicily and ancient Magna Graecia the offices of Venus or Aphrodite— always the sailor's goddess—have also been assumed by the Virgin.)

The town of Aegina has little to detain one except the museum, also good sea-food at the Miranda restaurant. There is one hotel, a rather crowded beach, and several reasonable tavernas. The museum is rich in specimens of ancient Aeginetan pottery, as well as bronzes and marbles which have come from the temple of Aphaia. Only a short walk to the north of the town lies the temple of Aphrodite, but no more than one column (without its capital) remains from this great Doric building. Built in tufa, it would in any case have only survived in a very imperfect state, but its ruin was hastened by Capo d'Istria, President of Greece, who had most of the stone used in building new quays at the time when Aegina was the seat of the Greek government.

Perhaps it is not illogical to take Aegina's history backwards, for the comparatively unimportant town which now confronts one has more connection with the first days of the new Greece than it does with that great Aegina which strove with Athens for

68

maritime supremacy, and which Pericles called a "speck in the eye of Piraeus." In 1826, the Council of the Greeks established their new centre of government in Aegina and for a brief two years the island regained something of its vanished splendour, becoming both the capital of Greece and the main commercial centre. Inevitably, it was soon dispossessed by its ancient enemy, Athens.

It was from Aegina that, on 30th November, 1827, the President of the Council wrote to the Admirals of the Allied powers, France, Great Britain and Russia, congratulating them on their success at Navarino—when the Turks lost two-thirds of their fleet and 6,000 men, in action against the coalition fleet under Admiral Codrington. Navarino more than any other action made Greece a free country, and it was not surprising that her new government should be fulsome in its praise. ". . . The Greek nation has seen with delight the triumphs which the naval forces of the three Allied Powers have gained over the enemies of Christianity and civilisation, and all Greece has re-echoed with acclamations which have been justly attributed to the ability and prudence of the accomplishers of this great enterprise. . . ."

Unfortunately, the allied Admirals were feeling far from well-disposed towards the Greek government. Pirates out of the Aegean—freebooters from Hydra, Spetsai, Aegina and other islands—had chosen the confusion of war as an admirable moment for recouping their own fortunes. It mattered little to them whether it was a Turk, a French or an English merchantman that they seized. It was for this reason that the allied Admirals had just been firmly remonstrating with the Greek government, and Capo d'Istria's letter continued, ". . . In proportion to this feeling of gratitude so strongly imprinted on the heart of every Greek, is the severe and profound regret occasioned by the receipt of your letter of 24th October; as by that letter the legislative body learnt how much you were displeased by the conduct of some 'cruisers'."

The allied letter which had secured this reply from the Council at Aegina is interesting since it shows how the old habit of piracy in the Aegean died hard. " Gentlemen—" wrote Admiral Codrington, "We learn with lively feelings of indignation that, while the ships of the Allied Powers have destroyed the Turkish fleet, which had refused submitting to an armistice *de facto*, the Greek cruisers continue to infect the seas. . . . Your Provisional Government appears to think that the chiefs of the allied squadrons are not agreed on the measures to be adopted for putting a stop to this system of lawless plunder. It deceives itself. We here declare to you with one voice that we will not suffer your seeking, under false pretexts, to enlarge the theatre of war, that is to say, the circle of piracies.

" We will not suffer any expedition, any cruise, any blockade to be made by the Greeks, beyond the limits of from Volo to Lepanto, including Salamis, Aegina, Hydra and Spezzia. . . . The armistice by sea exists on the part of the Turks *de facto*. Their fleet exists no more. Take care of yours, for we will also destroy it, if need be, to put a stop to a system of robbery on the high seas, which would end in your exclusion from the law of nations."

If this old correspondence deserves bringing to light, it is only because so much sentiment—and sentimentality—has been evoked by the Greek War of Independence. It is worth bearing in mind that there was another side to the relations between the allies and the Greeks. It was a side of life which Byron in the months before his death had grown to know only too well. No sooner had a success been achieved, than the Greeks fell out amongst themselves or—being individuals in a nation of individuals—each man hastened to ensure something for himself and family. They were aware, as Greeks have always been, that governments never fail to look after themselves, and that it is up to the individual to do likewise.

Aegina, incidentally, was one of the first places over which the Greek national flag was formally hoisted. It was different to the modern flag, being red and gold in colour. The flag that we know to-day owes its origin, it is said, to the white kilts of the Evzones and the blue breeches of the sailors. If this is so, then

England may be said to have played a further part in Greek history, for the first blue uniforms seen in the Aegean belonged to British sailors.

Prior to its brief moment of importance in modern history, Aegina had been remarkable for the great length of time it had remained a Venetian possession. It was, in fact, one of the last Venetian strongholds in the Levant, not being ceded to the Turks until 1718, at the Treaty of Passarowitz.

The ancient capital, **Palaiochora,** lies due east from Aegina, almost in the centre of the island. Like the medieval capitals of so many Aegean islands, it is a witness to the long centuries of piracy and anarchy when to live on, or near, the coast invited disaster. To-day it is a ghost town, coming to life only at the Festival of All Saints. The remains of chapels, monasteries and private houses, by far outnumbering the inhabited cottages of the modern peasants, are a legacy from the Venetian centuries. The island suffered its greatest disaster during this period when the famous corsair, Khair-ed-Din, known to the West as Barbarossa, landed on the coast in 1537, stormed the defences, and carried off most of the inhabitants into slavery.

Largely due to its position commanding the Athenian, or Saronic Gulf, Aegina's history has been more violent than any of the other islands in the vicinity of Attica. Romans, Aetolians, and Macedonians, all in their turn were quick to appreciate the importance of Aegina, and to seize the island as a base for a further extension of their power. How often, contemplating the wrecks and ruins of civilisations scattered over the Greek islands, one is reminded "Happy is the country that has no history!" Here, where the relics of ancient cultures are scattered like toys in the nursery, a sense of *taedium vitae* seems to rise like an almost palpable breath against the hot shimmer of the land.

In classical history, Aegina was the sea-power which rivalled Athens. Until the Athenians had secured either the friendship or the destruction of Aegina, they had no security for their own sea-routes. The struggle between the two seafaring powers was long and bitter, broken only by a truce during the Persian wars when Aegina joined with Athens to defeat their mutual enemy at sea, supplying thirty ships for the Battle of Salamis. In 458 BC Athens succeeded in inflicting a major defeat on her rival in two naval battles, in the course of which the Aeginetan fleet and those of its allies, Corinth and Epidaurus, were smashed. Athens proceeded to besiege the island and Aegina surrendered three years later. Its defences were razed, its ships handed over to the victors and the islanders became tribute-paying members of the Athenian confederacy. When the Peloponnesian War began, the Athenians, mistrusting the ancient enemy on their doorstep, expelled all the native Aeginetans, replacing them with Athenian colonists. Nearly thirty years later Lysander of Sparta, in recognition of the help Aeginetans had given Sparta during the war, restored them to their home.

Long before the classical period, Aegina had been a prosperous settlement of the Dorians. Before that again, it had been part of the Mycenaean sea empire. The island was first called Oenone, perhaps in reference to the wine made there. (If it was, or still is good, then I have been unfortunate—having filled a small cask here with some of the most unpalatable retsina in the Aegean.) There was a fountain nymph, called Oenone, daughter of the river Oeneus, who was the mistress of Paris before he rashly ran off with Helen. Oenone, who later committed suicide, has been identified with the goddess of wine. The current and classical name, Aegina, comes from one of Zeus's many mistresses, a daughter of the river god Asopus. Zeus stole her from her father, and conveyed her to the island where he lay with her in the form of an eagle. Aegina had a son by Zeus called Aeacus, who founded the island's fortunes and became famous for his wisdom. On one occasion, when the whole of Greece was dying from drought, Aeacus ascended Mount Panhellenius (Mount Elias) and implored his father to send them rain. Zeus complied, and Aeacus dedicated an altar to his father on the high peak, most probably somewhere near the modern chapel of Elias. A cloud has ever since settled on the peak of Mount Elias whenever rain is to be expected. It is quite true that, whenever the mountain pulls on his night-cap, one can confidently expect rain in the gulf and on the southern shores of Attica.

There are two ways of reaching the great temple of Aegina, either by boat to the bay of **Santa Marina** (with a stiff climb or a mule ride at the other end), or direct by car from the port. The temple, built in limestone, is wonderfully sited on the crest of a woody hill, with one of the finest views in Greece. From this north-eastern corner of the island one looks right across the gulf towards Athens and Piraeus. On a clear July day I have seen the Parthenon quite sharp against the dark sides of Lycabettus, while all the sea below me was traced with the snails' tracks of ships and sailing boats.

For a long time the temple was identified with the goddess Athena, but discoveries made in the past forty years have shown without a doubt that it was dedicated to the goddess Artemis Aphaia. It was as "Aphaia," the "not dark" that she was worshipped by the Aeginetans, this being the opposite aspect of the moon-goddess to Hecate, the "all-dark." Artemis Aphaia has been connected with the Cretan moon-goddess Dictynna, and it seems more than likely that she was the principal diety of the inhabitants of Aegina before the Dorian invasion.

Whatever the facts, it would be hard to find anywhere more inspiring as a temple site for a moon-goddess than this hill with the sea on both sides, set in an atmosphere scoured by the Etesian winds. (Modern man might choose it as the site for an observatory.) Over twenty Doric columns still remain, as well as part of the architrave. The whole temple was built on an artificial terrace which itself overlay the foundations of an earlier building. It was in this sixth-century layer that the inscription was discovered which linked the temple with Artemis Aphaia.

Special tours are sometimes arranged from Athens to visit the temple alone. Boats leave from Piraeus and sail direct to Vagia, about a mile and a half to the north of the site.

One can reach **Euboea** by car, train or boat. The largest island in the archipelago, it is ninety miles long and from thirty miles to a minimum of four miles wide. Technically there is no

73

doubt about Euboea being an island, yet somehow so near is it to the mainland, and so similar climatically and geologically that it bears little relation to the other islands of the Aegean. At its narrowest point, Euripo, opposite the town of **Khalkis,** the passage between Euboea and Attica is only 130 feet wide, and is spanned by a swing bridge. The Euripus, the southern end of the channel leading into the Gulf of Petali, is rightly named the "swift current," for the tidal streams can attain 7 or 8 knots, and even more after a period of bad weather. Since there is only a period of slack water lasting about ten minutes between the north-going and the south-going currents, and since these currents alternate as much as seven times a day, the passage of the Euripus is difficult even for steamships. Small boats and yachts are certainly advised to try and get a tow through the narrows.

It was in the **Bay of Aulis,** just south of the narrows beween modern **Vathi** and the Turkish fort of Karababa, that the Greek fleet bound for the siege of Troy was forced to wait for a favourable wind and tide. A north-easterly gale continued to blow, until Agamemnon's daughter Iphigenia, lured from Mycenae on the pretext of marriage to Achilles, offered herself as a sacrifice to Artemis. The site of this tragic act which precipitated the doom of the House of Atreus is reputedly the small whitewashed chapel to St. Nicholas on the west side of the bay.

"It was the policy of Boeotia," wrote Christopher Wordsworth, "contrived with more than Boeotian shrewdness, to make Euboea an island to everyone else but themselves. . . . They locked the doors of Athenian commerce, and kept themselves the key. This was the channel by which the gold of Thasus, the horses of Thessaly, the timber of Macedonia, the corn of Thrace, were carried to the Piraeus. Nor must we forget the importance of Euboea itself, which, from its position and its produce, its quarries, its timber, and its corn, was of inestimable value to Athens. The bridge was built over the Euripus by the Boeotians, 410 BC, and from that time the communication of Athens with the northern markets was either dependent on the fear or amity of Boeotia, or it was exposed to the dangers of the open sea. . . ."

This no doubt is the reason why the word "Boeotian" has come down to us through Athenian literature with such unattractive overtones. The fact remains that "Boeotian" should not be synonymous with peasant-like stupidity, but with astute cupidity. Like so many people, the Athenians tended to disparage those of whom they were afraid, by pretending that they were less intelligent than themselves.

There are two hotels in Khalkis, but I see no reason why one should linger there unless for the spectacle of the Euripus—better seen in any case from the island, or best of all from a boat. Over the sea-gate of Khalkis, the Lion of St. Mark is a reminder that this city like so many others in the Aegean once formed part of the Venetian empire. Khalkis, like Euboea itself, became important in history after the Fourth Crusade, that most cynical of all so-called "Christian" expeditions to the Holy Land, whereby Venice managed to secure for herself "a half and a quarter of the Roman Empire." Euboea naturally fell within the spoils of the old Eastern Empire and was divided between three Latin adventurers, Venice ultimately becoming mistress of all the profitable commerce of the region. In 1470 the great Sultan, Mohammed II, captured Khalkis, and the island of Euboea became part of the Ottoman Empire. In 1830 it was formally returned to the new Greek State, and in 1899 was thought important enough to be rated as a separate province. Another name for Euboea is Negroponte, The Black Bridge, dating again from the Venetian occupation.

The north of the island is by far the most interesting part. Here the remnants of one of the last great Turkish estates has been maintained by descendants of the Noël family (themselves descendants of the Byrons). It is a good example of what benevolent capitalism can do, if given the chance. (Something similar is to be seen in Sicily in the lands that have descended from Lord Nelson under the aegis of his title Duke of Brontë.) In this part of Euboea one finds sensible re-afforestation, good irrigation schemes, fat and healthy cattle, and a well-conducted agricultural system. Perhaps, one reflects, all that Greece needs is no more than capital to return it to those pleasant days when the whole of this area seemed an Eden.

The attraction of Euboea lies not in its history, nor in its architectural beauties (which are few) so much as in its scenery. The best of this is to be found along the western coast, where Euboea swirls away from the mainland, and where the mountains overhang the ten-mile wide Talanta channel. Despite its proximity to Athens, and despite the ease with which it can be reached, Euboea remains curiously lonely and remote. It is only just an island. But it is likely to remain, for a long time, one of the most unspoiled places in the Eastern Mediterranean.

CHAPTER 6

Poros

As the traveller begins to venture farther out into the Aegean, one thing he must be prepared for is the monotony of the food and, in many places, its poor quality. Those who travel in the comfort of cruise liners will not be faced with this problem, it is the traveller by island steamer or caique who must acquire a Spartan approach to food and comfort. Fortunately, however, much increased tourism may have changed the islands, it has certainly led to the building of a number of good hotels and an improvement in the cooking. There is a monotony about kid and goat, cucumbers, harsh olive oil, octopus and watery fish-soups, as the Aegean traveller soon finds out. But fortunately again, there is a quality about the Aegean air that may well have inspired the legend of the salamander—you can almost feed off it. In the islands, one's appetite becomes juvenile and undiscriminating.

Nowadays, with more and more people travelling by chartered yacht, the problems of feeding ashore in the remoter islands are simply solved—by staying aboard. Those who travel in their own boats, however, are well-advised to make sure that they are well-stocked and stored before leaving for the islands—and better still if they can store ship before reaching Greece. On a recent visit I left Malta with three months' stores of everything except fresh meat, vegetables, bread and wine on board. Coffee, tea, sugar— all such basic items should be remembered, for they are expensive in most parts of Greece and unobtainable in many small ports and anchorages. They have more value than currency. In many of the remoter places—Seriphos, Siphnos and Sikinos, to mention but three of the Cyclades—I found that barter was the best means of trade. "My coffee for your goats' cheese (often very good), "My corned beef for your cucumbers, eggs or melons . . ." and so on.

All manufactured goods are in short supply in the islands. Fortunately one needs little in the way of clothes for there is no reason to dress up, but swimmers, underwater fishermen and "schnorkellers" should take all the gear they are likely to need, and not expect that it will be easy to get replacements. While travelling around the islands, I myself gave up shaving. Those who like to maintain a smooth appearance would do well to remember that safety razor blades are very expensive in Greece, and often unobtainable. On the other hand, the village barber's shop, as in most parts of the Mediterranean, is a prime source of conversation and local gossip only to be equalled by the café or taverna.

This brings one to the question always complementary to food —drink. Water I have drunk in many islands—out of bucket, well, spring, and even tap—and never suffered any ill-effects. I must admit, though, that when travelling in the Eastern Mediterranean I have always had typhoid and T.A.B. injections, as well as fresh vaccination, a few months before going there. They are probably unnecessary; on the other hand they may, for all I know, have served their purpose.

Water, as the Aegean traveller soon discovers, becomes something of a fetish in thirsty and rugged islands. The cool glass of water that accompanies coffee, food or wine, symbolic in a way it can never be in rainy northern lands, is vital in the Aegean. I have known islanders with palates so fine that they could distinguish between different springs or wells. Water can also be a disputatious subject. In Syra a caique skipper almost came to blows with one from Santorin over the question of whose island had the best water. The Santorin man had the last word: "We may have little water and it may be what you say—but we don't need to drink it. We have the best wine in the islands!"

His boast was not far from true, the red wine of Santorin is excellent. In most places, though, the drinker will have to make do with retsina. Retsina, the Greek resinated wine, comes in many guises. The worst I have ever drunk was in Missolonghi. (I think it may well, especially if he was drinking it instead of his favourite Hock, have contributed to Byron's death.)

It is still something of a point of dispute between oenologists as to when the Greeks began resinating their wine, or whether they always did so. For those not familiar with retsina, the best principle is to dismiss all memory of "wines" as one has known them in the past. Retsina may be considered a different drink, and a very good one it can be. With a little water added, it is a good thirst-quencher on a hot day. Michael Yannis, a caique skipper met in Milo, a great wine-bibber and a carrier of retsina between island and island, gave me the following notes based on his experience. "To test if a retsina is good—pour a little in your glass, place your hand over the top and shake it. A good retsina will retain its characteristic wine-and-pine smell. A bad retsina will smell like vinegar after this treatment. Most retsina does not keep and must be drunk the same year, but some is good up to seven years old." The wine which we were drinking at that time came from the island, had been trodden out in the old way by foot, and the wine with resin added had been forty-five days in cask before it was ready for drinking. Retsina does not travel unless it has been sealed off from the air. This is done by pouring a little olive oil on the top, just filling up the neck of the bottle. I have done this myself with retsina in a demi-john, and found that it kept all right. The olive oil is removed quite easily by sucking it out through a straw, but once this seal has gone the wine will not travel.

After water and wine comes goats' milk. I prefer to boil it, but have drunk it fresh often enough without any ill-effects. Undulant fever, or Malta fever, which is carried in goats' milk, is an unpleasant complaint and used to be fairly prevalent in the Aegean. I have been assured by the Greek Tourist Board that it has now been stamped out, but I cannot vouch for this. Indeed I doubt if it could be completely eliminated without some form of control over the herds, which certainly does not exist in many islands. Sheep's milk I have never tried, although the cheese can be excellent.

Before we sail south to Methana and Poros one last word on the subject of drink and that concerns *ouzo*. If you like the taste of anis, and if you like Pernod or any of the other absinthe substitutes, then *ouzo* is your drink. It varies greatly from island to island and almost from bottle to bottle, unless you are drinking one of the labelled brands. Like most anis drinks it has a high alcoholic content but the after-effects can be depressing. *Mastika*, which I have drunk in Lemnos among other islands, is made from the mastic shrub berries and falls into much the same calibre as *ouzo*. Both are pleasant enough with a little cold water. An experience many years ago, during the war, reminds me that it is unwise to drink *ouzo* or *mastika* in traditional sailor fashion—neat and in large quantities. The story has it that this type of drink remains in the liver, or maybe it is the kidneys, for some considerable time and is reactivated by further liquid. I can vouch for having seen sailors the worse for the previous night ashore in Crete making for the water tap and, within quarter of an hour, regaining their Dionysiac mood.

" We go south," wrote Flaubert, "beyond the mountains and the great waters, to seek in perfumes the reason of love . . . the stars tremble like eyes, the waterfalls sing like lyres, intoxicating are the opening flowers; among those airs your spirit will grow wings. It is time, the wind is rising, the swallows are awakening, the myrtle leaf has fled away!"

It was from the temple of Aphrodite on the Acropolis that Phaedra, sick with love for Hippolytus, gazed southwards across the sea to Troezen, whither Hippolytus had been exiled. The dark hump of **Methana** just south of Aegina, with the peak of Mount Dariza breaking the sky, falls away into the sea at Cape Skylli. Just visible, on a day when the Meltemi have swept the haze off the sea, lies the gentle curved shape of Poros, half-way between Methana and the cape. Boats leave often, but irregularly for Poros and the Troezenian shore—often, in that there are plenty of them from Piraeus during the summer months, but irregularly in that sailing times seem to depend on such variable factors as whether the cargo has arrived, what arrangements the agent has made with the shipping line, and the state of the master's liver. It is best to inquire either at hotel, travel agency, or in Piraeus itself. A number of the boats call at Aegina first, then Methana and finally Poros. **Vromolimni,** the "Evil-

smelling Harbour" of Methana is rightly named, the pungent sulphur springs being unattractive to the nose, whatever they may do for the human system. Vromolimni is a resort and spa, with a number of hotels, villas and chalets available for rent in summer. A little north on the mainland, lies

the enchanting small harbour of **Epidavro.** Travellers in their own or chartered yachts will find this an excellent place to anchor while making the excursion inland to the Shrine of Asclepius.

Sailing south on a clear day, one has a magnificent view of the whole bay, with Cape Spiri to the north as purple as heather against the Bay of Megara, the small island of Kyra, and Angistri, half-way to Aegina, over whose head fair-weather cumulus clouds are usually grazing. **Poros** comes into sight, the two humps of the island dark-green with lemon groves. Beyond it the mountains recline like a giant sculpture, "The sleeping woman" they call her. Now, the town of Poros sculls itself up towards the sky out of a low breast of hill. A windmill spins on the shore, and the whole southern entrance to the bay flutters with the white sails of the ferry-boats. The wings of their lateens dip and soar like herring gulls over a shoal of fish.

As one sails in through the northern entrance, the extent of the harbour opens up. It is almost landlocked and one of the finest natural anchorages in the Aegean. Across the narrow neck of water at the southern end, the town of Poros sends up its brilliant pink, white, and blue houses like daylight rockets. On the mainland opposite, the village of Galata throws down white steps and dark alleys.

Poros is an island, but only just. Indeed, if one can accept the identification of Poros with the ancient Sphaeria, it was once possible to cross from the mainland by wading. This is far from true to-day, for the strait which gives Poros its name is deep enough for quite large merchantmen. Poros, for a long time, has been a summer resort for Athenians: a miniature Capri of the Aegean, where artists (genuine and otherwise), foreigners, and a leavening of eccentrics play at the not-so-simple life. For the same reason the Poriots, like the inhabitants of all villages which have become popular and internationalised, are not typical of Aegean islanders. It would be surprising if they had not become a little sophisticated. But I have yet to hear a Poriot sailor say—as I once heard from a fisherman in Taormina:—"I go to sea no more, now that the rich northern ladies come here for their holiday ."

There are several hotels, the Averoff and the Manessi among them, which are genuinely comfortable. There are also a number of pensions which, like those in Corfu, vary in degree, price, and quality. In Poros itself there are plenty of cafés, restaurants and bars. At the same time, the town has not become entirely redecorated for its summer trade, and those who like small dark tavernas and comparatively cheap meals can easily find them. Galata, reached in a few minutes by boat across the strait, is simpler and cheaper than Poros but has no hotels at the moment. They are sure to follow in the near future. Visitors who intend to stay in Poros are advised to book hotel accommodation well in advance. In recent years, quite apart from visiting Athenians, Poros has become popular with yachtsmen, while most cruise boats tend to call here at some time or other on their Aegean circuit.

"Across the blue water of the tranquil bay," wrote Frazer in *The Golden Bough*, "which it shelters from the open sea, rises Poseidon's sacred island, its peak veiled in the sombre green of the pines." **Calavria,** the sacred island, is connected to Poros by an isthmus. It is easy to reach by bus, but better to walk, for the path goes through the pine woods whose needly aromatic scent makes walking so pleasurable in Poros. The temple, or the sanctuary, of Poseidon lies on a ridge. It was excavated at the turn of the century, but little enough remains, and it is its situation that is rewarding. On the way there, one has a magnificent view of the mainland opposite, and of the narrow strait busy with life. Finally, from the far end of the high ground, there is a wonderful prospect of the Aegean, shining bright beyond the rich slopes of Poros.

The temple was the meeting place of an early maritime council, a body formed by Aegina, Athens, Epidaurus, Hermione, Nauplia, Orchomenus and Prasiae. It was also an inviolable sanctuary for all refugees and for the victims of shipwreck. It was here that Demosthenes, in flight from Antipater's soldiers, took refuge, trusting that not even the men of Macedon would dare profane so antique and famous a shrine. When Archias came with a troop of soldiers to take him, Demosthenes refused to be inveigled out of the sanctuary until—as Plutarch relates the story—he had had time to write a letter to his friends: ". . . He went into the temple, as though he would have dispatched some letters, put the end of the quill with which he wrote in to his mouth and bit it, as was his habit when he wrote anything. Then he cast his gown over his head, and laid him down." The soldiers now taunted him with cowardice and Archias himself came into the sanctuary and begged him to come out, saying that he would speak for him with Antipater and ensure the latter's friendship. While he was speaking, Demosthenes felt the poison that he had absorbed from the quill beginning to work and staggered to his feet, saying: "O Poseidon, now will I leave thy temple while I am yet alive and not profane it with my death." It was not to be. As he stumbled towards the door, the poison struck him down and he fell dead at the foot of the altar.

Demosthenes was the only outstanding figure whom history records as having been connected with Poros or its dependent

Calavria. Always, one suspects that this island pendent off the ear of Troezen, must have been fertile, favoured by mariners, and attractive to expatriates. It has little or no history, one reason perhaps why the island has such a mellow patina.

The architecture of Poros town itself is undistinguished, but it is not difficult to understand Henry Miller's enthusiasm, expressed in *The Colossus of Maroussi*, on sailing between Poros and Galata. It is not an illusion that one is sailing between houses; friendly faces do overhang the ship; while taverna doors belly forth the scents of retsina, *ouzo*, pine dust and fish. Casks of wine shadow the cool interiors, and along the waterfront where lie the smarter bars and cafés, the tables are clinking with dishes of squid tentacles, olives, chopped cucumber, chipped potatoes, lettuce and cheese.

In the bay of Poros itself, it can be hot and sultry at mid-day. But in the mornings the air is wonderful. As on parts of the Turkish coast, the pines run right down to the water's edge and the clean tang of pine greets you when you wake. I sailed into Poros one night just in advance of a heavy thunderstorm: wind from the north, lightning scissoring a sky that was purple-black like a grape. I dropped anchor in the small cove that lies just on the left, as you come in through the northern entrance. I shall never forget my morning awakening, with the sky rinsed clean by the wind and rain, the scent of pines, the dark varnished green of the lemon groves on the mainland, and the sight of the houses and the clock tower of Poros all shining after the scrubbing that the storm had given them.

The visitor to Poseidon's sanctuary should also make a point of walking down to the monastery about half an hour away. The path runs through the woods and in places becomes completely indistinguishable. It is best to go with a guide, or a friend who knows the way for, although the island is full of people, you are unlikely to meet anyone once off the beaten track. Greeks, in general, hate solitude. Brighton beach on a bank holiday would be perfectly comprehensible to them, and the preference of certain travelling strangers for solitude is usually ascribed to madness, some tricky piece of smuggling or sexual manoeuvre, or just plain drink.

The monastery has little to interest the architectural student but the site is charming, the water from the fountain is cool and good—so too the spoonful of rose jam which one of the monks gave me. The graves of one or two Greek admirals, distinguished in the War of Independence, lie in the courtyard. Poros harbour was an important naval base for the allied fleets during this war, and it was from here that Captain G. W. Hamilton of "His Majesty's Ship *Cambrian*, Poros on 28th January, 1827" wrote indignantly to General Kolokotrones:

"Sir—I inform you as a chief person amongst the representatives of Greece, formed at Castri, that one of the deputies chosen at Hydra has been demanded by me from that island as a pirate, who cruelly half hung an Ionian captain. I have not any doubt you will seize him if he ventures to Castri, and give him up to me." One is never far from memories of piracy in the Aegean and the Levant. For centuries these islands sheltered some of the hardest and most ruthless seamen in history. " But you are going on to Hydra," remarked a Poriot friend to whom I told this story. " Hydra! They're just the same there now as when that letter was written!"

Fortunately, I did not find it so. In fact, in the course of Aegean wanderings I have never lost a thing, finding always the most scrupulous honesty in the poorest of islands. Perhaps I have been lucky, but—if so—why have I been unlucky elsewhere in the Mediterranean, Sicily and Malta for instance?

The visitor to Poros must not leave without crossing to the mainland. An afternoon's sail takes one across to **Vidhi** where the ancient harbour of Troezen juts out from the shore like a fierce, tip-tilted beard. Its ancient name "Pogon" means no more than that, while its modern name Drapani, a sickle, reflects again the Venetian influence in this sea. Drapani is the same word as Trapani, the large port on the west coast of Sicily, and both recall the ancient Greek world where "Drepanon," a sickle, was a mariner's simple term for almost any sheltering peninsula.

The marshy land round Troezen reminded me of Missolonghi, but inland the fertile plain, rich with citrus fruit, stretches in a great swathe along the shore. Somewhere near here Theseus was born, and the unhappy Phaedra landed. It was here in Troezen that Theseus' bastard son Hippolytus raised that temple to Artemis which Aphrodite took as an insult to herself. Somewhere near here, as the newly-quarried stones were laid for Artemis' temple, Aphrodite conceived the plan of making Phaedra fall in love with Hippolytus. Here Phaedra, nursing her incestuous desire, watched the naked Hippolytus running and wrestling, and in frustration stabbed the leaves of a myrtle tree with her jewelled hair-pin so that they became jagged and perforated—as they remain to-day.

The rich plain and the sea off the Troezen shore seem to be unshadowed by these ancient tragedies. There are places, many places in Greece, where the past hangs as heavy as a cloak on one's shoulders. But certainly not in Poros. Coming back at night by car or bus from a mainland expedition, Poros seems to shine across the water like a miniature Paris. There is, maybe, a steamer coming in through the northern entrance and the lights of yachts and fishing boats are mirrored in the harbour. As you walk down through Galata to catch a ferry across, the sound of music comes across the strait. It is cheerful and exciting, a last contact with the world of sophistication—big cities, daily newspapers, and dancing on the twentieth-century volcano. If we sail eastwards across to Seriphos and Siphnos, or farther still to desolate Anaphi, we shall find another world.

CHAPTER 7

Hydra and Spetsai

Hydra is easy to reach, boats leaving Piraeus two or three times daily during summer, and once a day during winter—unless the weather is exceptionally bad. It is only 35 sea miles from Piraeus to Hydra, the length of the journey depending on whether the ship stops at Aegina, Methana or Poros on the way. After leaving Hydra, the ship goes to the port of Hermione on the mainland and then south again to Spetsai.

Unless one is young, or particularly anxious to test one's mental and physical stamina, it is best to travel first-class on Aegean steamers. The Greeks are great travellers, and "the sea unites but the land divides" is very true. Unfortunately, the sea also tends to separate man from the contents of his stomach.

Little can equal the chaos and nausea of an island steamer when the winds have put a good chop on the sea. If it is possible to get a cabin, make sure of doing so, but shipping agents are often unreliable, and cabins become increasingly uncertain if one is joining the steamer somewhere in the middle of her route, say at Poros. Bribery and corruption of stewards in such cases may sometimes pay dividends, and American dollars—if obtainable— can be an open sesame. Personally I prefer the upper deck, however wet and uncomfortable, to the groans and smells of small cabins packed with prostrate humanity. Not that the Aegean is by any means always rough, but there is an unfortunate section of the human race which can manage to be ill even before the ship has cast off her moorings and left harbour. The island traveller must prepare for some discomfort.

87

A barren rock, naked and waterless, **Hydra** lies four miles off the coast of Argolis. Only eleven miles long, with a total area of twenty-one square miles, Hydra has been best described in the epigram of Antonios Kriezes: "The island produces prickly pears in abundance, splendid sea captains and excellent prime ministers." In fact, out of this minute island have come some of the greatest sailors that the Mediterranean has ever bred. Admirals,

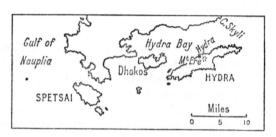

shipbuilders and fighters, their fleets drove the Turks out of the Aegean during the Greek War of Independence and were largely responsible for the ultimate liberation of Greece.

Archaeologically, Hydra has little to offer, for the island was unimportant in the days of Mycenaean or Classical Greece. After Aegina with its classical splendours, and Poros with its indulgent bay and fertile slopes of lemon and olive, Hydra is another world. Seen from the sea, it is a crested hump, bare and austere, disturbing the summer sky like the sharp statement of a caique's sail. The heart of the island is its port and harbour. A noble land-locked basin, sheltered by a mole from the prevailing northerly winds of summer, it is the harbour which has made Hydra famous.

The island first makes its appearance in history as Hydrea, "the well-watered," and so it may have been in classical times, for its position off the coast puts it in the track of any rain-clouds breaking on the mountains of Argolis. But centuries of felling trees without replanting, quite apart from the depredations of the goat, have left Hydra parched and barren. Earthquakes, to which the island is subject, may also have contributed to the drying-up of ancient springs. That it was still richly wooded when the Turks occupied Greece and the islands is borne out by its old Turkish name, *Tchamliza*, "the place of pines." To-day there are no fresh-water springs on the island, which is entirely dependent on the rainfall. In a bad year, water has to be imported by boat from the mainland. " But it is never as good as the water we catch ourselves on the island," a priest from one of the numerous churches remarked, with the true islander's patriotism.

The first thing that strikes one about the town and the harbour is its Italianate air. It is true that the colours everywhere are the Greek colours: white lime-wash and bright blue. It is true, also, that the streets are as clean as Naxos or Santorin, with house-holders busy with buckets of whitewash outside their doorsteps in the early morning. But the houses remember Venice. Their roofs, instead of being flat as in most of the Cyclades, are often gabled and tiled. A campanile fronts on to the harbour. Arched verandas, and square buildings reminiscent of miniature Renaissance *palazzi*, haul themselves up the rocks on either hand. Hydra was once a Venetian port and stronghold, and the Adriatic city has left her impress on this Aegean shore.

The visitor may find himself haunted by the impression that somewhere, somehow or other, he has seen these streets, these shadowed embrasures and dark doorways before. If he is a follower of continental films, he will indeed have come across them in Michael Kakoyannis's *The Woman in Black*, whose location was Hydra and whose tragic story might have been taken from any of the islands where small communities live cut off (except by visiting steamer) from the more liberal responses of the outside world. The painter Ghika at one time made his home on the island, and it is to his work that one should look for the best interpretation of the Greek island scene. Where other painters have given up in despair before the blinding clarity of the Greek light—where a detail on a building a mile away may be as sharp as something in the foreground—Ghika has cut to the roots of the islands. In his work he shows you the bones and the sculptural feel of these houses, shadowed alleys and rocks. "He can make a rock sing—" remarked a Greek critic, adding "—as indeed they do!"

An important event in Hydra's history was an influx of Albanian refugees during the sixteenth and seventeenth centuries. This stream of vigorous highland blood undoubtedly contributed to the island's later triumphs. Albanian, Venetian and native Greek became fused into a strain of indomitable seamen and patriots. The memory of Venice is preserved to this day not only in the architecture of the town, but in Venetian names among the Hydriotes and a few Venetian terms—especially in shipbuilding and sailing. The Albanian influence appears to have been slighter, although some Albanian words are to be found, and the name of the island's highest peak, Mount Ere, comes from the Albanian word for the wind.

The foundation of Hydra's greatness was laid in the eighteenth century, when the reviving commerce of the Peloponnese, coupled with the grain trade with South Russia, provided the Hydriotes with an outlet for their energy and ability. Hydra, once no more than a small port in the Venetian chain of empire, gradually became the dominant maritime power in the Aegean. "From here," as one of them exclaimed, "we ruled the Aegean! From this harbour our *sakturia* swept between island and island. We carried all the trade that passed between Asia and Europe!"

The *sakturia*, a fast and seaworthy small sailing ship of about fifteen tons, was the Hydriotes' great contribution to maritime progress. A memory of them can still be seen in the sailing caiques along Hydra's waterfront (although nowadays these have diesel engines and use their sails only as auxiliaries.) With the expansion of trade, the Hydriotes turned to building a larger type of merchant ship, the *latinadika*, a lateen-rigged vessel of about fifty tons. The Hydriotes now began to trade as far afield as Constantinople in the north, and Alexandria in the south. Soon they were rounding Cape Matapan and carrying the trade of the east to their former mistress, Venice. Trieste was another Adriatic port of call which came into the network of Hydriote trade, and soon Marseilles and the southern ports of France grew to know the hawk-faced, dark-skinned seamen of the Aegean.

Hydra, Spetsai and Psara (off the western coast of Chios) became known as the Three Naval Islands, and it was they who provided a large proportion of the Greek Naval Force during the War of Independence. All three, but Hydra in particular, had grown wealthy during the Royal Navy's blockade of Europe in the Napoleonic Wars. At a time when most of the merchantmen of the Mediterranean were in one way or another involved in the great struggle, the Hydriotes were able to trade with friend and foe alike, enjoying also a benevolent dispensation from the Turks. When Psara was attacked and practically depopulated by the Turks in 1824, Hydra, together with Syra, inherited much of the trade which their fellow Naval Island had previously enjoyed.

By the early nineteenth century, Hydriote trading vessels were carrying the produce and commerce of the east even as far as America. A census of 1813 shows that this small island was then supporting 22,000 people, 10,000 of whom were seafarers. In 1821, when the Greek War of Independence broke out, Hydra had a population of over 28,000. One family alone, the Konduriotti, was estimated as being worth £2,000,000 sterling.

Hydriote fleets and admirals, among them the great Andreas Miaoulis, immediately flung themselves into the struggle against the Turks. It is no exaggeration, as a Greek historian has put it, to say that "the final deliverance of Greece was mainly due to the fleets of Hydra." The island revolted from Turkish rule in April, 1821. From then on, throughout the many vicissitudes of the war and of the civil strife which distracted the Greeks from their main purpose, the seamen and shipbuilders of Hydra were constant in the struggle. After the death of Lord Byron, during the first and second sieges of Missolonghi, it was the Hydriote fleet which managed to keep the town supplied. "Victory," as Lord Wellington remarked of the Greek War of Independence, "must inevitably fall to the side that has command of the sea." This command of the sea was largely supplied by the men of Hydra.

Many of the most famous Greek seamen of this period were either Hydriote born or Hydriote residents. The Tombazes brothers were Hydriotes, and Jakomaki, the elder, was responsible for sinking the first Turkish line-of-battle ship after the War of Independence had broken out. Another brother, Emanual, is said to have been the first Hydriote to open up the trade route between Marseilles and the Black Sea—as a result of which the island's fortune was largely made. Another Hydriote Commander was Saktouris, who may have given his name to the *sakturia*. Saktouris—says one authority—"was rather given to piracy." The fact is that nearly all the Hydriotes were, and, as we have seen, the activities of the Hydriote "cruisers" caused many a headache among the Allied naval commanders. Andreas Miaoulis, greatest of all the Greek leaders and the most worthily respected, came from Euboea, but he too settled at Hydra. He was in command of the fleet in the successful action against the Turks at Chios in 1822. In 1825 he succeeded in relieving the garrison at Missolonghi in the teeth of a much larger Turkish squadron. Miaoulis died in Athens aged 67 in 1835.

To-day the fleets sail no more, and only the wealth of a few Hydriote families and houses remains to remind one of the island's astounding past. The population is half that of a century ago, and the majority live in the town of Hydra itself. There are three other small ports on the northern coast: Mandraki, Panagia, and Molo, but these are no more than fishing villages.

Hydra's wealth, which had depended latterly on the grain trade with South Russia, declined throughout the nineteenth century as the Russians took to building their own ships. It declined even further as the ports of Syra and then Piraeus gradually monopolised the trade of the Aegean. The memories of the island's great past are reflected in its houses and, Hydriotes being passionately patriotic, it is not difficult to secure an introduction to a family who will show you their house and possessions. In one house I dined off Maiolica plates, in a room lit by candles in English eighteenth-century silver holders, with wine served in fine Venetian glasses. Outside the windows, the harbour—from which

all this wealth had evolved—was quiet under the moonlight.
Only a lone caique was coming in, driving down from the north
under engine and staysail. Yet once, as my host reminded me,
the whole harbour and the bay beyond it had been thick with
shipping.

Nearly all the houses of the families who made their wealth
during the first half of the nineteenth century are like miniature
museums. The exterior of the buildings gives little indication of
their contents, for all, at first glance, appear almost identical.
At the Tombazes' house there is now established a branch of the
School of Fine Arts, where artists and students foregather.
Hydra, even more than Poros, has begun to take on the aspect of
something of an artists' colony. When I first sailed here some
thirteen years ago, I met one fisherman with a forgotten remnant
of "Brooklynese," but on my second visit a number of faces
familiar from London, Paris or the glossy pages of magazines
were in evidence among the bars along the waterfront. One
should not complain—for what may bring a moment's displeasure
to a passing traveller (anxious like so many of us to be completely
divorced from the world we have left) has brought a renewed
prosperity to the islanders. Hydra, which had sunk into the sleep
of centuries after its glorious past, has managed to regain something of the liveliness that its former sea-captains brought back.

For the casual visitor, the new tourism has meant an improvement in Hydriote accommodation. There are now half a dozen
hotels, the "Hydra" being in the first category (but not "de
luxe"), the "Hermis" and the "Poseidon" in the second, and the
pleasant, small "Sophia" in the third. Quite apart from hotels,
there are many houses in which the visitor can stay. I would
recommend anyone wanting to spend several weeks in the island
to make inquiries before leaving for Hydra—if possible with
Greek friends in Athens—and to find a private house in which
to stay.

There are many advantages to Hydra's new prosperity, for it
spells greater comfort, improved cooking—something not unimportant in the islands—and a tolerance on the part of the

inhabitants towards the eccentricities of dress which many visitors like to adopt as part of the "holiday mood." Do not expect that, in the less frequented islands, the bikini, or trousers on women, will escape notice. It is quite possible in many coves and bays to bathe naked, but I would not like to escort a bikini-clad or a tight-trousered female into the village of Livadhi in Seriphos —to mention but one small place. The Greek, male or female, has great respect and kindness towards the stranger within his gates and it is up to the stranger to reciprocate.

Apart from the houses of Hydra there is little to see, architecturally speaking. The church and monastery of the Dormition of the Virgin, which dominates the main square, is reckoned to be the oldest church in Hydra. Its date? 1808. That in itself helps to explain why this small fishing port has a unity not to be observed in other Aegean islands. It is almost entirely an eighteenth- and early nineteenth-century creation. Fortunately the Genoese and Venetian influence of an earlier period, coupled with a native skill in stone-masonry, has made Hydra a small jewel. It is an ideal place in which to drop anchor in a yacht. It is an ideal place in which to do little or nothing in the small bars and cafés of the waterfront.

For all these reasons, Hydra is not melancholy. Compared to many of the islands, it is still active in trade, and its fame as a shipbuilding centre has ensured that many a modern caique or inter-island schooner comes from Hydra. It is also a fine base from which to plan a series of expeditions to the other islands. A word at one of the bars or cafés, that you wish to visit such-and such an island, will usually result in an invitation to join a small trading boat that is going there in a few hours—or a few days. I travelled from Hydra to Syra, some 70 miles away, in a local trading schooner. She was about forty-five feet long and I formed part of a passenger-cum-cargo list that comprised one Greek priest, bound for his parish in Syra, one nursing mother, two widows who had been visiting their families, innumerable sacks and baskets, chickens in wooden cages, an old motor-bike, several jars of wine and olives, and a number of miscellaneous crates. Except for the motor-bike, she was a boat that might have sailed out of the *Odyssey*. Her captain, dark-jowled and naked to the waist, could easily have "doubled" for the wily Ulysses himself.

The island does not boast any special local delicacy, but visit the market on the main quay in the early morning. The men of Hydra are fishermen, and the best things in the Hydriote cuisine are fish dishes. In the cool morning light, stalls of red mullet, dappled soles and dabs, sea-green lobsters and the mottled arms of octopus gleam along the jetty. Near them are the vegetable stalls; the small cucumbers grown in the few patches of Hydra's arable soil, Cos lettuces, and plum tomatoes. Crisp piles of freshly baked bread compete with the scent of coffee roasting in the many tavernas along the quay.

For the early riser who is prepared to face a long climb before breakfast, **Mount Ere** or the second highest peak on Hydra, Mount Elias, provides a unique reward. Mount Elias, called after the convent which clings to its peak, was the place where Kolokotrones, the hero of the Greek War of Independence, was imprisoned. A tall pine, under which he is reputed to have sat, bears his name. But neither the convent, nor the pine of Kolo-kotrones, is the main attraction of the mountain. One should reach here early, in time to see the dawn lighten over the Aegean. To the east, Seriphos and Siphnos are just visible, outriders of the circling Cyclades. North lies the headland of Skyli, behind which Poros shelters. To the west the great bay of Hydra, and the attendant island of Dhokos, are shadowed by Mount Elias and Mount Ere. Southwards the sea is barren, all the way to Crete and Africa.

For bathers and underwater fishermen Hydra has plenty to offer. There is the small anchorage of Kamini a little to the west of the harbour, with a good bathing beach, and the fishing village of Vlychos not far beyond it. A tour round the island by *benzina* or caique is well worth making.

Sailors in their own craft should pay attention to the brief note in the *Admiralty Pilot* for this area: "During strong north-easterly winds, the high land causes heavy squalls from all directions in Stenón Ídhras. . . ." Stenón Ídhras is the strait between Hydra and the westward-lying island of Dhokos, and in this narrow stretch of sea one can run into some typical island squalls. The small areas of warm land rising out of the sea are their breeding ground: the mountains and valleys providing the springboard from which they are launched. Aegean seamen define them as "white squalls" and "black squalls". Those that run on dark feet, their passage marked by a blackening of the water, are not so dangerous as the white squalls which tear the whole sea into acid-bright splinters of foam. Torn sails, broken masts and disaster follow in their wake, unless the helmsman has his wits about him.

Hydra is to-day—as it was in its past—a place from which to make a departure, and a place to which one is glad to return. The very fact that it has grown a little sophisticated can make one eager to leave. Equally, after days, weeks or months in more remote islands, one can dream of it as of a miniature metropolis.

The narrow alleys, the houses pristine as snow, the shadowed coolness of the waterfront tavernas, and the sight of the fishing boats and coastal traders gliding in and out of the historic harbour, these stay in the memory long after other, and more famous, delights have faded. At night, when the lights begin to twinkle along the rocky shore, Hydra looks like a ship. The island slants into the sky—a sail alert for the first breath of wind. As the captain of the caique that took me to Syra boasted: "Wherever there is an ocean you will find a man from Hydra!"

One of the reasons for sailing to **Spetsai** is that it is a communications link. From here one can get to Nauplia—for Argos and Mycenae—or south again to Monemvasia. Spetsai is little in itself, although there is a good hotel in the Poseidon, good by most Aegean standards that is to say. A rocky island, the area in which the town is situated is the least attractive. Sail round Spetsai and you will find that the southern and western shores are, like parts of Poros, redolent and green with pines. "The climate is exceedingly healthy," one authority states. It may well be. I never had the chance to investigate this, and to find out about a climate, requires weeks or even months.

Like Hydra and Psara, Spetsai was one of the Naval Islands, furnishing a large proportion of the ships and men in the War of Independence. Like Hydra and Syra, it declined with the emergence of Piraeus as the seaport of Greece. It still has its trade, though, mostly between the islands, Nauplia, and the country inland. It was in Spetsai that I saw a Venetian *trabaccola*, those apple-cheeked, bluff-bowed ships designed for the shallow waters and the raging Bara of the Adriatic.

It is curious how, the world over, local types of ships seem to reflect the architecture of their homeland. The *trabaccola* looked very Venetian and out of place alongside the quay of Spetsai with Mount Elias, crowned by its small white church, away in the distance above her thick pine mast. The summer prosperity of Hydra and Poros is just beginning to catch up with Spetsai, but the island is too far for most Athenians, and it is the Naupliots who tend to have their small summer houses here, or in the country outside the town. I doubt whether Spetsai will be able to emulate the success of the other offshore islands. It lacks their charm and, as the manager of the Poseidon remarked: "We have neither the civilisation of Athens nor the windmills of Mykonos." It is a good harbour, though, and a good staging post for small boats bound up to Nauplia.

CHAPTER 8

Andros, Tinos, Zea, Kythnos, and Syra

"Andros, the northernmost and one of the largest of the Cyclades, is mountainous throughout, the watershed being chiefly on the south-western side, with spurs or ridges extending north-eastward. . . ." Thus the *Admiralty Pilot*, with its usual succinct accuracy. On the day that I first came here it was spring, and the regular winds had not set in. I had had an awkward crossing from Cape Colonna for the prodroms, the forerunners of the Etesian winds, are variable in direction and strength. All across the forty-mile-wide Zea Channel it had been a succession of squalls, first off the land of Attica, then white squalls down from Euboea, and then the wind shifting and changing to blow in my teeth from the long blue back of Andros.

All the way from Makro Nisi, near Cape Colonna, I had seen the bulk of Mount Kovari, a few miles south of Port Gavrion, with its twisted peak trailing cloud like sheep's wool caught on a rubbing post. I had intended to make for **Port Andros** on the eastern side of the island, but the look of the clouds, the strength of the squalls, and the way the sea was siphoning through the Doro channel north of Andros, put me off. Chance—and so often it is only chance that can lead one to unlikely coves and anchorages in the Aegean—determined me to make for Port Gavrion.

The Athens boat does not call at **Port Gavrion,** but it is easy enough to get to Andros itself. The steamer drops anchor at Batsi, a few miles south of Port Gavrion, and then rounds the

98

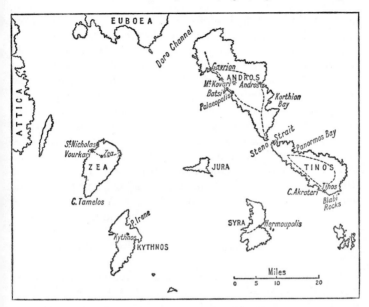

island to call at the main ports of Andros and Cordion Bay, both
on the east coast. One reason perhaps why Andros is one of the
least visited islands is that it is likely to be a rough crossing—
85 sea miles from Piraeus and about eight hours in the boat.
There are daily sailings both in summer and winter by steamers
making the round trip, Andros—Tinos—Syra and back to
Piraeus again.

Port Gavrion is protected from the south by a fringe of islets
and there is something reminiscent of a coral reef about the way
they circle the bay and define its blue limits. One of them is a
perfect small sugar loaf. On the day that I came here it was
wreathed with white spray, for the squalls whipping down off
the mountain were all that I had been warned to expect—
"baffling when the wind is moderate, and heavy when the wind is
strong." Perhaps that is the best way to arrive at one of the
Aegean islands—tired out, slightly scared, and delighted to find

99

shelter in the lee of the land, to see houses with smoke rising from them, and to find the company of other ships at anchor.

To visit the Aegean without some eye for the lines of a boat is rather like going to Ireland without any appreciation of horses —a lot of the conversation and many of the arguments and enthusiasms are going to be meaningless. On that day in Port Gavrion I had three other vessels near me, all sheltering from the wind, and all eager to engage in that pleasantest of harbour recreations—ship visiting. They were all what might be called "caiques," but this is a generic term that covers a multitude of sins, as well as virtues. One of them was a *varkala*, single-masted with a graceful counter-stern. Gaily painted and deep-loaded with metal drums, she came from Hydra. A *varkala* or "small boat" is perhaps the commonest type around in the Aegean—the lines varying greatly from one area to another according to the traditional designs of local shipbuilders. Usually they have quite a high stem, and lovely flowing bulwarks, rising towards the stern. Significantly, the word is Italian, a reminder—as so much else in the Aegean—of the centuries when Venice ruled these waters. Near me a larger boat, also of wood construction, a *trackonderi* wallowed in the swell. With a canoe stern and the high poop that is a legacy from the old sailing-trading boats of the Mediterranean, the *trackonderi* is a maid-of-all-work. She trundles about this sea laden with everything from iron ore to sponges, crated goods, wheat or old scrap iron. Her skipper rowed over to me and assured me that with nightfall the wind would die. He, like myself, was bound through the Doro Strait for the town of Andros. "We shall leave in the morning, about dawn," he said, "before the day's wind starts."

The third boat was a *meen*, about sixty tons, very tubby with ugly thick bows and a squarish transom stern. She looked just what she was, a container built to hold any and everything, and to press callously through the sea under the power of her large diesels. There are many like her nowadays in the Aegean, and they are as ugly as the *varkalas* can be beautiful. I was assured by her captain that she was an American design. He found proof of this in the fact that she was so ungraceful, awkward at sea, and had no other purpose than to make the maximum amount of profit for her owners! I suspect that American dollars had probably gone to build and engine her, but that she was an attempt on the part of former *varkala* builders to copy the lines of a Liberty Ship in wood.

Next morning I heard my neighbour start up his engine and motor past me. He shouted something but I declined to follow. I had no intention of going round to Andros immediately. During the previous evening I had had time to read a little about the island, and I had realised that I was only a few miles north of **Palaeopolis,** the ancient city and capital. Palaeopolis, incidentally, is easy to reach from Andros town and the drive is worth the trouble; the road passes through the island's deep valley of Messaria, with the mountain of Kovari (snow-capped until late spring) overhanging it. Approaching Palaeopolis by sea, on the other hand, one sails in towards the base of the mountain where Thiakon Point, a spur of Kovari, juts out from the north.

Palaeopolis is a place to visit if you like to find a most beautiful site with no guides, very few ruins, and little but the place itself to remind you that the Greeks were perhaps the most brilliant "site-choosers" in history. Over and over again one finds this— whether at Selinunte or Syracuse in Sicily, at Crotone in Italy, or in the native islands themselves. Imagine the good fortune that gave men of impeccable taste and sensibility the chance to operate in an almost virgin world! "Survey the world from China to Peru," and to-day the architect will find that others have been there before him. But, for the ancient Greeks, there was the archipelago itself, the western coast of Greece and its islands, outhern Italy and Sicily—all clean, unsullied canvases on which to build their temples, their theatres and their cities.

They clearly chose Palaeopolis, or the small bay between the capes of Thiakon and Thouridha, because it was facing towards the mainland as well as the other Cyclades, and because it was secure from everything except a south wind. (The south wind, in any case, is the least prevalent, and the least to be feared, in this part of the world.)

There is little to see in Palaeopolis to-day, a small fishing village, the remains of the ancient city-wall, and a gateway. The few pieces of statuary, pottery and metalwork are either in Andros Museum or, like the "Hermes of Andros," in Athens. Under the shadow of the mountain, looking south towards Jura, Zea and Syra, the old city had a wonderful command of the whole strait. One wonders why the later capital was built on the east coast, and can only assume that it was sited to accord with its trade. And the Venetians quite naturally used Andros as a staging post across the Aegean between Samos, Chios, and Turkey. The reason why I had gone there myself was to cross to Nikaria and Samos by the shortest route. One of the advantages of sailing the Aegean in a small boat is that one very soon begins to appreciate the reasons why such-and-such a bay was chosen as the site for a town, or why a classical harbour became unused during the Middle Ages. At Palaeopolis there are the remains of what must once have been the ancient breakwater. I made fast alongside it and amused myself skin-diving to see whether a marble head or at the least a pottery jar might reward me. I have no doubt that they are there—Andros was not unimportant 2,000 years ago—but they await more fortunate and more skilful divers than I.

The island itself, some twenty miles long by ten wide, is geographically and scenically an extension of Euboea. In Andros one can find deep sheltered valleys and never know that the sea is no more than a few miles away. The ability of islanders to look inwards is the quality that saves them. Without that ability they would become hypnotised gazing outwards at the sea that is always, and never, the same. An island is a microcosm—platitude enough, but how often it is forgotten by those who should know better. An Englishwoman in Rhodes remarked, "But it's so small," pointing at a farmer's half-acre of wheat, "—And they call that a field!" I reminded her that American farmers from the Middle West were amused by the miniature size of English wheat fields. Quantity means nothing, and that is something one should always bear in mind when visiting the islands and the islanders of the Aegean. The fisherman in Palaeopolis who talked to me of Andros town sounded like an English countryman talking of London. The minute compass of an islander's life is still big enough, and one needs little space in which to be born, procreate one's kind, and die. In an island like Andros, an inland farmer has to make something of an expedition to get to the sea. In one island (not Andros in fact, but Kythnos) I met a peasant farmer and his wife, living under six miles from the sea, who had never been down to it.

The town of Andros lies on the east coast at the end of a small cove, and it is here that the boat from Athens calls, and the traveller disembarks into a rowing boat. The northernmost of the Cyclades, Andros was settled by Ionians, and it was they who founded Palaeopolis. Probably the present port and capital was always inhabited because of its situation facing towards Ionia. But it was in the Middle Ages, and later during the Venetian occupation, that Andros with its fortress and its battlements became the island's capital. Mulberries brought the island its medieval fame, when the silk of Andros was known as far afield as western Europe. It is not an island for the architectural student, but for the visitor who wants to bathe—there are fine sandy beaches near the town—who wants to do little or nothing, or who wants a few weeks or months in which to come to terms with himself. It is not impossible to have some comfort, even though Andros does not have the facilities of Hydra or Poros. There are three hotels—the Triton, Paradissos, and the small Aigli. I have stayed in none of them, but have good reports of the Paradissos (B class by Tourist Bureau ratings). I have eaten at the Korthion in **Korthion Bay:** good fish, drinkable wine and excellent figs. I would recommend it as a place to stay, although Korthion Bay does not to my mind equal Palaeopolis or Gavrion. There is an hotel at **Batsi,** the Avra (rated C and unvisited). But its proximity to Palaeopolis should make up for any defects. Fortunately, however simple and rough the ingredients of island cookery, the standards of cleanliness are no worse than most western kitchens—better, if anything. Many of the islanders are somewhat akin to the Scots in their passion for scrubbing and tidiness. Mainland Greeks, on the other hand, are often what the Scots say that the English are.

Tinos, some fifteen miles long by five broad, is separated from Andros by the narrow Steno Strait. The same steamer service which runs to Andros also calls at Tinos once a day. The capital lies on the south-western side of the island and looks across towards Syra, only ten miles away. South again, divided by the narrow Mykoni Channel lies Mykonos, and the heart of the islands—Delos and its attendant, Rheneia. What Delos was to the ancient world, Tinos is to modern Greece. This is the heart of Orthodox piety, containing the miraculous wonder-working ikon of Our Lady, the Panayia. On March 25th and August 15th pilgrims come to Tinos from all over Greece and the Aegean, for it is on these two days that the ikon is carried out from its shrine. The sick and the crippled are borne to the church of Our Lady of Tinos, and innumerable are the cures attesting to the power of the Panayia—as the multitude of gold and silver votives bear witness. It is somewhat curious that this stronghold of the Orthodox faith should be found in Tinos, for a great many Tiniots are Roman Catholics. The island was occupied by the Venetians longer than almost any other place in the Aegean, with the result that there are more Catholic families here even than in Syra, that other great stronghold of Roman influence.

Tinos has been called the Lourdes of Greece, and a somewhat similar commercialism has undoubtedly crept into the islanders' attitude towards their visitors. At Andros I was warned against the men of Tinos—"They will rob you of all you possess"—but fortunately I did not find it so. One should always beware of paying too much attention to what one islander says about an-other. As in classical Greece, patriotism is strictly regional.

The fact that the island attracts a great number of visitors is reflected in its hotels. There is the large and comfortable Tinion Palace, the Gallini, the Avra and the Flisvos, the last

On Syra

Mykonos

three all rated category C. There are also a number of pensions as well as private houses which produce bed and breakfast. Anyone visiting the island during the two great religious processions should make quite sure of accommodation well in advance. At these times the island is packed to overflowing, and any kind of bed is a luxury.

Tinos, like Andros, was an Ionian settlement, and it was here that Poseidon was worshipped in his role of "snake-killer." Legend has it that the island was overrun by snakes until Poseidon intervened by dispatching some storks which devoured them all. Here, as so often, one can probably detect beneath the simple story the conflict of two religions. The word "Tinos" has been held by some authorities to be the Phoenician word for "Snake." It seems quite probably that, if there was once a Phoenician settlement here, a snake goddess was worshipped, who was ultimately dispossessed by the sea god of the new conquerors, the Ionians.

The town is not architecturally of any great interest, but it is remarkably attractive in the way it spreads itself along the waterfront. The accent is on white—stark dazzling white, with only in a few places an odd touch of the second Greek national colour, blue. From the sea, Tinos looks like crystallised foam, and there is something lace-like and delicate as spray about the white chapels, the dovecots, and the tiled towers. Crowning the town is the great church of the *Panayia Evangelistria* or *Tiniotissa* (She has many names), approached by a broad avenue that leads up from the port. The church itself is undistinguished, but the courtyard and the entrance are delightful, cobbled mosaic-work contrasting with the austerity of the blinding white of the building.

The wonder-working ikon of the Madonna of Tinos was discovered in 1822, and the two great feasts of the Panayia have been celebrated annually in the island ever since then. In recent years the importance of these celebrations has increased rather than diminished. The *Panayia Tiniotissa* has taken on something of the aspect of a national shrine, ever since the Greek cruiser

Elli was torpedoed off the port on August 15th, 1940. This action by an Italian submarine, two months before Italy declared war against Greece, has somehow twined the two threads of Tinos together—the wonder-working Madonna, and the old conception of the sea god who could only be appeased by sacrifice. The unfortunate *Elli* was lying peacefully at anchor in the roadstead, dressed overall with flags in honour of the Panayia, when the Italian torpedo struck home. Her dead are commemorated in the church by a shrine decorated with the old cork lifebelts from the cruiser.

Tinos is rich in villages, may of them accessible on the local bus, and nearly all of them cubist abstractions in white and blue. **Borgo,** the old Venetian capital, is one of the strangest places. It can only be reached on foot or by mule and, like so many of the *castra* or citadel capitals of the period, its situation is an historical tribute to the pirates of the Aegean. The peak of Exoborgo overhangs modern Tinos, and on this bare crest of rock one finds the ruins, still partially inhabited, of the old citadel and capital. Below Borgo on the eastern side there is a Catholic convent and on the other side the French Ursuline College.

One finds in the islands, as elsewhere in Europe, a certain snobbishness on this question of religion—Venetian names and descent, as well as an adherence to the Catholic Faith, often being considered proof positive that one comes from the upper classes. On the other hand, there is practically none of the English snobbishness of birth to be found in Greece. There is a great respect for success, certainly. But, as for breeding, did not the Greeks decide when they formed their first constitution that they would have no titles—"Because all Greeks are noble"?

Lutra, deep in the folds of a rich valley, is one of the most attractive villages in Tinos. Its Venetian houses and fountains confirm that it was here the merchants had their country residences. Pyrgos, another small village, boasts a School of Fine Arts where sculpture students are welcomed. At Kinara there is the residence of the Roman Catholic bishop. The large bay of Panormos on the north-east coast is grand and imposing, but not always friendly to the swimmer, since the north wind blows home and there is often a heavy, breaking surf. St. Nicholas Bay, on the other hand, is a fine place for swimming and fishing, and an excellent anchorage for small boats. Tucked just round the south-eastern corner of Tinos, between Blabi rocks and Cape Akroteri, it is a delightful place, but sailors and fishermen need to watch out for the heavy squalls which whip down off the land whenever the Meltemi are blowing strongly.

Together with Syra, three other islands complete the northern-most group of the Cyclades. One of them, Jura, is little more than a rocky hump, harbourless and uninviting, lying due north of Syra. Zea or Keos, commanding the approaches to Athens from the north, is craggy and mountainous, with a high spinal ridge running right down the eastern coast. There is only one harbour in Zea where steamships call on their way south to Seriphos and Siphnos. This is the port of St. Nicholas, on the north-western coast, looking across towards Makro Nisi. It was once quite a busy little port, a coaling station for ships on the Black Sea route, but now even this small prosperity had departed. There are, I believe, less than 3,000 inhabitants in this ten-mile-long island, most of the young men leaving as immigrants or merchant seamen, or going to swell the unemployed in the sad shanty towns on the outskirts of Athens.

The town of Zea, like so many other capitals in the islands, lies about two miles back from the harbour, and clings for security to the hillside. From the sea, it has the same enchant-ment as do all hill towns glimpsed when one is on passage—an invitation, as it were, to "put the oar over one's shoulder" and walk inland, find some quiet white cottage with a vine and shadowed courtyard, and stay for ever. But one passes by because, if one has ever tried to live that life, one knows the ennui that lies heavy as dust in those streets. One knows that it is they, the dwellers in the small white houses, who look out, see the boats passing—and wish that they were on them.

The island has two long sand beaches; one of them by the village of Vourkari attracts a number of summer visitors.

Vourkari is a pleasant fishing village, lying on the southern half of the bay, about half a mile from the port. Round the southern-most tip of the island, Cape Tamelos, one comes into sight of its neighbour, **Thermia** or Kythnos, another harsh and mountain-ous island which derives its name Thermia from its warm springs. There is no regular steamer service to Thermia. Coming down to it from the north, it lifts a vulture's bald pate out of the sea—uninviting, and yet, for those who sail there, **Port Irene** makes a pleasant anchorage. "Port," the word suggests something that it certainly is not, but this fine sheltered inlet on the north-east coast is ideal for those who like peace and quiet. The warm springs with their thermal establishment are a little to the north of here, but in Port Irene itself there is nothing but a hamlet—village is too big a term—of five or six houses. One of them belongs to the lighthouse keeper, who every evening can be seen rowing out to tend the lamp which signals the opening to the harbour. He also keeps the only bar and general store. His *ouzo* was good, and so were the fried eggs, cucumber, island bread, and goats' cheese. I have eaten many worse meals in big cities—and without having the pleasure of Port Irene outside the open door.

One needs time for the islands, and there is never enough of it. It is ideal to travel on your own, in a small boat, and cut time to your own measure. But even then there is always something constraining, or making demands upon one's lessening reserve of days, weeks and even hours. I could happily have stayed in Port Irene for several days, but I had friends to meet in Syra. I remember the conversation of my Greek acquaintance, that lighthouse keeper-cum-bar keeper-cum-general storeman. One finds many like him in remote places. He earned about thirty shillings a week for his lighthouse duties and less still from the bar, for there were only three other families in the port. Two of the houses were deserted—owners gone to America. The shepherds and goatherds came down occasionally from the hills but, other than them, he saw no one save a rare Athenian tourist, a wander-ing yachtsman, or a caique sheltering from bad weather. At the back of his house he had a pocket handkerchief of a garden,

108

immaculately kept, where cucumbers and tomatoes grew. He had also two goats, his rowing boat and fishing nets, and a wife and small son. I would not say that he was content—who is?— but he seemed as cheerful and well-balanced as anyone I can call to mind.

The village of **Kythnos** lies about a mile and a half inland, south from Port Irene. The village repays a visit—not that it possesses anything unusual, but because it is typical of so many of these island villages. It is "a duty" to see at least one of the ordinary, unspectacular and unwritten about places. It helps one to understand the life that is going on in all those other villages that one will never visit, but only remark—far away and white in the hills—from a steamer's deck, or through the saloon windows of a passing cruise ship.

A bare mule-track leads from Port Irene, jagged with stones. Seaward the barren rocks stretch away, and on the landward side there is thin grazing land for sheep. On a distant ridge are the silhouettes of munching goats. Round the village thin cornfields cluster, and the women in their dusty dark clothes are reaping and stacking. When the stranger passes them they gather the corner of their shawls into their teeth. The men—and it is they who ride the donkeys—are more forthcoming and ask the stranger who he is, where he comes from, and what he is doing in Kythnos. Island curiosity is insatiable and a wallet full of family pictures is an invaluable asset.

Kythnos surmounts a hill, a sugared cake of houses, with clean streets where even the pavements are whitewashed. Yet this is no Capri, no international tourist resort. Windmills are spinning on the crest of the rise, their canvas sails reefed well down to-day, for it blows hard. Everything is blue and white, even the church. The bearded Pappas escorts me to a shop to buy vegetables and then takes me to a taverna. (Here, as in many islands, I found my beard was a kind of passport to priestly good will—almost an old school tie.) There was only one old man in the bar, passing his time over a glass of water and a necklace of amber beads. Everywhere in Greece one hears the click of beads, those distractions for the restless hands: "And cheaper far than tobacco for the nerves!" They have, incidentally, nothing to do with the Christian Faith (as many Roman Catholics, equating them with rosaries, suppose). They are a legacy from the Turks. On the bar there was a two-day-old paper from Athens and a silent radio.

It was dark when I stumbled back down the toothed track to Port Irene. The moon had not yet risen, and the sea to the east was only just distinguishable by being a little darker than the land. Out in the bay there was a glimmer of light from the small lamp at the entrance. Only the lighthouse keeper's house and bar gleamed in the darkness. I joined him over a glass before rowing back to the boat. It was nothing much of a day, and yet it remains in the memory. There are many days like that in the Aegean.

It is strange really that Delos was accounted the still heart of these spinning islands, for **Syra**—geographically at any rate—is nearer the centre. Hilly and cultivated, with the mountain of Pyrgo dominating it, one might have expected Syra to have attained considerable importance in classical times. Yet, curiously enough, there seems to be almost no mention of Syra in ancient history. The philosopher Pherecides, the teacher of Pythagoras, lived here and legend credits him with a cave-home in the north known to this day as "Pherecides' cave." Eumaeus, the faithful swineherd of Odysseus, was a Syriot who had been captured by pirates as a child, and then sold to the king of Ithaca. "The soil is good, and there is pasture for sheep and cattle, and it is rich in wine and wheat," he says, nostalgically remembering his old home.

Approached from the east, the twin-breasts of the city's hills distinguish Syra from the other islands. Crowned with their white houses, these hills dominate the fine harbour which brought the island prosperity. Upper Syra, the hill on the left, with its clustering houses and its cathedral of St. George, is a Venetian foundation dating from the thirteenth century. The harbour of Syra was naturally not ignored by Venice, neither was the geographical position which made it an ideal staging post for the east-west trade of the Aegean. For administrative purposes, the island came under the Duchy of Naxos and was the seat of a Latin bishopric. In the seventeenth century Louis XIII took the island under his protection, at the instigation of the Capuchins who had settled here. It was this French interest in Syra which largely contributed to the island's later prosperity. At the time of the Greek War of Independence, Syra—unlike the other Naval Islands of Hydra, Spetsai and Psara—remained neutral under the protection of the French fleet. In 1822, when Psara and Chios were devastated by the Turks, refugees from these two islands came to Syra and established the second of its two townships, **Hermoupolis**. The Chiots and Psariotes were skilful traders and seamen. With the aid of their ships and business acumen, the port of Syra gradually became dominant in the Aegean. Hermoupolis was named after Hermes, ancient god of Traders, but —as a native of Hydra once pointed out to me—"You should not forget, when you go to Syra, that Hermes was also the Protector of Thieves!" Hermoupolis is the modern town which now spreads all around the waterfront of Syra. The second hill, the one to the right of Upper Syra is the Orthodox hill and is known as Vrontadho. Left and right hillocks confront one another, Orthodox and Catholic, and confer a decorative distinction on low-lying Hermoupolis.

There are direct steamer services to the island from Piraeus, while it is also on the Andros–Tinos route. Hotels are more abundant than in most of the Cyclades—The Kikladikon and the Hermes being the best (rated B by the Greek Tourist Office). There is also The France, as well as several others which are clean and unpretentious.

About 20,000 people still inhabit the town—a huge population compared to most of the Cyclades where, for instance, an island like Kythnos (bigger than Syra) has a population of little more than 3,000. Hermoupolis to-day, despite its decline as a trading centre, is still the capital of the whole of the Cyclades.

Seventy-nine miles from Piraeus, Syra is little more than ten miles long by six wide. It is the best place from which to find caiques bound for the other Cyclades, for it is still the meeting point of inter-island trade. There are plenty of steamship sailings—not only between Syra and Piraeus—but between everywhere else in the Aegean. From here, one can find ships or schooners bound for Rhodes, the Dardanelles, Lemnos, Chios, where you will. It is also an agreeable place in which to pass a few days while waiting for transport. The port is partially sheltered by a natural breakwater, the Isle of Asses, and partially by the long artificial arm which protects the harbour from the east. Cafés, restaurants and bars of every description abound. From **Hermes' Street,** which opens out from the harbour esplanade, one reaches the main square—a strange, half-ghostly place overshadowed by memories of the island's vanished greatness. On some occasions—especially if there are several ships in, or if it happens to be an island festival—the square has an atmosphere of Italianate gaiety. At other times, and particularly if rain clouds lour over Syra, the square is reminiscent of an Edwardian or Victorian watering place. It is Latin, though, in character and this gives it, even on its most desolate days, a certain charm.

Unlike so many of the smaller and poorer islands, Syra is quite well off for motor transport—buses and taxis that will take one to most of the interesting places in the island. Episkopeion is a charming village within easy reach, and it is only a short walk from here to **Kini,** the fishing village below it. Kini has a good sandy beach and a cheerful crowd of fishermen who will hire their boats for excursions or fishing trips round the island. Della Grazia, on the western coast, is much like any small summer resort, and it is here that the prosperous Syriotes tend to have their summer villas. The beach is good but there is little else to be said for Della Grazia, except that in autumn and spring this part of the coast is the local sportsman's paradise. Going to, or returning from northern Europe, both doves and quail alight on this side of the island.

The centre of Roman Catholicism in Greece, Syra is in some respects a little like Corfu, in the days before international tourism began to revitalise the Ionian island. Syra is unlikely to share in these particular favours, for it does not possess the romantic quality which endears Corfu to northern visitors. The port has a charming, but slightly faded air. Where there should be fifty ships at anchor, there are only five. Tavernas that should be riotous with sailors spending their pay, nourish old men with long memories. "My family were shipowners," a Syriote told me. "All through the last century we had ships, just like Onassis has them to-day. Even as late as 1920, we still owned two merchant ships. But then—ah, what an accident of fortune!—the English coal strike broke us. It was the end of our money, and of our ships." He said it without a trace of bitterness. What's done, cannot be undone. In the Aegean, just as in southern Spain, the influence of Islam lingers on, not so much in the architecture as in the manners. "*Mekhtoub,*" says the Arab and shrugs his shoulders. "What's done, cannot be undone," says the Greek—but prepares immediately to see what can be salvaged from the wreckage.

There is reasonable retsina to be drunk in Syra, the vegetables are good, the fruit excellent, and the climate dry and healthy. *Loukoumi,* or Turkish delight, is one of the island's exports, and even those who may shudder at childhood memories of gelatinous stuff covered with icing sugar should try the original sweetmeat. Scented with roses, stuffed with nuts, or flavoured with anis, it dissolves on the tongue like a memory of the sultans. It is an Ingres of sweets, and not to be despised even by those whose taste is for savoury things. So too is Syra itself. It is not a "typical" Aegean island. Flavoured by Venice and Genoa, fashioned to some extent by the Pope and by France, it is something of an exotic.

CHAPTER 9

Mykonos and Delos

There are daily boat services to Mykonos from Piraeus, and the island is easy to reach from other ports in the Cyclades. It is just over ninety miles by sea from Athens, but the ship often calls at other places on the way and reaches the island after dark. Night is perhaps the best time to catch one's first glimpse of Mykonos. Under the giant summer moon, the whitewashed houses—which are blinding at midday—achieve an ethereal beauty. They shine like soap bubbles, lit it seems with some interior radiance. They give the illusion that they might burst and dissolve in a light cloud of spray.

The town rises on the sloping shoulders of its hills in a natural amphitheatre, a half-moon city that is without doubt one of the most enchanting in the Aegean. There are other towns in other islands that appeal more to the purist, but no one can refuse Mykonos its claim to be the white and shining town—*I Lefki Mykoni*. For these reasons it has become a resort for Athenians, and for many foreign visitors an ideal "Siren Land." Like Hydra and Poros, the fact that tourism has made an impact here means that food and hotels are better than elsewhere. Again, too, it is a fine point of departure for other and less accessible islands, and one to which the traveller can happily return. After an absence of some weeks, it is pleasant to come back to Mykonos and see what new patterns the kaleidoscope of human relationships has assumed during one's absence.

The town lies sheltered on the west side of the island, at the end of the **Bay of Turlo.** Cafés and restaurants abound along the curving arm of the harbour—a bad one, incidentally, for small boats. Although protected by two breakwaters, terrific gusts whip over the water during the strong Meltemi. Small boat sailors are well advised to anchor a little to the north, and outside the breakwaters. This, indeed, is what the island steamers usually do, and the passengers are brought ashore in rowing boats.

There are plenty of hotels and pensions. There is the Leto

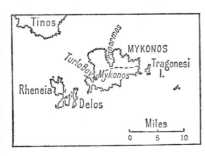

(category A) and built, so I was told, solely for the benefit of Americans! There is the small Delos, and the Apollo (both D) and both clean and comfortable. Best of all, for those who intend to spend a certain time in Mykonos, are the many private houses which let rooms during the summer season.

Bona fide artists can stay at the Mykonos branch of the School of Fine Arts which is open throughout the summer, but they must first make sure of their reservation before leaving Athens—or preferably, some time in advance of their visit to Greece.

At the entrance to the harbour stands a blue-domed chapel to St. Nicholas. Nearby, one is likely to find the famous pelican of Mykonos. I have no idea of the life-span of a pelican, but I suspect that when this one dies from over-feeding a substitute will be quickly found. The pelican of Mykonos is the subject of a story which gives one an insight into the character of the islanders. One day, so the tale goes, a flight of migrating pelicans was passing over Mykonos when one of them collapsed exhausted on the beach outside the town. The fishermen and one in particular named Vassilis, looked after the bird and adopted him as a mascot. They gave him the name of Petros. Innumerable were the photographs taken of him during the fifties, and this sleek and fish-gorged bird became almost a symbol of the new-found prosperity of the island. Then one day, restored in strength and spirit, Petros took off—feeling perhaps a migratory pull towards the north. After only a short flight he found himself over Tinos, about half a dozen miles away and, remembering perhaps the fleshpots of life ashore, made a landing. He was once more adopted. The Tiniots, so say the fishermen of Mykonos, are a notorious race of thieves, and had long coveted Petros. Imagine then their delight when this bird alighted on their island! They, too, had a tourist attraction similar to that previously enjoyed by rich Mykonos. It was not long before the men of Mykonos heard about this friendly bird which now graced the harbour at Tinos. It was the rape of Helen all over again. A fleet of Mykoniot boats put off towards Tinos to recapture their paragon. Petros was hidden before they landed, and the Tiniots refused to hand over their property. "He is a pelican, yes." They said, "But we know nothing about yours! This one came down to us from the skies." Reluctantly the men of Mykonos returned to their island. But, not to be defeated over so important a matter, they then sailed over to Syra and took their case before the Chief Magistrate of the Cyclades. The latter, envisaging perhaps a pleasant short holiday in Mykonos, agreed to come over to the island and pronounce judgment. The Tiniots, he said, must bring the bird to Mykonos and must agree to a test that he was about to make. So Petros arrived with a boatload of fishermen from Tinos, and all waited for the magistrate's verdict. "I understand," he said, "that when a certain pelican lived here in Mykonos he had a special friend in a fisherman named Vassilis?" All present, including Vassilis, nodded assent. "Now," said the magistrate, "Petros will remain in the company of these men from Tinos and a number of you are to stage an attack on Vassilis —in full view of the bird!" Vassilis was set upon in a mock-assault. Within a few seconds the pelican bounded away from the Tiniots, and with a croak of rage proceeded to lay about Vassilis' attackers with his great beak. "It is proof enough," said the magistrate. "This is clearly the bird that Vassilis befriended, the bird which was known to the people of Mykonos as Petros. Here he must stay!"

It is the town of Mykonos which is the island's real attraction, for scenically it has very little to offer. Unlike Andros, Tinos and Syra, Mykonos has few distinctive features. Barren and granitic, its hills are low mounds, and its vegetation is sparse. The vine flourishes, however, and ancient coins of the island show Dionysus and a bunch of grapes as emblematic of Mykonos. Lying almost in the centre of the Aegean, Mykonos is exposed to the full scend of the sea when the north wind, *Vorias* (the ancient Boreas), is blowing. The rocky and attractive bay of Panormos on the north coast makes a fine spectacle in midsummer, the boom and the sizzle of the surf more reminiscent of the Atlantic than the Aegean. But there are other bays and beaches sheltered from the prevailing wind, the most popular being at Tourlo just outside the town, while several quieter and more secluded ones lie in the south.

The traveller who has reached the island under the still spell of moonlight will be dazed by Mykonos at midday. It is the most white-washed town in all the islands, and the glare and razzle-dazzle of the streets is almost blinding. Dark glasses are no affectation here, and the incredible purity of the light in this part of the Cycladic world makes one wonder how much the ancients suffered from opthalmia. But then, they lived a simple life—rose at dawn, took a siesta no doubt in the afternoon, and worked again until sunset. They did not tire their eyes with many books, nor weaken them with cigarette smoke, and artificial light. It was in Mykonos that I met an old woman who told me she was ninety-two. She was busily doing needlework in the sheltering embrasure of a doorway; and she needed no glasses, dark or otherwise, to thread her needle.

The houses in Mykonos are not unlike those with which one has become familiar in Poros, Hydra and elsewhere. They are the same simple blocks, plastered and whitewashed, the only difference here being that one finds many more two- and even sometimes, three-story houses, than elsewhere in the Cyclades. Unlike Syra, the town has no real central core. The meeting ground and the place for the evening promenade is the water-front. Here one also finds the Museum of Antiquities with its good collection of vases—Cycladic, Geometric, Attic, Corinthian and Rhodian. A muscle-bound "Hercules" is the principal piece of sculpture. More interesting are one or two of the cups, particularly a red-decorated, two-handled bowl with a design of dancing figures. But Mykonos, one feels—and few of the pieces in the museum are Mykoniot products—has never been a home of the arts. Somehow Mykonos seems too charming to play host to the clear-sighted Apollo, or to the raging Dionysus.

It is a maze of streets, pleasant and inconsequential, yet often so attractive in its unthought-out design, that even the most dedicated disparager of "prettiness" will be forced to cry out— "Poh-poh-poh!"—that Greek exclamation which can convey everything from delight to frank incredulity. Mykonos is reputed to have 365 churches, one for every day of the year, and certainly their numbers are staggering. The **Paraportiani,** the "Church beyond the Walls," is one of the strangest—a pyramid-shaped group of family chapels that would look like a confectioner's dream gone mad were it not redeemed by the austerity of its steps and verticals. How often in the Aegean one finds the marriage of Byzantium and the classical world, and marvels that so different a mingling of dogma and outlook has produced such fine offspring. Quite often in Mykonos one can find, where plaster and lime have peeled away, fragments and antique blocks of marble built into the houses. These are a legacy from the centuries when the Mykoniots sailed across to desolate Delos and helped themselves from the ruined houses and temples of the sun god's island.

There are few trees on Mykonos, and most of them, other than olives, are to be found in the town itself. Rounding a corner, one suddenly comes upon a tree leaning crazily out of a cube of whitewash—a tree that seems curiously important. Trees in the Aegean, like wells and springs of water, assume an archetypal significance. Under the acid light, a single tree growing out of the barren island seems a miracle that reveals to one a Blake-like vision of the earth. The Square of the Three Wells, *Ta Tria Pigadia*, is a good example of what Mykonos has to offer. It is "pretty," but not in a cloying "chocolate box" kind of way. The austerity of its colouring—pure white with only here and there a dash of pale pink or blue—and the geometrical simplicity of the houses redeem it from the quaint.

From the ridge behind the town, known as the High Hills, where the windmills stand (little used to-day since most of the grain is sent to the mainland for milling), one has a fine view of Mykonos. Beyond the town lies the bay, with one small brown islet asleep on its surface, and beyond that again is Delos with the hump of Mount Cynthus dark against the sky. For those who aspire to an even finer panorama of the islands, a two-hour mule ride takes one to the summit of Mount Elias. From here the whole of Mykonos is visible, with Delos and Rheneia away to the south, and the bulk of Tinos filling in the northern horizon. Ships and caiques trail across the windy sea and the Mykonos channel is usually scuttering with small white waves as the current pushes down from the north.

There are several beaches near the town, easy to reach either by car or boat—Aghios Stephanos is the most fashionable, about three miles by road from Mykonos, and a good place for swimming and fishing. Along the south-eastern coast there are several delightful coves and bays that can only be reached by sea, for which reason they remain comparatively unvisited even in midsummer. Spelaeologists should hire a boat and make an excursion to **Tragonesi islet,** just off the eastern tip of Mykonos. Here wind and weather, and the steady scouring of the Aegean, have hollowed out innumerable caves, some Gothic and macabre, others filled with shimmering blue light. There are others, too, where, with all the grace of Nereids, families of seals have taken refuge.

"No visitor," says one Greek Guide, "will fail to acquire after a few days the 'Mykonian' look . . . an irresistible attraction to the summer visitors of both sexes." The peasant weave is, in fact, an attractive island product, but the raw colours and the

simple patterns do not sit happily on all figures. It is an unfortunate fact that the "Mykonian" look seems to appeal most
strongly to those visitors who should at all costs resist it. One
island speciality which must be recommended are the almond
sweetmeats, small cakes of almond paste that smell as good as they
taste. *Louza*, a kind of smoked meat with a lot of seasoning, is also
worth trying.

From Mykonos it is only five miles by boat to **Delos,** the heart
of the Aegean. When the Meltemi permits, crossings by boat take
place every day in summer. But quite often the traveller Delos-
bound will find that he has to wait a day or two in Mykonos for
the seas to moderate. It is as well, when embarking from
Mykonos in one of the local boats, to be prepared for an enforced
stay in Delos. There is a Tourist Pavilion on the island with food
and accommodation during summer.

The caiques come alongside the remains of the ancient mole in
Delos harbour. "The best anchorage," says the *Admiralty Pilot,*
"is in the northern part, known as Limin Dhilos, in depths of
from 9 to 12 fathoms, good holding ground of dark sand, mud and
weed." I can confirm this, having sat out a gale here in a ten-ton
boat. In normal weather I would recommend to yachtsmen the
small bay just south of the ancient mole and anchorage, under the
lee of **Mount Cynthus.** It is poor holding ground, but beautiful
silver sand, and I stayed here once for two days and nights. In
the clear sand every link of the cable, two fathoms beneath me,
was as distinct as if under a microscope. There are few occasions
in life when one can say with absolute conviction, "Now, I am
happy." For me Delos provided a full forty-eight hours—a kind
of euphoria which, if prolonged, would prove unendurable.

Delos, the hub round which the Cyclades (Kukloi—rings)
radiate, was formed by nature to be the focal point of a seaman's
world. If one is tempted to ask why so small an island, without
any natural resources, ever became what it did, then the answer
can be given by any sailor. Delos is the last, and best, anchorage
between Europe and Asia. To the east it is shielded by Mykonos,
to the north by Tinos, and to the west by Rheneia. Looking at a

One of the windmills of Mykonos

Delos. *Above*, the Lions of Delos; *below*, detail of a mosaic floor in the House of the Trident

chart, it is easy to see how the direct sea-route between the Gulf of Nauplia (with Argos at its head) flows straight across the latitude of 37° 10′ North of Patmos and Samos. Exactly in the centre of this trading route lies Delos. At the same time, it is almost in the centre of the trading route between the Dardanelles and Crete. Religious centres may sometimes, as at Rome or Lourdes, attract trade and commerce. But more often one will find that where the trade is, there also are the temples. Merchants then as now, are eager to purchase security in both worlds.

Leto, daughter of the Titans Coeus and Phoebe, was one of Zeus' many mistresses. It is said that when they coupled, he transformed both the maiden and himself into quails. "Artemis," writes Robert Graves, "originally an orgiastic goddess, had the lascivious quail as her sacred bird. Flocks of quail will have made Ortygia a resting place on their way north during the spring migration. . . ." Mr. Graves identifies Ortygia with **Rheneia,** a likely supposition since Artemis is presumed to have been born in Rheneia and then to have crossed the narrow straits to Delos, where she assisted her mother at the birth of Apollo. Quail still alight on Rheneia and Delos in spring, and it seems possible that some earlier god or goddess, connected with the quail, or with birds in general, was once worshipped on the island.

It was the natural jealousy of Hera which led to Apollo and Artemis being born in Delos and Rheneia. Pursued throughout the world by Hera, Leto was borne on the wings of the south wind until she found herself over Delos, "the wandering island" as it was called, because it had drifted throughout the Aegean since the dawn of time, waiting for the birth of the miraculous twins. Poseidon, in one of his rare moments of generosity, struck Delos with his trident and anchored it firmly to the bed of the sea.

Leto, after giving birth to Artemis on the island of Rheneia, crossed the straits and it was in Delos, on the north side of Mount Cynthus, that she gave birth to Apollo beneath the shade of a date palm. Immediately the barren island was transformed, flowers and fruit burst from the rocks, the Bird of Dawning

121

crowed his delight at the sun, and swans circled the sacred lake. The palm tree became sacred to Apollo, and his worship was clearly established on the island before the Trojan War (or before the writer of the *Odyssey* told of it) for Odysseus says of Nausicaa that he can only compare her beauty to "a young palm tree which I saw when I was in Delos growing close to the altar of Apollo."

In the seventh century BC the island was a protectorate of Naxos, and the religious centre for the Ionian league of islands. Athens was not long in seeing the importance of Delos as a trading centre, and also as the mainspring of Ionian tradition, religion and culture. Shortly after 540 BC Pisistratus performed the purification of the island shrine by ridding it of all sepulchres. From henceforth, Delos was declared a consecrated and virgin island, not to be defiled by human birth or death. It was an island outside of time and time's creatures, for which reason anyone in danger of dying, or a woman nearing childbirth, was ferried across to Rheneia to avoid the long and involved purification ceremonies which would otherwise have been necessary.

A further and more elaborate lustration followed in the year 426 BC, and again in 422 BC, after which date all the remaining native Delians were expelled from the island and sent to Ionia. The island's first great period of prosperity was immediately during and after the Persian wars, when its position in the centre of the Aegean made it strategically and commercially important. During Macedonian times, Delos had its second and greatest period. The island was independent and rejoiced in a secure position as something akin to a "free port" for the trade between east and west. The Romans again granted it a number of commercial privileges, although they restored the control of the Delian worship to Athens. In the third year of every Olympiad, on the anniversary of the god's birth in May, the great festival of the Delia took place. A convoy of ships set sail for the island, full of priests, sacred choirs, and bearing oxen for the slaughter. Leading the way went the sacred ship itself, the Theoris, with the head of the Athenian delegation aboard. Disembarking near the Sacred Way, the priests, choirs and other principals went in procession to the temple of Apollo. Here hymns to Leto and her two children were sung, and—after ritual sacrifices—games and competitions took place. The whole festival was something of a mixture between a pilgrimage to Lourdes, a Salzburg festival, and an athletics meeting. It is difficult perhaps for us to visualise to-day, but very typical of the way in which the ancient Greeks fused together all the various sides of human nature.

If the weather is suitable, the caiques from Mykonos usually land their passengers in the sacred port, a little north of the ancient commercial port. The latter is easy to recognise from the ruins of old warehouses, granaries and quays which fringe its side. The temple of Apollo lies about 150 yards inland from the ancient jetty, with the Agora of the Competaliastaes to the right near the commercial port. The **Sanctuary of Apollo,** in which the temple lies, is a great square impressive in its size and silence. Little remains intact, and only the base of the great statue of Apollo just in front of the temple still exists. A fragment of the torso can be seen near the temple of Artemis, one foot is in the British Museum, and one hand is in the Delos Museum. The statue was a gift of the Naxians, and made of Naxian marble as the inscription on the base bears witness: "I am of the same marble, both statue and base." It needs an effort of imagination to visualise the sanctuary as it once was, with the giant bronze palm tree over-shadowing the colossal figure of the god, the temple bright in its colours, and the treasuries of the various states rich in carving and gold. But fortunately Delos provides many spurs to the imagination. It is one of those rare places where one can feel the past in the palms of one's hands.

Leaving the sanctuary and going 200 yards to the north, one crosses the Sacred Lake, now dried and dusty under the sun. Against a sky of blinding blue the lions shout into the wind. They are long-bodied, lean archaic lions, with a trace of panther in their ancestry. Made of Naxian marble, these were the guardians of the Shrine. Their open mouths, in contrast with their white heads and bodies, seem like tarry caverns from which only the deepest of voices could issue. They roar above the shining ridge and their flanks lean to the dry earth achingly, as though they hungered for dampness and rain. Out of the nine which once protected the lake, only five remain. A sixth was taken away by the Venetians in the seventeenth century, and now guards the arsenal in Venice. Cresting their ridge of stone and flinty tussocks they turn an indifferent eye on the modern intruder— "Get out, Alexander, you are standing in my sunlight!"

A few hundred yards south of the Sacred Lake is the Delos Museum with its many household objects excavated by the French from the commercial quarter. There is a fine archaic sphinx from Naxos and there are also a number of archaic statues, but little from the classical period. Vases, statuettes, terra-cotta masks, and two kneeling satyrs which once formed part of the altar of Dionysus are among the many treasures of the island. The museum is interesting and well arranged, yet the real wonders of Delos are outside. The broken marbles, the barley grass, the small golden thistles, all are surcharged with the wonderful Apollonian radiance. Delos has sometimes been compared to Pompeii, but I cannot agree. Pompeii is a submerged Roman Blackpool, Delos is one of the sacred pulses of the earth. The one is a tombstone to human hopes, lusts and fears, the other is a navel of light, where one can feel the pulse of life that sustains the world.

Birth and death may not have been permitted on this sacred island, but the spring of life, the act of love itself, is celebrated. Facing the museum, at the north-east corner of the great sanctuary, is the small **Shrine of Dionysus**. Outside it stands several choragic monuments with marble phalli, white and triumphant over the broken skyline. Around the base of one of them is carved a charming light-hearted representation of a bride being carried to her new husband's home. On another monument one sees Dionysus with a Bacchante dancing in attendance. The marble phallic bird, symbol of the body's immortality in the seed of the body, dominates this corner of the sanctuary. It is poignant amid the dust, the silence, and the heavy weight of the past, to find these celebrations of wine and love-making.

One reason why one feels the past so vivid in the air of Delos is, perhaps, that the island is still as devoid of the beginnings and ends of life as it has ever been. No one really lives here. During the summer, the curator of the museum and his wife stay in Delos. A few shepherds and goatherds cross from Mykonos and Rheneia to pasture their animals, but that is all. In winter it is unvisited, given back to a silence that seems more potent than any speech.

In the small bar outside the museum, the wife of one of the summer museum attendants talked with nostalgia of Mykonos. And how was it? And the cafés and the lights at night? She had not been there for several months, and she longed to hear again the chatter of friends and the gossip between one doorway and another. She sighed, thinking of the evening promenade and the half-moon harbour sparkling with its lights.

I would advise anyone who can spare the time to spend a night in Delos. One is made free of the island when the caiques from Mykonos have gone back again with their cargo of visitors. Walk south from the sanctuary to the "House of Dionysus," on the way to the theatre. Here, as in several other of the more important houses in Delos, the columns have been re-erected and a roof has been put on to protect the mosaic floors. After so much of the crude work which one finds in other cities of the ancient world, the mosaics of Delos are a revelation. They have a delicacy and brilliance that is unsurpassed. The House of the Trident, the House of Dolphins, and the House of Masks—all lie in the area between the commercial port and the foot of Mount Cynthus. The colours seem as vivid as if the mosaics had been laid yesterday. A dolphin twines his body round a sea-wet trident. Panthers and birds and melting fruit surround an eternally empty and silent floor. Fish, flowers, and leaves combine to form a pattern as intricate as any Persian carpet.

The theatre itself, dating from the second century BC, is one of the few disappointments on Delos. Unlike most Greek theatres, it is not carved out of the natural curve of a hill, but is built up in massive cyclopean blocks. One compensation is the view to be gained from the summit of the theatre: the blue channel,

Hecate Island, and then Rheneia. It is the perfection of island scenery. "Everything flows," as the "Dark Philosopher" remarked. And yet, beneath the appearance of flux—or so I have felt looking over that channel from the theatre—everything at the same time remains unchanged.

As the sun goes down beyond Rheneia, the low forehead of Hecate Island becomes suffused with colour. The scrub and scree on Mount Cynthus seem to catch fire, and now one sees how perfect—how "ideal" a mountain it is. During the bright noon hours, Mount Cynthus seems of little importance, a harsh granitic rock and no more. But with the sunset, its sculptural form is revealed. It is the quintessence of all mountains, even though it may be little less than 400 feet high.

The **Sacred Way** mounts the hill by an easy pathway of steeps and inclines, passing the shrines of the Syrian and the Egyptian gods. In front of the temple to Serapis stands a headless statue of Isis. Her own temple lies in ruins nearby. The Serapion itself is one of the best preserved temples on Delos, a delicate structure of Ionic design. A little to the north lie the cisterns where the sacred fish of the Syrian goddess Astarte were kept. There are a number of ancient cisterns on the island, some having been of secular use and others designed solely for purificatory rites or—as in the Serapion—for the preservation of sacred animals. At sunset, and in the still, cool hours that follow, one hears the voice of the island. From innumerable underground cisterns and caverns (where they have been preserving their shiny liveries from the blazing afternoon), the bullfrogs begin to croak. Now from all sides one hears that classic "Breka koax koax!"—a sound at first laughable, and then somehow sinister. Here in the Serapion, where the orgiastic rites of Astarte were once celebrated, some Syrian priest heard, as he fed the sacred fish, the booming voice of the frogs. Through him, as through all of us in our brief span, "the gale of life blew high. . . ." Booming out of the stagnant water, the yellowing weeds, and the hollowed places where palaces and temples once stood, only "Breka koax" survives.

126

I have climbed Mount Cynthus at sunset and watched the westering light over Syra and all the sea beyond that island, but dawn is the time to climb the mountain. If you have once seen the sun come up over the Aegean and the islands quicken into colour and shape, you have a memory that can be taken anywhere in the world. The Aegean is a landscape which one revisits in sleep, in dreams, and in the midst of great cities. One can be re-absorbed into it, and—although I have travelled in many countries—I know no other region into which one can slip back so happily.

It is a gentle climb up Mount Cynthus, for the Sacred Way was not necessarily designed for the young. At dawn the frogs are silent, but the lizards are still awake. I had nearly forgotten the lizards. I am no expert on reptilians, but nowhere else in this sea (except in Rhodes) have I come across lizards the size of those to be found on Delos. They are, I would guess, of the Family *Varanidae*—Monitors—for they seem to be more active at night than during the daylight hours. They confront you with cold stares at the windings of the pathways. They are not quick-silver, and nervous, like most Mediterranean lizards, but im-placable. It is not until one is right on top of them, that they give a wag of their fat tails and move sideways into the scrub. They seem always to be watching. Once, as I stepped inside the dark entrance to the sacred cavern, one of them crept inside behind me. As I slipped and slithered in the bat-dung on the floor, and as the bats rustled their scaly wings over my head, I noticed the lizard. He squatted there, quite still, just keeping me under observation.

At the Villa Albani in Rome there is a bronze copy of Pheidias' statue, "Apollo Sauroctonus," Apollo the Lizard-slayer. In the Louvre there is yet another marble copy. The god has a soft, almost effeminate figure, resembling to some degree the "Diony-sus" of Praxiteles at Olympia. One thing that appears to have troubled scholars is the lizard which clambers up the tree against which Apollo is leaning. "Apollo Sauroctonus" becomes immedi-ately clear to anyone who has visited Delos. I suspect that these

127

large lizards may have been especially imported to the island from their native North Africa to minister to that component of Apollo's godhead which was connected with a totemic lizard-worship.

The **Sacred Cavern** below the peak of Mount Cynthus is clearly a natural fault in the rock which has been turned into a small, dark temple. It is an alarming place at dawn, when the early light makes a *grisaille* of the interior. Huge granite slabs form the roof and the whole place—unlike anywhere else in Delos —has a heavy sombre atmosphere. This old rock temple, older perhaps than anything on Delos, was probably the shrine of some darker god or goddess than the bright Apollo and his silver sister. Here, one feels, the return of spring was ensured by the blood of a chosen youth. The rough granite still growls for its ceremonial wetting, for the shrill cry, and the razor-sharp stone.

The straits between Rheneia, Hecate and Delos begin to tremble under the growing light as one climbs the mountain at dawn. Finally one reaches the buildings of a more enlightened age. The summit of Cynthus has been carved out as a platform for the shrines of Zeus and Athena. Curiously enough, this place which should certainly have been dedicated to Apollo seems to have been neglected by his priests. A minor shrine to Artemis has been uncovered, but nothing to the sun god.

It is on the peak of Mount Cynthus that one understands and feels the whole of the Aegean. To the north Tinos is dark against the pale sky, and to the east Mykonos sleeps upon the sea. Westward lie Syra, Zea, Kythnos and Seriphos. They are revealed as the night clouds begin to peel away from their craggy summits. South, across a fifteen-mile channel, lie Paros and Naxos—Byron's "beloved Naxos" to which he hoped one day to retire. Their cheeks are bearded with cloud. Away over the eastern sea, invisible behind Mykonos, the other islands circle—Nikaria, Furni, Patmos and Samos. Rock and thyme, sage, olive and vine, they scoop their circlet of land out of the water—stepping-stones between Europe and Asia.

CHAPTER 10

Seriphos, Siphnos, Milos

The western chain of the Cyclades, running down from Zea or Keos at the top, to Kythnos, Seriphos, Siphnos, Kimolos and Milos, has less obvious attraction than the islands in the Gulf of Athens, or off the mainland coast. They are all on shipping routes from Piraeus, but sailings are less frequent than to many other islands.

Less distinguished in history than the central and eastern islands of the Aegean, they are ideal places for those whose mood is to escape the newspaper and the radio, and to scratch the surface of an unfamiliar world. As with all islands, though, the traveller can do no more than "scratch the surface"—unless he is proficient in modern Greek, and has the time to spend several weeks in one place. In Seriphos, Siphnos and Milos, the ex-Brooklyner, the "Howdy" man, with his half-remembered American and (if the roads permit) his battered taxi, is rarer than elsewhere. There is more obvious tragedy in these islands, more stark poverty to be found than anywhere else that I know, except parts of Calabria and some of the mountain villages of Sicily. One virtue though, that the poor island Greek has over his Italian counterpart is the greater cleanliness of his home and his village. There is something in the scouring Etesian winds that produces an attitude reminiscent of the island Scots. But Seriphos, Siphnos and Milos—for those who intend to stay more than a few hours before rejoining the steamer—are best visited by yacht or charter boat. There are few comforts, and little in the way of hotels.

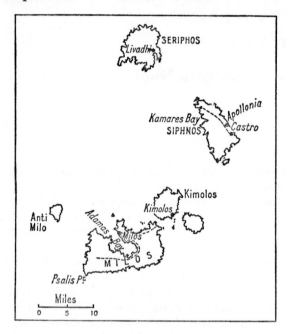

Seriphos is almost a perfect sphere, the Chora, or high town, lying inland on a strange peaked hill beyond the gulf of Livadhi on the south-east corner of the island. Entering the deep blue gulf one sees a snow-capped ridge of houses rising on the inland hills. Snow in midsummer! It is the houses and streets which give this illusion. They are among the purest in all the islands.

Livadhi itself is a lovely and land-locked harbour, open only to the south, with a sand beach straggling all around its head, and a small village of about 200 inhabitants. It is from this deep bay, reminiscent of Norway rather than the Aegean, that the iron ore of Seriphos is shipped. Around the bay are the sad stains of the iron mines which just—but only just—manage to keep Seriphos from being a deserted island. Seriphos is beautiful but sad. It was here that an iron-worker told me that his pay was "A little under £1 a day for ten hours' work. I work six days a week. With the high cost of living one cannot feed and clothe one's family." It is little wonder then that the inhabitants of Seriphos have been emigrating steadily over the past fifteen years.

It is easy to be romantic about Greece, a natural error to observe only the golden skin. But to meet a miner from Seriphos is to comprehend "the tragic sense of life." With little or no modern equipment, to work as men worked 2,000 years ago, underground in a mine with little safety equipment, is the lot of the men of this place. As I wrote a good many years ago, "It is little wonder that most of the men emigrate or go to join the unemployed in Athens. Always there is a bitter edge to one's enjoyment of the Greek world: always, unless one is abnormally insensitive, one must be conscious of the starvation that lurks only just below the surface."

To the visitor, though, **Port Livadhi** itself is a delightful place. In the distance there is a bone of hill crowned by windmills, in the foreground the white shore, with clear water right up to the edge of the beach. I had been told in other islands that the men of Seriphos were unfriendly and prone to violence. But when I first dropped anchor here, half-a-dozen small rowing boats immediately put out from the shore to welcome the stranger. With them came the Pappas, who insisted that I go ashore and enjoy the local wine with him.

Mega Livadhi, the town of Seriphos, is as pleasant as it looks from the bay. There are no hotels, but the stranger would have no difficulty in finding a family prepared to offer him a room for the night. Just on 1,000 people inhabit the town, but their numbers are rapidly declining. It is a silent place at night, one without memories of historical greatness—only of the ruinous hand which history lays upon the small and unimportant. A friend of mine once thought of staying here for six months to complete a philosophical work upon which he was engaged. After a few weeks he retired defeated—"I felt that I was being absorbed into the silence."

The trouble about Port Livadhi in the summer is the heat.

Surrounded on all sides by an amphitheatre of rocky hills, it burns like an oven during the midday hours and, even at night, the temperature hardly drops. The rocks around absorb the heat, and throw it back in great shuddering waves as soon as the sun is down. But as a harbour for small boat sailors I can recommend it, and it would be hard to find a place more remote from the modern world. Here is a diary entry from Livadhi in mid-June:—

"Midday is electric with the high shrilling of the cicadas. We lie sweating under an awning and fan the flies away. My new friend the harbour-master has retired to bed 'until about six o'clock.' The fisherman who has an English diesel engine in his boat, similar to my own, has long since rolled himself under one of the thwarts. Only a bare foot, sticking out into the sunlight, reveals his presence. In the shack bar on the foreshore the proprietor slumbers in a basket-chair (his wife has pulled the curtain across their room at the back and gone to bed.) Nothing moves. Even the cats—and, like most ports in Greece, this one is alive with cats—are invisible. . . ."

In the summer one must be prepared for the sun and the heat. The islands are pin-points of fire, and everything is stark and shadowless. After a time, the light seems to get right behind one's eyes, a blinding feeling as if one has become all spirit. It was on days like these that the Maenads ran mad upon the hills, and the panthers of the God were unleashed. Blood as well as wine was spilled along the upland ridges. The sea was burning and even the shadow of the boat on the seabed looked warm.

Eight miles from Port Livadhi, across a windy channel, lies **Siphnos.** Steamers from Piraeus call here, anchoring in Kamares Bay on the western side—a pity, for it means that most travellers see only the island's least attractive aspect. The eastern side of Siphnos is green and cultivated in terraced vineyards, with a straggling line of bleached villages running from crest to crest. Kamares Bay, on the other hand, is barren and uninviting. On the left, a mining village spouts fire and smoke, and on the right a post-war village has sprung up, which—unlike almost anywhere else in the Aegean—has houses without character and streets

132

without cleanliness. I came in here one evening and viewed the shore with disfavour. Perhaps I was prejudiced, having left Delos only the day before, and my mind still being inhabited by those images of peace and silence.

Just as I was on the point of saying "Oh well—it's only for a night," the unexpected happened. All the small boats on the beach were run down into the water, and the villagers—men, women and children—scrambled aboard them. They rowed out into the bay and circled our boat, laughing and asking those inevitable questions, "Where do you come from? Why do you come here?" Then suddenly, from one boat after another, the women and children began to sing. Strange that sound of singing coming across the evening water! Many of the girls had flowers in their hair, or round their necks. While the men rowed, they trailed their hands in the water, leaning their heads together and singing softly.

It was in Kamares Bay that I first came across this gracious habit, the evening row around one's native cove or bay, the islanders' equivalent to the "promenade" of Mediterranean cities. Here, where there are no tree-lined boulevards and no cafés on broad sidewalks, the people take their evening "stroll" by boat, relaxing on the sea as the cool night wind begins to draw onshore. The village priest, resplendent in his dark robes, with flowing hair and patriarchal beard, sailed slowly past, sitting back in the sternsheets of his boat as grand as any Doge of Venice. He passed under our bow and waved a hand in greeting—only to remember that these strangers had not yet been ashore in his village. Nothing would satisfy him until we had joined him in his boat and been ferried back to the jetty. *Ouzo* and dishes of cucumber and cheese were quickly set out on the café table. I agreed with him that it was certainly a good *ouzo*. "Of course it is," he said. "It comes from Siphnos, that's why."

I asked whether I could buy some retsina for the boat, and the proprietor who had joined us explained that they had no spare bottles in the village. If I brought my own ashore he would fill them. Bottles are hard to come by, and highly valued, in most of the islands. Shamefacedly, I thought of the dozen or more I had tossed over the side rather than have them littering up the cabin.

It was nearly dark when we got back on board. The boats were still circling the bay, the singing clear across the water. There is a sad lilt to those old songs and even the ones that tell of love or humour seem to ache with the harshness of life. Lamps began to flicker in the windows of the new village. On the far side of Kamares Bay the furnaces still smoked and flamed.

In the morning, the villages behind Kamares Bay flared along their hill-tops. Going ashore, I found that not all the village was as dilapidated and unattractive as it had first seemed. The architecture in Siphnos is, in fact, as good as any in the Cyclades. But to see it at its best, one must either take the road from Kamares—a long climb on a hot day—or sail round to the other side of the island, where Castro Bay lies below the old capital. If you take the road, you will pass the twin villages of **Appollonia** and **Artemona** on the watershed of the island. They straggle into one another, in much the same way that the religious territories of Apollo and Artemis once overlapped. Individually, the Siphniac houses are better proportioned and more attractive than those of Mykonos, but the two villages which undulate along the island's spine seem to lack a heart. One does not carry away the same immediate impression of grace that one does from a town like Mykonos.

Castro, the old capital, on the other hand, is one of the most attractive places in the Aegean. It lies on the eastern side of the island clinging like all these old townships to its protective hill, and hedged round with a fourteenth-century wall. Unfortunately, like the Castro of Zea, its glory has departed, and many of the Venetian buildings are collapsing in ruin and the streets have an abandoned air. The most distinctive houses are those built into the wall itself, and facing across the sea towards Paros and Anti-Paros. Here, unusual in the Cyclades, one finds enclosed wooden balconies (somewhat reminiscent of the Maltese-type balcony) built out beyond the walls. Following along the main street one passes under small bridges, thrown out by the houses to connect them with the higher ground where the next street runs.

Castro has a medieval air, and there is something faintly reminiscent of Rhodes about it, although the Knights of St. John never, in fact, extended their influence this far to the west. Perhaps the Venetian Corogna family, who were responsible for building the walls, were familiar with the Island of the Knights. The harbour, on the other hand, can never have been suitable for any large-scale activity, even though it is deep enough. It is a summer anchorage only, and would be untenable in the hard winds of winter. In classical times, when Siphnos was among the richest of the islands, this would not have mattered much, since the galleys were always hauled ashore in the autumn.

Castro is built on the same site as the ancient capital of the island. This was the Siphnos described as "rich in gold and silver" and adorned with Parian marble. But the mines were worked out, or submerged by a volcanic change in the sea-bed, during classical times. Pausanias attributes the destruction of the mines of Siphnos to the anger of Apollo. The people of Siphnos had been accustomed to offer Apollo an annual gift of a gold egg. But on one unfortunate occasion they attempted to deceive the god by presenting him with an imitation gilt one. No doubt there was an efficient assay-master at Delphi, for the ruse was at once discovered. Hence, so legend has it, the anger of the god and the destruction of the mines of Siphnos.

Undoubtedly many remains of the ancient city lie beneath the Venetian houses, or are built into the walls of Castro. Just above the harbour, in a shady ravine, I came on two muleteers watering their animals from a marble trough. On closer inspection, it proved to be a fine marble sarcophagus with a rich swag of grapes and other fruit decorating the side. The past lies heavy in Castro.

> *Tutto è pace e silenzio, e tutto posa*
> *Il mondo, e più di lor non si ragiona.*

Leaving Kamares Bay on the west of Siphnos, the steamers from Piraeus have a twenty mile crossing to Adamas Bay, the seaport of **Milos,** and one of the finest natural harbours in the Aegean. Whatever it may have been in antiquity, Milos is not a beautiful island to-day. Barren and blinding under the summer sun, it is volcanic like Santorin. The great harbour was probably once the peak of a volcano which, long before the memory of man, blew itself to pieces and let the sea rush in. Except that the island has not the same fertile natural beauty, it is somewhat reminiscent of Ischia—where, again, a volcanic peak has disappeared to create a great deep-water harbour. Like points of brilliant white fire, the chapels and shrines of Milos glitter on the peaks of the hills that surround the deep bay. Coming in to anchor one sees the dark mouths of caves against the white of the land, below the village of Adamas itself. Once, no doubt, troglodytic dwellings, they nowadays serve as boathouses for the fishermen.

The "Aphrodite" of Milos, the "Venus de Milo," was found in 1820 in the ruins of the ancient theatre. This lies to the north-east of Mount Elias, the principal hill behind the modern capital of Plaka. Plaka, which is on the northern side of the harbour, boasts one small hotel and is the seat of local government. It is a comparatively uninteresting village with a population of only one thousand. It is uninteresting, that is to say, after other towns in the Cyclades—although, if one came upon it after a wet and foggy northern winter, it is possible that it might seem like paradise.

Theophrastus in his work *On Plants* writes of the island: "There at Milos they reap apparently thirty or forty days after sowing, wherefore is a saying of these islanders that one should go on sowing until one sees the sheaves. . . . However, it is said that pulses in their country do not grow like this, nor are they abundant. Yet they say that the soil is wonderfully fertile, for it is good both for corn and olives." I found the retsina very poor (maybe I was unlucky), but the figs and olives excellent.

Above Plaka rises the peak of Mount Elias, where the ancient acropolis stood. It was a hot day and I shirked the climb, although assured by one toothless ancient that it would be possible to view the mountains of Crete from the peak. They are ittle more than seventy miles away, and I have no reason to doubt that in the sparkling air of midsummer those "blue, remembered hills" would be visible.

Milos might prove a good harbour for the small boat sailor in which to winter, although it has the disadvantage of being so large that, even when I was there in July, the breath of the Meltemi was raising a small sea inside the bay. It is a good harbour, though, to rest in if bound westwards for Kithera and Cape Matapan, or equally if destined for Crete. It is only about seventy miles from Psalis Point at the south-western end of Milos to Suda Bay. Milos, as might be expected from its proximity to Crete, once formed part of the Minoan Empire. The British School at Athens has excavated at Philacopi, about two hours by mule out of Adamas, and has uncovered the remains of two Minoan cities.

When I was last in Milos there was great excitement in the town, for rumour had it that the missing arms of the "Venus de Milo" had just been discovered. They were found by a restaurant owner, Mr. Kyritsis, "hidden in a small hollow inside a wall and resting on a bed of leaves." Unfortunately I could not get to see them, as the Milo museum authorities were brooding over them, before sending them to Athens for examination. The local story has it that in 1890, when the French sailors were loading the statue aboard ship for dispatch to Paris, a fight broke out between them and the Turkish garrison troops, in the course of which the statue was broken. A French writer, Jean François Icara, claimed to have seen the arms of the "Aphrodite" before they were taken away by some local inhabitants. In his account, one hand held an apple, while the other clutched modestly at her falling robe. It will be interesting to see whether the arms now in Athens match his description. It will be difficult, in any case, to eradicate from millions of memories the image impressed on them by those sepia prints in uncountable school rooms of the armless "Venus de Milo."

CHAPTER 11

Paros and Naxos

Whether you come to them from the north, direct from Piraeus, or whether you approach from the south, winding up through the Sikinos-Ios channel, the blue humps of Paros and Naxos are inspiring. The largest islands of the Cyclades, they contrive to seem all of one piece, sculptural and impressive. Both are dominated by massifs in the south-east, from which the land slopes away evenly to fertile plains. Mount St. Elias on Paros, and Mount Zia on Naxos, two-and-a-half thousand feet and over three thousand feet respectively, are like the twin pillars or gates to the sea. This feeling is even stronger if one is sailing south, bound into the southern Aegean for Santorin or Crete.

Paros is flanked by a sister islet, Anti-Paros, of which I know nothing except that it contains a cave famous for its stalactites. But there are caves all over the world, and I doubt whether most travellers, with only a few days to spend on Paros and Naxos, will be tempted into some bat-befouled cavern. There are regular sailings from Piraeus, and both islands are easy to reach from the other Cyclades. But if one is travelling from any of the islands that lie to the south, one is quite likely to be delayed. In midsummer, when the Meltemi are blowing hard, the narrow channel between Paros and Naxos can run like a mill-race.

Paros, some ten miles long by seven wide, is about half the size of Naxos, yet in its way it is more impressive. Where Naxos has a romantic beauty in its valleys and folds, Paros is all of one piece. It would be pressing the analogy too far to say that Paros

138

is Grecian form and Naxos Gothic form, nor would I entirely agree with Blake: "Grecian is Mathematic Form: Gothic is Living Form. Mathematic Form is eternal in the reasoning memory: Living Form is Eternal Existence." But Paros is certainly sculptural, which is appropriate enough for the island from which came that lovely, coarse-grained marble. "Lych-

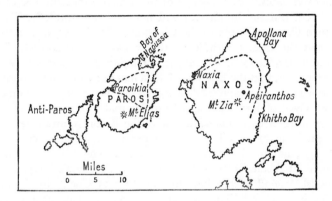

nites" Parian marble was called, "won by lamplight," for the quarries on the northern slopes of the mountain were subterranean.

Paroikia, the capital, lies on the north-western side of the island in a deeply-indented bay. Like Mykonos, it is a town by the water and, like Mykonos again, it has the sparkle of life that always revolves around ships and boats, nets, engines and sails, arrivals and departures. There are several hotels, the Xenia and the Pandrossos among them, at both of which one can find adequate comfort and reasonable food. The lobsters of Paros are good, and the local wine—heavy, and dark—is a refreshing change after some of the retsina in other places.

The town does not have the distinction, perhaps, of Mykonos, but it is pretty and unspoiled. Alleys wind and shine off the waterfront, and one comes upon curiosities like the medieval tower which is built largely from the drums of classical columns.

Tucked in between carved blocks of marble, the old columns protrude like giant cotton reels.

Paros is distinguished by the finest church in the Aegean, the **Katapoliani.** Most scholars seem to agree that the word means no more than "On low (or lower) ground" but other argument runs that the word is a diminutive of Hekatontapyliani, "The hundred gates." Ninety-nine of them have reputedly been discovered, but the hundredth will not be found until the Turks return Constantinople to the Christians. No doubt, as is nearly always the case, the duller of the two versions is correct. The church itself is far from dull, it is magnificent. It was here, so legend goes, that the Empress Helena had her vision of the finding of the True Cross, and made a vow to build a great church on the site. Cyril of Jerusalem and Eusebius make no mention of this story in their accounts of the life of the Empress, and it did not become current until the fourth century and then, curiously enough, not in Greece but in the West. The Abbey of Haut-villiers at Rheims claims possession of St. Helena's body, while English legend makes her the daughter of Coel, our familiar "Old King Cole." The church of the Katapoliani, at any rate, was not built until two centuries after St. Helena's death.

It is, in fact, three churches all under one roof: the main church, cruciform, and partially restored in seventeenth-century Baroque; the smaller basilica of St. Nicholas; and the baptistery. The latter has a large cruciform font for baptism by total immersion. The columns in the basilica come from a Doric temple, probably sixth century BC, and there is a fine early seventeenth-century stone screen. Badly damaged during a great earthquake in 1773, the Katapoliani has only just been restored. Much of its early simplicity has now been given back to it, although I can well believe that there are those who regret the loss of some of its former darkness and mystery. Restoration, however, has revealed an early tessellated pavement and the bases of four columns which date from a much earlier and smaller church. It is not impossible that they belong to the original church in which the Empress had her vision—or perhaps to the church which was founded on the site before Justinian sent his architects from St. Sophia to build the present Katapoliani. The church is the focus of a great pilgrimage every year on August 15th. Yet, despite its far greater antiquity, beauty and interest, the Katapoliani does not seem to have anything like the same appeal for the Orthodox as does the Tiniotissa.

About five miles north-east from Paroikia lies the **Bay of Naoussa,** approached through a lovely green valley, heavy with vegetables and vines. One can reach it on foot or mule, or by boat—but Naoussa Bay is no place to be caught in when the Meltemi are boiling the sea at the base of the steep cliffs. In the inlet on the north-east side of Naoussa there is room for a small boat to anchor, and the swimming is perfect. Too often in the Mediterranean the sea seems tired and languid, but here it is quick on the skin, oxygenated by the silver breakers that roll past the small headland. The village of Naoussa, with a small stream running through the heart of it, is delightful.

Inland from Paroikia, the country everywhere has the calm and sculptured feel that is distinctive of Paros. This is an island which would cure the jangled nerves of city-dwellers, for it is peaceful without being enervating. The Parians, in fact, are a cheerful breed of islanders—less commercialised than the Mykoniots and not so dour as the men of Siphnos. The inevitable *bouzouki* music, heard everywhere in the islands, seems to have a gayer and more astringent lilt in Paros.

Paros was traditionally colonised by Arcadians, and later by Ionians from Athens. Archilochus, the satirist, was born here in the mid-seventh century BC. Prior to Archilochus, Greek poetry had been restricted to the epic hexameter and the elegiac metre, but to the Parian must go the credit for the invention of iambic poetry—so suitable with its light quick rhythm to the satiric muse. Only fragments of his work remain, but Hadrian referred to his verses as "raging iambics." He seems to have kept his rage mostly for verse, for he was banished from Sparta for his cowardice and licentious character. I have an affection for Archilochus, at least he was an honest man. He admitted that, on one occasion in a fight against the Thracians, he threw away his shield and fled. No wonder the Spartans had little use for him. But he seems to have lived only to prove the truth of the old adage about "he who fights and runs away," for he was killed in a battle against the Naxians. His conqueror, a Naxian called Korax, was thereupon cursed by the oracle of Apollo for having slain one of the favourite servants of the muse.

The Parians of antiquity had rather an unpleasant reputation. They sided with the Persians during the Persian wars, and even sent a trireme to help them at Marathon. In retaliation, the Athenians dispatched a fleet under Miltiades to besiege Paros and to secure 100 talents as reparations for their "Medism." The expedition was unsuccessful, Miltiades (as Herodotus tells the story) breaking his thigh while jumping over the palisade that surrounded the temple sacred to Ceres. Gangrene set in, and Miltiades died on his return to Athens. Not content with their earlier treachery to the Greek cause, Paros also sided with Xerxes. But this time they were not allowed to get away scot-free, and Themistocles exacted a heavy fine from them.

Like the other Cyclades, Paros became subject to Venice after the Fourth Crusade, and then fell to the Turks in the siege of 1537. The island now forms a province of Greece together with Naxos, and both islands share the same bishop. The famous quarries are no longer active, not because they are worked out, but because world demand for marble has declined and there are other and larger quarries (such as Carrara) which can produce suitable marble more cheaply. This is a great pity, for the Parian marble with its granular texture and its almost transparent whiteness is singularly beautiful. Exported to all corners of the Greek world from the sixth century BC onwards, Parian marble was the medium in which Praxiteles worked. It was in this native marble that the famous Parian Chronicle was cut. This outline of Greek history, consisting of 93 lines in the Attic dialect, is now among the Arundel marbles at Oxford, and only a copy is on view in the small museum at Paroikia. Whoever was the author of the Chronicle, he showed a proper disrespect for the

142

achievements of politicians, most of the recorded events being the births and deaths of poets, the dates of festivals, and the dates when different kinds of poetry were introduced. "Important political and military events," says one authority rather sadly, "are often omitted. . . ."—a pleasant change from modern chroniclers.

Largest and most fertile of the Cyclades, **Naxos** lies only six miles away from Paros, across the blue, fast-running strait. One enters the harbour with Vakkhos (Bacchus) islet on the port hand. The islet takes its name from an old temple to Dionysus, the ruins of which are still visible, and it is connected to the shore by a small causeway at Vakkhos Point. It was here, perhaps, that Dionysus met the beautiful Ariadne.

I approached the island on a fair day, when the green lemon- and olive-groves looked as if they had just been varnished, and when the small white city of the Dukes glittered gem-like under the sun. The story of Ariadne was fresh in my mind. Ariadne seemed to me then—as she does still—the most attractive of all Greek heroines. Her sign still gleams in the sky for all to see— the *Corona Borealis*, or "the Cretan Crown," that chaplet of stars which Dionysus hung in the heavens as his wedding gift to her. Ariadne was the daughter of Minos, King of Crete, and of Pasiphae. Aphrodite, who had taken Theseus under her protection before he sailed south to kill the Minotaur, arranged that Ariadne should fall in love with the hero. It was with Ariadne's help (and with the magic ball of thread given her by Daedalus before he left Crete) that Theseus managed to penetrate to the innermost recesses of the labyrinth and slay the Minotaur, Ariadne's monstrous half-brother. Ariadne, now passionately in love with Theseus, fled with him from the Cretan capital. The first place that their ship visited on the way to Athens was Naxos. It is at this point that the story becomes mysterious. Although he had appeared to be equally in love with Ariadne, Theseus left her asleep on the foreshore, hoisted sail, and set off to Athens. Ancient writers had many and varied explanations for the hero's behaviour. One was that he had fallen in love with another woman, Aegle, a second that he was fearful of his reception in Athens if he arrived with the daughter of their ancient enemy, King Minos, for bride.

While Ariadne slept, and while Theseus pursued his voyage to Athens, a ship bearing Dionysus crept northwards towards the island of Naxos. It was a ship which had formerly belonged to Tyrrhenian pirates, who, ignorant of Dionysus' divinity, had captured him intending to sell him as a slave. But the god made a vine grow up from the deck, while ivy twined around the rigging, the oars became serpents and he himself was transformed into a lion. The pirates immediately jumped overboard leaving the ship to Dionysus, now restored to his normal graceful form, and to a phantom crew. The ship came on steadily over the water towards Naxos, while the air was filled with the sound of flutes. Stepping ashore on the island, the first person Dionysus saw was the sleeping Ariadne. He fell in love with her, and she with him. Certainly she did not long regret the vanished hero, Theseus, who, while her marriage to Dionysus was being celebrated, was bearing down on Athens with his ill-omened, dark sail hoisted. Ariadne seems to have been happy with the god, and bore him many children.

Ariadne, whose name most probably means "The Very Holy" was associated with the moon goddess and was also considered the personification of spring. I think it was spring when Dionysus came to Naxos and when, in his role of Dendrites, "the tree-youth," all the trees of the island burst into leaf, the birds returned singing from the south, and the whole world was filled with desire.

The harbour town of **Naxia** has no memories of its classical past. Its interest lies in its Venetian ancestry, for Naxia's greatest period was during the Middle Ages when "all the qualities o'th'isle The fresh springs, brine-pits, barren place, and fertile" belonged to its Venetian Dukes. Naxos was captured in AD 1207 by Marco Sanudo, an energetic and enterprising freebooter, who established the Duchy which remained in existence until the island fell to the Turks in 1566. It was during those 300 years that the town of Naxia assumed its present form, with its battlements, much of which still remain, dominating the harbour, and the palace and retainers' houses of the Dukes forming the main block of the upper town. One must not look for important medieval or Renaissance buildings in Naxia. What one finds, to remind one of the Dukes of Naxos, are charming and irrelevant touches—a coat-of-arms over a house-front, or a Venetian gate juxtaposed with a Cycladic "square-box" cottage.

Naxia rises up from the harbour in a series of terraces, steep alleys, and white houses that look like children's toys. It has the atmosphere of a "penny-plain, twopence-coloured" theatre, and there is a feeling that it could be taken home and put in the toe of a child's Christmas stocking. Everything seems miniature: windows, shop fronts, doorways, and rooms all look as if they had been made for a race of dwarfs. In summer, these narrow streets, these whitewashed rooms and scrubbed floors are cool. In the winter, on the other hand, their miniature windows can be boarded up, and there are no broad avenues through which the wind can howl.

Robert Liddell in his *Aegean Greece* wrote that he found Naxia dirty: "Both upper and lower towns are filthy. Walls hopefully ask you not to throw rubbish against them. . . ." Perhaps times have changed (although the first time I visited Naxia, shortly after the war, I found it reasonably clean). On my last visit I noted: "Here, as in many other islands, the pavements are whitewashed twice a day. It is difficult to describe this atmosphere of cleanliness except to say that, when you step ashore, you find yourself looking at the soles of your shoes before setting foot in the main street."

It is not as clean as Hydra or Poros, but after the skin-destroying dirt of London, or the paper-blowing winds of New York, I found it almost surgical. The shops were golden with the Naxian lemons, and green with cucumbers and lettuces. A cool scent lifted off them—a compound of night dew, rain, and sunshine. Bread shops in the upper town exuded that crackling smell which always reminds me of a frosty day in Paris, and outside the butchers' stalls—with their clean boards and razor-sharp cleavers—the sad carcasses of kids hung the odour of blood on the air. Roasting over charcoal fires were those long skewers twined with sheep and goats' guts, and stuffed with herb-flavoured meat. These ancestors of the homely sausage should not be despised by the Aegean traveller.

Like so many islands which were for a long time under Venetian rule, Naxos has many Catholics among its people, though less than one finds in Tinos or Syra. The Catholic cathedral itself is of little interest, and there is more of the old Latin heritage to be found in the lintel over a doorway, or a mouldering coat-of-arms.

The wine of Naxos is quite good, but has hardly enough quality to commend it to a modern follower of Dionysus. There is one drink, though, unique to the island which must be tasted. This is Citron, not to be confused with any French soft drink, but a miraculous distillation of lemons. It is a liqueur, and not an apéritif. The acidity of the lemon and the sweetness of the sugar are admirably counterbalanced. In the words of a Naxian: "In Citron you hold within your mouth the quintessence of a lemon grove, the pale breasts of the fruit, the dark green of the leaves, and the perfume that rises from the bruised peel. . . ." It is a pity for Naxos, perhaps, that no commercial firm has discovered this excellent liqueur and put it on the world market. Naxos, which once exported thousands of lemons to England and America, has lost most of this trade in recent years, and many a Naxian lemon grove has been ploughed up to make more mundane pasturage.

The interior of the island is one of the few places in the Cyclades where the folded valleys are remote enough from the sea to have a distinct life of their own. Like Euboea and, indeed, like parts of Andros, it is possible in Naxos to feel that one has lost contact with the sea. But, whereas Naxia itself has some comfort to offer the visitor—two hotels, the Neon perhaps the better—it would be unwise to expect anything except a rough bed anywhere else in the island. Between the northern and southern mountain ridges, a graceful valley leads through to the village of Apeiranthos, and a daily bus can be found to take one over to the eastern side of the island for the night. One of the most pleasant places, the **Bay of Apollona,** is almost inaccessible by land. A marble colossus, unfinished and abandoned in the quarry, dominates Apollona. It is worth remembering that the sculptors of Naxos rivalled those of Paros in their time, and that it was the Naxians who originally took Delos under their protection.

Naxos was visited by the youthful Byron during his first pilgrimage to Greece. It was a place which he never forgot, one which he often described during his years of success and disillusionment, and the "dream island" to which he often expressed the hope that he would return.

With its easy communications with Piraeus, and its variety of scenery—from the narrow lively streets of Naxia, to the silences of Mount Zia or Khitho Bay on the south-east coast—Naxos offers the expatriate a potential island-home where ennui would not too soon overtake him. Unfortunately I must record that, in my small experience, the Naxians are not the pleasantest of islanders. It was in Naxia that an officious harbour-master delayed my sailing by insisting on copying out all my ship's papers —most of them were in English script and therefore competely incomprehensible to him. I was anxious to get under way to Ios before darkness fell, and therefore naturally indignant at such a waste of time. All over the world, however, one must expect to meet with ignorant jacks-in-office, and in Greece, fortunately, they are rarer than in Italy or England. After an hour's hard labour the harbour-master joined me over a Citron at the shanty bar a few yards from his office. His face bore so worried an expression that I accompanied him back to assist in his duplication of my papers. I did not sail for Ios until dawn next morning.

CHAPTER 12

Ios, Amorgos, Sikinos

Ios is one of the most delightful of all the lesser-known Cyclades. More fertile than the "dry islands" of Amorgos, Sikinos and Pholegandros, it has a most attractive small harbour. One enters by a winding bay from the south, with the church of St. Irene serving as a leading mark. The village lies at the far end, with a landing place where passengers disembark from the rowing boats that bring them ashore off the steamer. There are no hotels here, but one or two cheerful tavernas, and it would not be difficult to find a room in the *chora* of Ios which lies about half a mile back from the port. The steamers from Piraeus bound for Santorin usually call in at Port Ios. Amorgos, Sikinos and Pholegandros, on the other hand, are more difficult to reach, services to them being irregular.

Seven cities are recorded as having claimed to be the birth-place of Homer, but Ios is one of the few which claims to be his burial place. "Homer's tomb" lies on the northern slopes of Mount Pirgos, the main peak of which dominates **Port Ios** from the east. There could be few more suitable places for the poet's bones to lie than on the green sides of this mountain, where the northerlies rustle the grass all summer, and where the eye instinctively turns eastwards towards Asia and the distant plains of Troy. It may be some Greek patriarch, a Turkish warrior, or even a wandering Crusader who lies beneath the tomb which the people of Ios claim as Homer's, but it matters very little. Here is as suitable a place as any in the Aegean.

Ios is rich in churches and the brows of the hills and the green

148

troughs of the valleys are encrusted with their domes. On a summer night they glow like moonstones. The church of St. Irene, at the head of the bay, is a delightful example of the best in Greek island churches. This is not because it contains any fine ikons, nor because of any architectural peculiarity, but solely for its simple perfection of dome and arched belfries. It sets the mood

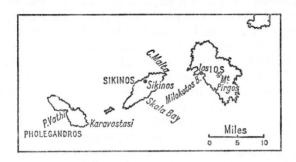

and tone for all of Ios, one of the cleanest places I have ever visited. Even the small harbour village is free from the odd scraps, forgotten fishbones, frayed ropes and broken crates which haunt most waterfronts. In this small harbour, anchored less than a cable from the church, I spent one of my pleasantest evenings in the Aegean. It was not unique certainly, but typical of those evenings which one remembers elsewhere, and in later years, as containing something of the essence of the good life.

I was lucky enough to arrive when a shadow play was being held. Karaghiozi, that Rabelaisian patriot, was up to his usual antics—antics which, unfortunately, get rarer and rarer as the cinema establishes its hold over the Aegean. I could hear the cracked voices from behind the screen as I rowed ashore. I was just in time to find one of the comic Jewish puppets—Jacob, I think it was—complaining that Karaghiozi had made off with all his money and a string of sausages to boot. Among the spectators there were a number of old men in the Turkish trousers and faded embroidered waistcoats which one sees less and less each year in

149

the islands. They had a Cretan look, some of them with those grizzled, half-moon beards which again are reminiscent of Crete. The Pappas was there, a giant of a man, well over six feet with shoulders proportionately broad. After the show was over, I was introduced to him formally by the owner of the taverna, outside which the Karaghiozi play had been performed. The Pappas was married, he informed me, and the father of three children. "All males," he said with pride, "all males." (On account of the dowry system, it can be disastrous to be the father of girls in Greece.) He struck his beard with a patriarchal gesture and beamed at the sea as we sat down and called for coffee. The pine-topped table was scrubbed like a yacht's deck and our glasses of water shone in the lamplight. Although it was after midnight the harbour was still festive, for a number of people had come down from the surrounding hills and from the high town to see Karaghiozi. Some of them were dancing, suddenly and inexplicably the way Greeks will—all on an impulse. One young man was waltzing dreamily with a chair for partner.

One cannot understand the islanders, or any Greek for that matter—until one understands his passion for water. I love to see those tumblers sparkling on the table. In the Aegean, water—like almost everything else—takes on a primal and elemental quality. The drying-up of a spring can mean death to a farm or vineyard. Our state-given water, medicated as it often is with chemicals that the Government has decided are good for us, and flowing through the same mass-produced pipes, can never have any of this quality.

The dew was falling by the time I got up to go. All around, the night air was becoming perceptibly damper and cleaner. It was not too difficult to visualise the tired grasses on the hills and the flowers and vegetables in the plots around the bay lifting their leaves and heads at this dampness—at this so necessary water. A single-cylinder petrol engine started up with a raucous bang as I said good night to the landlord. " Our charging plant," he explained. "I have the only wireless down here in the port. My batteries ran down some weeks ago and the engine was broken.

It is only to-day that a caique has come in from Piraeus with the spare parts."

The high town itself is enchanting. I have been unable to find out anything of its history, except, of course, that like the rest of the Cyclades Ios was formerly a Venetian possession. The town shows less traces of Venice in its architecture than Naxia, but it is neater and more sparkling. A dust road runs from the port to the town, made pleasant even in high summer by the carefully-worked small fields that border it. The town is as snow-white as the villages of Apollonia and Artemona on Siphnos, but it has a coherence and a related structure which those two lovely villages lack. The architecture of Siphnos is a little finer than that of Ios, and the mouldings of windows and doorways are more detailed. Yet, all the same, I think I prefer the *chora* of Ios to almost any other small town in the islands. One could be happy here.

Perhaps because the Pappas and the landlord had sent on advance word, I found a warmth of welcome that has ever since predisposed me towards the island of Ios. I suppose, being an East Anglian born and bred—from a smaller village than Ios even—I treasure the Greek friendliness towards the stranger, all the more for the fact that in Norfolk a stranger is a "furriner" for all his life. The same of course is true in many parts of the world, in Greece too, but the hospitality due to the visitor at the gates is rarely forgotten in the Aegean. As a journalist in Corinth once remarked to me, "There is still one god of the old religion who is respected everywhere in Greece—Zeus Xenios, Zeus who protects strangers."

Behind the town of Ios there is a bare ridge chiselled out of the hill. It is cut into threshing floors and backed by a double line of windmills. Unlike the much-photographed windmills of Mykonos, the windmills of Ios really work, for the island is too far away from the mainland for it to be practical to send the grain over for milling. The mills catch the north-easterly wind as it siphons between the valleys from the eastern side of the island. The great difference between the windmills which one used to see operating in East Anglia when I was a boy and those in the Aegean, is that the Greek mill—unlike the post mill or the Dutch mill—is static. Because the winds which will drive it are almost constant from the north, it does not need to be made revolvable (the post mill revolves on a central post, and the Dutch mill revolves at the top). The sails also are much simpler than those of the North, being no more than triangles of canvas attached to between eight or twelve thin arms.

When all the sails are furled, the Greek windmill has a bare look like a dandelion-head from which all the seeds have gone, but when it is in action, revolving against that dazzling sky, it looks like a large white daisy gone mad with sunstroke. Each sail can be individually reefed, the canvas rolling around the arm in much the same way as a yacht's mainsail is roller-reefed around the boom. The Greek mill, however, has other variations to accord with the wind's strength. The miller can set—out of possible choice of ten sails—six only, or eight perhaps, but each half-reefed, or six all at full stretch. It is a simple and ingenious mechanism but I have been unable to find out when or how it first reached the Aegean. It seems, though, as if the windmill originated in Germany or the Netherlands sometime before the twelfth century. In Crete, pumping windmills are common (on the high plateau of Lassithi there are reputed to be over 12,000), but in the Aegean the true corn-grinding windmill is fast disappearing. It is a great pity, for when, as in Ios, they spin above a white Cycladic town their Pythagorean circles give a lift to the heart.

From the town of Ios there is a fine view of the surrounding island and of the bright bay where the small port lies. There is a good beach for bathing on the east side of this bay, but by far the best in the island is to be found just south of Port Ios in Milokotos Bay. At the head of Milokotos there is a sandy beach where I anchored one day when the Meltemi was blowing a gale. Even with the bulk of the island sheltering me from the wind, the dust and sand were whirling off the foreshore, and twigs and parched grasses were sailing seaward. Milokotos is a pleasant place: rocks and bushes, barley grass, white sand and shingle. I was debating whether to row ashore and walk over to Ios town, for I had run out of bread, when suddenly two boys appeared. One was about ten and the other sixteen or seventeen, both astride donkeys, and surrounded by a herd of goats. Seeing an unfamiliar vessel in their native cove they began to wave excitedly and shout. I caught nothing but the one word "cigarette." Before I had time to think about putting the rowing boat in the water, the elder of the two had stripped off his clothes and run naked into the sea. "An image of ancient Greece! But," as I remarked to my wife, "for heaven's sake, don't let him see you. The modern Greek is more bashful about his body than his forefathers. He hasn't noticed yet that there's a woman on board."

It was only when the youth was up to his armpits in water that I realised he could not swim. He made a good effort at it, striking out time and again, and half-drowning himself in the process. I got the dinghy into the water, took some cigarettes with me and went ashore. I believe that if I had not decided to row in, he would have gone on until he had either drowned or had learned to swim. The Greeks can be like that—crazy but determined. The two boys had a little bread with them, which they insisted on giving me in return for the cigarettes, also some goats' cheese. I rowed back to the boat again. Under the declining light, the scene took on a strange, timeless quality. The young boy had now stripped off, and was paddling and throwing stones, while the other youth was running naked up and down the beach. The shadows of the mules were long on the sand, and the goats were browsing on the thin grass that edged the cove. All the time there was the hollow sound of the wind over the island.

After Ios, **Sikinos,** its barren neighbour across the eight-mile channel to the west, seemed a little disappointing. Sikinos has no harbour, and the only anchorage of any size is the Bay of Skala on the south-eastern side of the island. There is a small lighthouse on the point which shelters the bay from the prevailing wind and sea—a useful light if one is sailing through the Sikinos-Ios channel after nightfall. The bay itself is well-sheltered but rather bleak, although it has a pleasant small beach at its head. The narrow pathway which leads from the bay up to the town follows a dry stream-bed, and is edged with olives and oleanders.

The small town lies on a ridge near the north-western coast. There is only one other village in Sikinos, and the total population of the island must be less than one thousand. On the only occasion when I visited the town of Sikinos I was told that it then held about 400 people and the village of Vouni less than 200. Sikinos is poor and parched, a place for exiles (some Communists were sent here after the last war), a place far out of this world. All the same I did not find it uncheerful and, although it was not so clean as Ios, I had a good meal here—mullet, tomatoes, and some drinkable retsina. Walking back to Skala Bay, I thought that the island seemed as barren as Malta in midsummer, but unredeemed by the noble architecture of the Knights of St. John. Curiously enough, looking at the chart before I left Sikinos, I noticed that the prominent cape at the northern end was known as Cape Malta, *Kavos tis Maltas*. I can only assume it got its name from some British sea-captain or hydrographer during the nineteenth century who, nostalgic perhaps for the security and fleshpots of Grand Harbour, found something familiar in the tawny slopes of Sikinos.

Pholegandros, which lies about six miles west of Sikinos, seems to be one of those islands which I am destined never to visit. It would appear to be more interesting than Sikinos, with a small town that sounds as if it might equal that of Ios. James Theodore Bent, the author of *The Cyclades* (London 1885), came here and described it.

I can do no better than recommend his book to other Aegean travellers, an impertinence perhaps to recommend Bent, but too few people nowadays seem to be acquainted with his work. (It is time that it was reissued.) It is the classic of Aegean travel in English and will never be superseded, for one good reason that Bent was lucky enough to visit the islands when they were still, as it were, intact, and only just waking out of the sleep of centuries. A Yorkshireman, Bent was one of those hardy and indefatigable Victorians who make the modern traveller feel somewhat ashamed. Accompanied by his wife, herself an expert photographer, Bent spent a long time in the Aegean, the fruit of which was his book *The Cyclades; or Life among the Insular Greeks.* He later distinguished himself in archaeological work in Asia Minor, and then—having, as it were, exhausted the ancient world— he spent most of his remaining years in the Persian Gulf, the Hadramaut, and South Africa. He was the first European to make a detailed examination of the ruins of Zimbabwe and the ruins of Axum in North Abyssinia. Bent died in 1897, from malaria contracted while on an expedition in South Arabia.

If my inability to land on Pholegandros has done no more than introduce some new readers to Bent's book, it has been worthwhile. I have tried twice to visit Pholegandros, on the first occasion dropping anchor in Port Vathi on the south-western coast. It blew a strong northerly, and within an hour the squalls sweeping down from the hills made landing impossible. On the second occasion I anchored in Karavostasi, having been told by a caique skipper in Syra that this was the only safe anchorage. Karavostasi lies on the south-east coast, facing towards Sikinos, and is another insecure anchorage if the Meltemi are strong. I found so heavy a scend setting into the bay that, although I waited twelve hours—mocked by the sight of the people on the shore, the gleam of the church of the Panayia high above me, and Bent's description of the town—I was forced to leave without going ashore. I think Pholegandros must be easier to visit by island steamer, although on both these occasions I do not believe any ship would have been able to land its passengers. Theoretically, at any rate, the steamer from Syra and Piraeus calls at Pholegandros once a week. One day I still hope to visit the island. But it is one of the pleasures of Aegean travel that the islands are inexhaustible, one is always hearing of coves, ports and inland villages, that one has missed. The Aegean is a microcosm of the world's richness, and a whole lifetime would hardly be sufficient to explore it thoroughly.

Seventeen miles east of Ios lies **Amorgos,** the outermost of the Cyclades. It is suspended in the centre of the Aegean by a small

necklace of islets, Heraklia, Echinosa, Kupho and Karos, all
hanging below the throat of Naxos. Nearly all these islets are
uninhabited, although goatherds pasture their flocks on Karos in
summer. Passing it under sail one day, I saw a small rowing boat
with two men in it. They were quietly fishing, seemingly careless
of the suck and swallow of the swell under the island's venomous

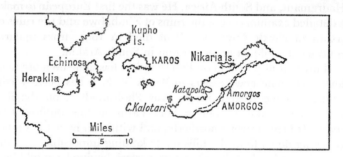

cliffs. Unlike Pholegandros, Amorgos has a fine natural harbour,
Port Vathi or **Katapola,** on the west coast. One comes into it
through sheer and frightening cliffs (but safe enough in fact, for
all are steep-to), and drops anchor in beautiful firm sand. A
steamer comes here weekly and is, I suspect, a good deal more
reliable in its arrivals and departures than at Pholegandros.
Katapola is a secure place in all weathers. Not that the squalls
do not scream down when the wind is high, and quite a big swell
sets into the bay.

In Katapola itself there is one small hotel—perhaps hotel
conjures up too grandiose an impression, "inn with beds" is more
accurate. It is clean and cheerful, and the food was reasonable, or
perhaps I was lucky for they happened to have fresh lobster that
day. Small though Katapola is, it is quite lively and there is a
pleasant little arcade along the front. The people are nearly all
fishermen or farmers, for there are no mines or other industries
here.

Lean as an eel, some twenty miles long by only three miles
wide, Amorgos is a place where one can never forget or ignore the

ea. Even on a quiet and windless night, one hears the "uncountable laughter" of a million waves lipping at its high cliffs or
breaking round **Nikaria islet,** which lies just offshore to the
north. "A wreckers' island," I had been told, and certainly the
men of Amorgos had a bad reputation as pirates in the past—but
no worse than the Hydriotes, or, if it comes to that, almost any
other islanders one likes to mention.

The women of Amorgos are reputedly famous for their beauty:

> *Go your ways, O go your ways*
> *I choose another mark*
> *Girls by the seashore*
> *Who understand the dark. . . .*

Unfortunately I did not remark any notable beauties—some
fine eyes perhaps, but then one sees fine eyes everywhere in
Greece. A great deal was lost to the islands when the local costumes were superseded by drab imitations of western clothes.
Regretfully also, I think: "But what's become of all the gold?"
and I am thinking of the island jewellery which in Amorgos, as
elsewhere, once used to decorate ears, arms and throats. One
must conclude that it has long since gone into the melting-pots
of jewellers in Athens. It is a sad pity, and one must go to the
Benaki museum in Athens to gain any idea of how "the white-
skinned women of Amorgos" may once have looked. Poverty,
the Moslem influence, and the rigid tenets of the Orthodox
Church have between them contrived to make the island woman
a somewhat dull and colourless creature.

Amorgos can lay claim to only one famous figure of antiquity,
the poet Simonides. He was a native of Samos, but later became
known as Simonides of Amorgos since he founded a colony on the
island. He wrote iambic satires and seems to have hated women.
At least, the largest fragments of his work which we possess are
unflattering comparisons of women with various types of animals.
I can only imagine that Simonides was unlucky with the local
beauties.

The island is one of the finest of the Cyclades. It justifies the
adjectives "grand and noble" for its cliffs alone, while its fertile

157

valleys are delightful in their contrast with the bleak mountain ridges. The main peak, Mount Elias, lies north-east of Port Vathi, almost in the centre of the island. Amorgos was originally a Cretan colony, and Minos or Minoa seems to have been the principal city, set in the middle of Amorgos, with two smaller towns at either end. Only at Minos have any interesting remains come to light, an Ionian temple to Apollo, and a gymnasium. The modern capital—a title somewhat disputed by Katapola— is called **Amorgos** or Castro. It is not unlike Ios, but less well cared-for and in itself hardly justifies the hard climb that it costs to get there from the harbour. The *Guide Bleu* gives it as "Four hours' walk" from Katapola but I think that can only refer to a very hot day. No great walker myself, I made it in an hour, although I would not deny it is a fairly stiff climb. Chora is worth visiting because one can stop here for refreshment, before setting out along the cliffs to the Monastery of the Panayia of the Presentation. This takes almost as long as the walk up to Chora, but more than repays the effort. The site of the building is magnificent. It hangs in the sky like a wind-hovering hawk. The cliff towers above it, the sea shines at its feet, and the monastery, surrounded by a herb garden, is like a pendant in the ear of the island.

The ikon of Our Lady reached Amorgos in one of those mysterious boats (like the Holy Face at Lucca) which seem to have been constantly errant on the face of the Mediterranean during the Middle Ages. It is almost indistinguishable and stained by time, but its potency is vouched for by the numerous ex-votos that surround it. It would be difficult to be more "cut off from the world" than here. Clearly this is a condition that men desire less and less in our century, for the monastery, which might well be served by many monks, had only two resident in it. I am always hearing of people who wish to dedicate their lives to contemplation, and to leave the futile struggle behind them. Where could one do it better than here, with the scent of thyme from the garden, the sea at one's feet, and all the sky above? But I can only conclude that contemplation and the service of God

re harder taskmasters than that "rat race" about which we so
often complain.

In the Hymn of Callimachus, Delos is described as "Windy
and waste and battered by the sea," but I think that the description fits Amorgos better than anywhere else in the Aegean. It is a
strange island. It has a quality and a dignity that is lacking,
perhaps, in some of the more gentle and fertile places.

There is a fine cove at the southern end of the island. About a
quarter of a mile to the east of Cape Kalotari, the western point
of Amorgos, the land dips in to reveal a sandy beach and a huddle
of cottages. This is the hamlet of Kolofana, well-sheltered from
the prevailing wind and sea, where I have spent a happy day.
I fished and swam, and watched the white seas beyond the point
as they ran booming all the way to desolate Anidro, and beyond
that again to Santorin.

CHAPTER 13

Santorin

One comes to Santorin through a great circular bay whose shore are formed by Santorin itself, and by the islands of Therasia and Aspronisi. The bay is a volcano's heart, and the water which glows like a sapphire beneath the boat's keel sinks down and down—a thousand feet to the heart of the ancient crater Santorin takes its name from St. Irene, the island's patron. Prior to the Fourth Crusade, when the island became part of the Duchy of the Archipelago, it was known by its ancient name Thera Pronounced Phira, it is still commonly so called by many Greek anxious to revive the classical name for their home. In legend the island originated from a clod of earth presented to the Argo nauts by Triton, and it was then known as *Kallistae*, the Very Beautiful.

Beautiful it still is, but it is an exotic that has more than a little of the monstrous in its nature. To say that it is differen from the rest of the Cyclades or the Sporades (to which geo graphically it belongs) is a wild understatement. Santorin i not "like" anything, or anywhere else in the world. Once, a geologists agree, the whole of the bay (eighteen miles round it inner rim), was covered by a huge volcano. At some time during the Mycenaean age—suggested dates range from 1000 to 1500 BC —there was a vast eruption, accompanied by the subsidence o the central massif. It has even been theorised by more than one scholar and geologist that the explosion of Santorin may have generated a tidal wave which devastated Knossos. Certainly the explosion of Santorin may have rivalled that of Krakatoa and

The volcanic island of Santorin. *Below*, a precipitous mule-track leads up to the town of Thera (*above*)

Thera, on Santorin

may have been caused in the same way—an inrush of sea water into a submarine cavity giving rise to explosions of superheated vapour. Krakatoa produced a wave fifty feet high which destroyed towns and villages hundreds of miles away. Santorin is only sixty miles north of Crete.

In historical times there is plenty of evidence of volcanic activity. Strabo records an eruption in 196 BC, when flames and smoke arose out of the seabed between Santorin and Therasia for four days, and a small island was thrown up. In AD 726 another island appeared in the centre of the bay and in 1570 the island of Mikra Kaumene, and in 1707 Nea Kaumene arose. The most recent earthquake was in 1956 when parts of the island, but in particular the town of Pyrgos at the south-western end of Santorin, were badly damaged.

As you approach from the north and enter the great bay between Santorin and Therasia, you see ahead of you the smoking tumuli of **Palaia, Mikra and Nea Kaumene**—Old, Little and New "Burnt Island." The latter is still changing shape and increasing. The *Admiralty Pilot* wisely advises one not to navigate in its vicinity—and it would be a brave man who would dream of doing so. I have always found a berth of a mile or so alarming enough, for the sea is charged with freshly-minted pumice and the water warmer than one would reasonably expect even in the midsummer Aegean. These sinister boils breaking the smooth skin of the sea have the malignity of all blind crescent things. To a seismologist, no doubt, they are as fascinating as a cancer to a surgeon.

There are three boats from Piraeus and Syra every week, and almost every cruise liner calls at Santorin. In addition, many caiques and local coasters come here to load with pumice or with wine. It is an easy place to visit and I would recommend anyone who can spare the time to stay for several days. There are two hotels in **Thera,** the capital, both of them clean and pleasant. The Atlantis is the most comfortable and, for those who want to wander farther afield, it would not be difficult to find a bed for a few nights or more in either Pyrgos or Oia, the village at the northern end of Santorin. It is here, at Oia, that the steamers stop before sailing on to Thera, three miles away. They cannot anchor at Oia, but make fast to a large buoy lying just off-shore, for the depth of this great harbour is 1,200 feet in places.

The cliffs stoop down sheer to the sea, fascinating but frightening. I came here on my last visit at sunset, when the volcanic rocks were assuming the most fantastic shades of colour. The

cliff wall on my left by Oia was cleft by a vivid band of arsenic green. Above and below it, the rock was tinged with purple. Clumps of rose-madder lifted strangely out of acres of tufa, and the sea all around was full of pumice. Large lumps of it floated about and jarred against the hull. Yet even the pumice of Santorin is unlike those grey and respectable lumps we handle in our wash-basins at home. Some of the pieces are the softest shades of pink, others streaked with red, and one which I picked out of the water had a bar of cobalt on a field of pale green.

As the sun set behind Therasia, the village of Manolas, surmounting the island, was caught by the light and its square houses and white churches gleamed like a row of teeth. **Merovigli,** the old Catholic town on the ridge between Oia and Thera, straggled along the knife-edge cliffs, leaning over like a potential suicide. Here and there, the slumped heaps of ruins showed where some buildings had already succumbed to vertigo.

> *A savage place! As holy and enchanted*
> *As e'er beneath a waning moon was haunted. . . .*

Santorin is "romantick." To walk the silent streets of Merovigli on a moonlit night is to feel the Byronic mood at its strongest. There is something about Santorin which reminds me of the paintings of James Pryde—those diminutive figures at the base of threatening walls. Santorin is not Corfu or Rhodes and, if it is at all Wagnerian, it is *Götterdämmerung*, not *Parsifal*.

After Oia the steamer slips down the bay and secures off

Thera, where the passengers disembark by boat. Small ships and yachts can anchor close inshore below Thera, where a shallow ledge of rock juts out opposite the small jetty. For the steamer traveller it is the usual Aegean disembarkation—shouts and cries, mislaid belongings, crates of chickens, and, inevitably, one or two still suffering from *mal de mer*. There is a small tourist office and a bar on the jetty. I can recommend both, the bar sells the good wine of Santorin, and the tourist office has a small counter for the sale of the local cloth. Most peasant-weaves are a little too "arty-crafty" for my taste, but the Santorin cloth is as distinctive as the island. The colours, as always, are rich and bold. The patterns are executed with a stiff elegance in silk and gold threads, on backgrounds of purple, blue or mossy green. The wine, too, has quality. Unresinated and slightly, but not over sweet, it reminds me of the wine from Alcamo in Sicily. It has something of the fullness of Marsala, but with none of that cloying heaviness.

I spent a pleasant evening on this jetty, sitting with the young man and his mother who ran the bar and the tourist shop between them. Both spoke excellent French, for Santorin is something of an outpost of Gallic culture in the heart of the Aegean. There is an Ursuline Convent on the island, and the Sisters run a small school. Before the last war, there were many French speakers on Santorin, but their numbers have declined in recent years. The disappearance of the Alexandrian French, some of whom owned summer houses in the island, has no doubt contributed to this. The old lady's son was entertaining on the subject of the Italian occupation of the island during the war.

"They were not bad men," he explained. "Very home-sick, and unsure of themselves. Oh, but how neat they were! The officers, I mean——" He fluttered his hands and examined his fingernails intently. He hit off exactly that gesture of Italian dandyism—a kind of physical "prissyness" which either entertains, or appals, the rough Northerner or the Greek.

Nine hundred feet above the landing place, the town of Thera swings into the air. If you lean back on the jetty and crane your neck you can just make out the white towers and houses. I would never for a moment attempt the climb on foot, at any rate during the day. There are 800 broad steps zigzagging all the way up to the town. I did it once at night, because there were no mules available, but even in the cool hours it is an exhausting climb. Whenever a ship comes in, however, all the muleteers are ready at the bottom to embark the visitors. At which point, for those unfamiliar with it, a word about the basic Greek saddle. Unless it is well-cushioned, or rather, heavily-padded with plenty of old sacks, it is folly to attempt to ride astride. A tent-shaped structure of wood, it is really designed for riding side-saddle. You hang on to the wooden pommel, get both feet over (it does not matter which side) and slump your body towards the centre for balance. In this way the bony ridge of wood in the centre is taken under the bend of the knees, and the pain is almost endurable.

The terraced path of steps winds backwards and forwards. If you lean over carefully, and look down as you come to a bend, you will see the previous slope some thirty feet below. On one blue morning I made the climb with a reluctant mule and a surly young muleteer. Just as we were turning the corner from one zig to another zag, incensed at the mule's slowness, he caught the poor brute a great clout between the legs with his stick. The mule leapt forward, the saddle slipped, and I found myself hanging over the vertiginous slopes, gazing straight down at the water some four hundred feet below. "Our armies swore terribly in Flanders," cried my uncle Toby. "But nothing to this. . . ." It took a number of glasses in the first taverna at the top to restore my interest in Thera and its architecture.

The town is a comparatively modern foundation, built mostly during the mid-nineteenth century when the old Venetian capital at Skaros, a little to the north, became untenable through earthquakes. It is pleasant and clean, with an unbelievable eagle's-eye view of the world, and the air has all the rinsed taste of the wind. Along the bony spine that runs north to Merovigli,

164

chapels, houses and churches clamber like goats on a mountain track. The narrow streets crackle with that intense light which one only finds in the Aegean. So vivid-clear is it, that the moulding over a window a hundred yards away is like a detail under a magnifying glass. A painter friend of mine spent a week in Santorin once, and nearly went mad. "I can't do it!" he would shout, hurling down a canvas. "I was trying to get a landscape on the east side this morning, and all the time I was working on the figures in the foreground, I was noticing a carved lintel on a doorway about a mile away!"

The small main street of Thera is whitewashed throughout. No animal traffic, as the Mayor explained, is allowed to use it. I tried to imagine a main street anywhere else in the world that was reserved solely for the use of pedestrians. How noiseless the island seemed on that particular June morning. Wander, as I did along the ridge from Thera, where the houses run towards Merovigli and Skaros. There are places where you find yourself wrapped in a cocoon of silence. Under the vaulted ceiling of a Venetian arcade my footsteps sounded like the tramp of an invading army. This was near the Catholic Cathedral, a place heavy with the feeling of a vanished world. A French acquaintance, a happy exile with a young wife and children, took me here first. After the austerity of Greek churches, this sudden dive into the Latin, or Venetian past, was strangely moving. Outside the Cathedral, when we looked eastwards, the other face of Santorin revealed itself. Here the land slopes away in fields and vineyards, rich volcanic earth that is in marked contrast to the scarred sides surrounding the ancient crater.

Like the land around Etna and Vesuvius, the fields of Santorin are potent breeders of the vine. No doubt the experts can explain it in scientific terms, but in all these places something of the soil's fiery nature seems to be communicated through the roots of the plants, so that every grape contains a pinpoint of fire—a minute, imprisoned explosion. The coloured headkerchiefs of the women dipped and stooped among the terraced landscape like butterflies. Men on mule-back threaded their way through the dusty lanes, dark and active as scarab beetles. Like a vase painting come to life, I saw a group of women winnowing—separating the grain from the chaff. They flicked the wheat in the air and a golden smoke of husks drifted away before the wind. It powdered the nearby road and settled like pollen over an adjoining vineyard.

From Thera you walk along the spine of the island, a mile or so, to Merovigli and Skaros. If you are staying in Thera, I suggest the best time is in the early evening after a siesta—in that way you catch the best of the light over the bay and the island. If you return after dark, take a torch, or try and pick a night when there is a moon. The streets and alleys of the island are uneven and curiously unrecognisable. It can be more than disconcerting to turn a corner and come on a sharp drop to the sea, or walk down some steps and find yourself in a ruined house that suddenly disappears in a crumbling slope—where only an old chimney, sticking up out of the cliff, reveals that once there were other houses on this steep face.

Cycladic and Venetian architecture is jumbled side by side with nineteenth-century memories of Athens and Paris. Mostly, the small houses are as white and bony as the spine of the island. Sometimes only the curve of a roof or the trembling smoke from a chimney reveals their presence, for many of them are excavated from the tufa itself, and often lie below ground level. Wood is as scarce as water on the island, and the roofs of houses are often made out of old barrel vaults. The shortage of wood has also meant that furniture has acquired a special significance in Santorin. On the way to Merovigli, where I stopped for a coffee and a glass of water, the daughter of the house pointed proudly to a pair of carved chairs—"They have always been in the family!" The fact that they were most probably seventeenth-century Venetian meant nothing to her: they were real, wooden chairs, and most comfortable. Seats and settles, side tables, and even beds for children are often carved out of the rock at the back or sides of the rooms.

I praised the water which was soft as silk and she smiled and told me that it came from their own cistern. Like nearly every-where else in the island, they caught the rainfall in tanks below their houses, diverted by pipes from the flat roof. There are no springs in Santorin and, sometimes after a dry winter, water has to be imported. It is an island where wine is of less account, and far easier to come by, than water.

Merovigli, which slopes down to decaying Skaros on the left and runs into Vourvoulo to the north, is the old Catholic quarter. It is sinking slowly into the stone from which its houses were quarried—disintegrating drop by drop into a fine powder com-pounded of time and tufa. Shadowed doorways open upon empty courtyards, and the grass grows round the ring bolts where once the mules were tethered. A boarded window creaks as the wind rises. Along the cliff face the dust spills away in cloudy veils and drifts above the precipitous sides. At noon the cicadas shout from silent courtyards. In the small piazza, so high that even Thera looks hundreds of feet below, a few pale trees grow, and there is a miniature promenade with iron railings through which one views the eastern sea. The stone-flagged square has the air of an opera house that has not been used for centuries. It was here that I found a delightful small taverna. I am ashamed that I have no record of its name, but there is only the one. Thirty feet long by twenty wide, with a lofty ceiling, it was cool and pleasant, with a proprietress as hospitable as she was broad in the beam.

In the far corner, backed by two wine casks, was the bar. Behind a faded curtain was the family bedroom. The floor was surgically clean and the walls freshly whitewashed. I had eggs, bread and a cucumber salad. It was while I was waiting for these that I noticed the screen—English, of that there could be no doubt. A pair of sentimental cats gazed into a roaring coal fire. A coach and six on the Brighton Road. Queen Victoria, Byron and Palmerston—a curious company. There were fashion prints of 1880, Christmas cards, and late nineteenth-century drawings from *Punch*. "It belonged to my mother!" said my hostess proudly but beyond that she knew nothing of its history. What exile, I wonder, passing the winter evenings over months-old magazines, banished the orchidaceous quality of this island by constructing a thing so homely, so inartistic, and so essentially English?

After the stillness of Merovigli, after the grassy courtyards and the crumbling Venetian mouldings, the bustle of Thera seems as exciting as a visit to a big city. Men are active about their trades; animals stumble beneath bales of fodder and casks of wine; the local newspaper has just come out and is being eagerly passed from hand to hand. A steamer has arrived in the bay and her passengers and sailors are spending their money in the Vulcan, the Theoxenia, and the other bars and cafés. In the Vulcan I met the Mayor of Thera, a delightful man, eager to practise his French on a foreigner. It was on a par with my Greek so that, whenever the conversation moved out of the practical world into abstractions we had to fumble between the two languages. He was born in Thera and had lived here all his life.

"You must think that sounds dull?"

I deny it. It would be difficult for this island to be dull—bizarre or macabre, but hardly dull.

"It is quiet here in the winter," he went on. "Often we see no strangers for months on end. But, like everywhere else, we have our own life, and there is always plenty to do. In the summer a number of Athenians come down here, also foreigners like yourself, and then there are always the cruise boats and the island steamers."

He offered to sell me a four-roomed house—four rooms, not counting kitchen and cellar and an out-building—fully furnished, for seven hundred pounds. Of course one could find an inhabitable house much cheaper than that, and I know that fully furnished in Santorin means very little.

Fish, vegetables and wine are the cheap things here. The tomatoes, lettuce and cucumbers, raised on those eastern slopes or in tiny plots behind the houses, are first class. The wine needs no further advertisement, and the few meals I have eaten ashore here compare favourably with most places in the Aegean. Even as far afield as this, something of France rubs off on the native indifference towards the table, and Santorin is one of the few islands where I have had a really good herb omelette.

The museum in Thera must not be forgotten. There are some fine geometric vases, as well as a certain amount of Minoan ware. The Hellenistic and Roman period of the island is well represented and there is also a good collection of inscriptions. There is a weight-lifter's weight, possibly from the Olympic Games (and, therefore, one assumes a Santorin champion) which bears the inscription "EUMASTES LIFTED ME." It weighs about half a ton. Santorin, despite its pleasant hedonistic atmosphere, could clearly breed athletes. Which brings one back to its history and to the fact that this island was a pioneer of colonisation. Colonists from Sparta, and Minyan refugees from Lemnos, came here originally led by a certain Theras (who gave his name to the island). They, in their turn, planted one of the most famous of all Greek colonies, **Cyrene,** on the north coast of Africa, from which modern Cyrenaica takes its name. It is not perhaps so surprising that the founder of the Cyrenaic school of philosophy should have come from Santorin. "Our modes of being affected —these alone are knowable," said the Cyrenaics, maintaining that pleasure was the only good for man. They have often been attacked by those who have only taken a cursory glance at their system, but it should not be forgotten that some of Aristippus' later disciples decided that true pleasure can even consist in self-sacrifice. It was Hegesias who reached the formidable, if logical, conclusion that real pleasure is impossible, and that only suicide can ensure the absence of pain.

I can think of two English writers who would have appreciated Santorin although, despite certain points of resemblance in their natures, they might not have made the best of neighbours, Ronald Firbank and Walter Pater. Certainly, Firbank would have found scope for his comic genius in the inhabitants and their doings, for Santorin is a baroque island, as fantastic in its way as the dwarves and hunchbacks of the Villa Palagonia. Cardinal Pirelli would not have seemed so very out of place here and, for that matter, Pater's conclusion to *The Renaissance* has a Santorinian ring about

"Not the fruit of experience, but experience itself, is the end. . . . Not to discriminate every moment some passionate attitude in those about us, and in the very brilliance of their gifts some tragic dividing of forces on their ways is, on this short day of frost and sun, to sleep before evening."

One requires a certain amount of stamina to visit ancient Thera for it is about three hours on mule-back, although nowadays one can at least drive as far as **Pyrgos**. Badly damaged as Pyrgos was in the last earthquake, it is still quite an attractive village, with a lacy white tower that recalls some of the delicate pierced stonework of Tinos. On the way, in the middle of one of the vineyards, one passes what, so I have been told, is the only completely intact antique temple in Greece. It is not imposing, a tiny shrine from the third century BC, crowned now by a Cross and dedicated to St. Nicholas. From Pyrgos, by foot or mule, one follows the road to Mount Elias from the peak of which one can see the mountains of Crete. From here the track circles down along the barren flanks of the mountain to ancient Thera, which lies on the eastern coast and faces across to desolate Anaphi.

This was the capital of the Dorian settlers, sited on a ridge about 1,000 feet above the sea. Inscriptions show that the settlement was in existence at least as early as the ninth century BC. The ancient harbour was immediately north of the town, near the beach of Kamaraea, a poor place one would think when the Meltemi were blowing—but then, in midsummer, the boats could always retreat to the south of the island and in the autumn, in any case, they would be hauled ashore. On the main terrace of the ancient capital was the Festival Ground for the celebration of the Gymnopaidia in honour of the Dorian Apollo. This was the Apollo Kourotrophos, "Rearer of Boys," and patron of the palaestra. We are a long way here from the Delian Apollo, and in a simpler, harsher world where one feels the shades of Arnold and Thring approving the Public School spirit. Here the youths danced and sang, and here are the inscriptions so carefully recorded by Hiller von Gartringen, the German archaeologist, who at his own expense excavated the ruins at the turn of this century. The inscriptions bear the names of handsome boys, recorded by their admirers.

> *These too, these veins which life convulses,*
> *Wait but a while, shall cease to bound;*
> *I with the ice in all my pulses*
> *Shall sleep as sound.*

(A. E. HOUSMAN)

Cyrene, the African city which was founded by settlers from ancient Thera, is connected with a strange legend about Apollo. The nymph Cyrene was a virgin huntress like Artemis, and Apollo, seeing her out hunting one day, immediately fell in love with her. The wise Chiron prophesied that if he took her to the Libyan desert and consummated the marriage on the bridal couch of virgin sand, she would bear a divine son, a second Apollo —undefiled and immortal. In due course she gave birth to a son, who was brought up by Chiron and the Centaurs. He was given the name Aristaios, "The best of all" and, as such, became the patron of hunters and herdsmen. Carl Kerenyi in *The Gods of the Greeks* describes his other attributes: "In his honour the Etesiai, the trade winds, blow for forty days on end. He invented the beehive and beekeeping, the oilpress and the making of cheese. He is said to have been the first to lay snares for wolves and bears, and to have freed the island of Sardinia from wild birds."

The ruins of a Byzantine church lie next to the Sacred Way, as one walks from the temple of Apollo north-westwards towards the Sanctuary of the Egyptian Gods. There is little here to compare with the Eastern sanctuaries on Delos, but across the square in the direction of the temple of Dionysus, there are the ruins of several houses of the Hellenistic period. The caretaker pointed out an engraved phallus on the wall of one of the houses nearby. On the scroll surrounding it is the pleasing inscription—"To My Friends."

Ancient Thera is not the real reason why one should visit Santorin. There are many, and more interesting, temples and remains elsewhere in Greece and the islands. The things that I remember best from my visits to this island is the moment when the sunset flares along the rim of Santorin, just before the light dips below the backbone of Therasia; the smoking islands sinister in the twilight; and the sight of the volcanic ash as it blows sadly away from the ridges below Skaros and Merovigli. In cave dwellings just north of the landing stage the fishermen mend their nets, hooves clatter on the 800 steps up to the town; and on the eastern slopes the vines shudder under the Meltemi. Santorin and Delos are the two poles of this Aegean world. In the Apollonian light on Mount Cynthus it seems as if life is only just beginning. The "Burnt Islands" in the centre of Santorin Bay speak with a different voice—"This is the way the world ends." Between Delos and the Kaumene we have a choice to make.

CHAPTER 14

Skiathos, Skopelos and Skyros

The Sporades, the scattered islands of the Archipelago, fall into two groups—the northern Sporades lying a little to the north-east of Euboea, and the southern Sporades off the south-western shores of Asia Minor. The latter formerly belonged to the Turkish vilayet of "The Islands of the White Sea." Both groups are less visited, and consequently less sophisticated, than the Cyclades or the islands off the Peloponnesian coastline. These scattered or "sown" islands have always lain somewhat out of the mainstream of history, one reason why in some of them old patterns of life and culture have lingered on.

Skiathos, Skopelos and Skyros have one thing in common, which immediately distinguishes them from most of the Cyclades —they are well-wooded. Coming upon them after a visit to the sun-tawny "dry islands," one's first feeling is likely to be one of amazement, if not perhaps of relief, at the sight of the wooded slopes, dark green even in summer. One of the best ways of visiting the islands is to take the weekly steamer direct from Piraeus, which does a circuit of the northern Sporades, going up the east coast of Euboea, calling at all the group on its way, touching at Volos, and then returning via the Euripus Channel to Athens. Alternatively, in summer there are three sailings from Kumi or Kymis Bay, on the north-eastern coast of Euboea facing towards Skyros. Pullman coaches go direct from Athens via Khalkis, and then across Euboea to Kumi. The drive through Attica, the crossing at Khalkis, the views of central Euboea, all make this route the most pleasurable for those who take a Johnsonian view of sea travel. From Kumi to Skyros is only a twenty-mile crossing.

The main group of the northern Sporades, which includes Skiathos, Skopelos, and Khelidhromi (the ancient Ikos), runs out in a sickle shape from eastern Pelion. It is a sickle, that curves towards the north, so that the outermost islet of the group, Psathura, is less than thirty miles from the tip of the Chalcidic peninsula. From here, Mount Athos is less than forty miles away, due north across one of the most windy stretches of sea in the Archipelago.

There are various ways of getting to Skiathos and Skopelos, either by caique from Volos at the head of the gulf, or from one of the small villages on the eastern coast of the Pelion peninsula. The islands lie across the mouth of the deep gulf of Salonika, and the views from sea are magnificent, Pelion and Ossa thrusting their shoulders against the western skyline, with craggy Euboea to the south, and the islands marching out in shadows of green and blue towards the open sea. Unlike the northern end of the gulf, where the city of Salonika stands, the islands are cooled by the Meltemi. Farther up the coast, on the other hand, in the waters between Olympus and the Chalcidic peninsula, the humidity and airlessness can be oppressive.

All the area from Mount Ossa down to the southern tip of Euboea is awkward for small boats, for the sailor is on a harsh and unfriendly shore. It is worth remembering that between Cape Sepias, opposite Skiathos on the mainland, and Mount Pelion to the north, this coastline of Magnesia was the graveyard of Xerxes' fleet. Here is the story as told by Herodotus in Aubrey de Sélincourt's translation:

"The Persian fleet . . . made the Magnesian coast between Casthanea and Cape Sepias, and on its arrival the leading ships made fast to the land, while the remainder, as there was not much room on the short stretch of beach, came to anchor and lay off-shore in lines, eight deep. In this position they remained during the night; but at dawn next day the weather which was clear and calm, suddenly changed, and the fleet was caught in a heavy blow from the east—a 'Hellespontian' as the people there call it

174

—which raised a confused sea like a pot on the boil. Those who realised in time that the blow was coming, and all who happened to be lying in a convenient position, managed to beach their vessels and to get them clear of the water before they were damaged, and thus saved their own lives as well; but the ships which were caught well off-shore were all lost; some were

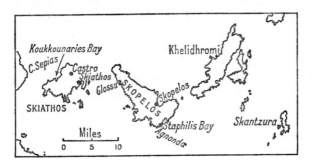

driven on to the place called the Ovens at the foot of Mount Pelium, others on to the beach itself; a number came to grief on Sepias, and others, again, were smashed to pieces off the towns of Meliboea and Casthanea."

It is a wreckers' coast, and I have no doubt that in later centuries there have been many Magnesians similar in fortune to Ameinocles whom Herodotus describes as picking up "a large number of gold and silver drinking cups which were washed ashore and included among his finds Persian treasure-chests and innumerable other pieces of valuable property." Four hundred ships were lost in this three-day storm and the Athenians were so overjoyed at the result that they promptly dedicated a shrine to Boreas, the north-east wind, on the banks of the Illissus. But if the Magnesian coast is to be treated cautiously by the sailor, the island of **Skiathos** has one of the safest and most delightful harbours in the sea. Here the steamers come in to anchor, and here a whole fleet could ride in safety.

The modern town lies on the southern coast of the island, with a large harbour divided into two main arms by the small promontory on which the town stands. Delightful in its white walls and (here one immediately notices a difference from the Cyclades), its red-tiled roofs, Skiathos is built on two small hills. Behind it rise densely-wooded hills, and at its feet are innumerable small wharves occupied by fishermen and their families, nets, boats, fish-traps, and all the paraphernalia of the sea.

Caiques are still built in Skiathos, in a lagoon at the head of the eastern harbour, but far less now than they were twenty years or so ago. The Piraeus, with its commercialisation of caique-building, has put many of these small island shipyards out of business. But here, in Skiathos, is as good a place as any to watch the building of these graceful and traditional vessels. At some time or other every Aegean traveller ought to visit a boat-yard, and get the resinous tang of pine-shavings in his nostrils, and see the ribs of a new boat shining in their fresh-cut whiteness. A lot of Greece, of the Aegean, and of the cultures which have risen out of this sea, becomes more explicable after a visit to a working boat-yard. A new dimension is given to the *Odyssey*, to Thucydides, to Byzantium even, and to the Venetian Aegean.

On the foreshore of this lagoon I watched them building a twenty-five-foot caique. Nikos, the master-builder, showed me the beautiful half-model which he had made before the work was started. Here, as in eighteenth-century England, a model of half the vessel is hand-cut out of wood, to serve as the blue-print for the workmen. Two or three men were at work on the vessel, shaping the ribs, and paring the stem with adzes. Like all the old hand-instruments—scythe, plane or axe—the adze evokes from its operator a satisfying and beautiful rhythm. The arms swing, the wrists twist, and the body sways deeply. It was here, too, that on another visit I saw the launching of a small fishing boat. Just before she went down into the water, Nikos brought a cockerel out of a basket and gave it to one of the men. With a deft stroke of his adze he severed the cockerel's neck against the stem-piece, and then, with the stump of the neck, made the sign of the cross on the stem and stern posts. Every vessel must be consecrated and, in

176

Greece just as in England, they have the same expression: "Every ship must have a life." The cockerel is a substitute. No doubt, centuries ago, a human life was required, just as in Fiji every new war canoe used to be launched over human rollers.

The town of Skiathos was built in the early and mid-nineteenth century, when the increasing trade of the Aegean and the liberation of Greece had coaxed islanders all over the Aegean to come down from their hillside Castra, and to build again at the water's edge. It is an interesting fact that throughout the Cyclades, the Sporades, and indeed all the islands of this sea, the classical capitals were almost always on the water. This is proof that not only were the inhabitants seafarers, but that a certain security obtained in classical times. Under the Roman, and later the Byzantine empires, anti-piracy patrols secured the freedom of the sea for those who passed upon it "on their lawful occasions." Then, for something like one thousand years, the Aegean reverted to a pre-classical anarchy, and the pirates of the Archipelago became a byword throughout Europe. Life in the islands retreated from the shores, and went up inland to the mountain Castra, or fortified places. The ancient harbours decayed and silted up, becoming no more than havens for coastal fishermen, or landing points for the raiders.

It is important to remember that, during these lawless years, it was not only the Turks and the Moslem corsairs who menaced the islanders and the coast-dwellers of the Archipelago. One of the most notorious Aegean pirates of the sixteenth century, El Louck Ali Fartax, was a former Dominican brother. He turned Turk, and achieved such success in his bloody profession that Sultan Suleiman the Magnificent secured his alliance to the Grand Porte, and made him one of his admirals. The Aegean during those centuries became a haven for renegades from every faith and nation. It was not until the comparative stability of the Aegean during the nineteenth century, and the development of Russian trade between ports like Hydra and Syra, that the islanders began once more to build beside the water. For obvious reasons they often chose the sites of their classical ancestors. In Skiathos to-day, as in so many other islands, the port has become the capital, and the ancient capital, Castro, has declined to a ghost town.

Not all of the Skiathians are native to the island, many of the fishermen having come here as refugees from Smyrna and Chesmé after the disastrous Greco-Turkish war of 1921. After 1923, when the Greco-Turkish convention arranged for the compulsory exchange of Moslem and Greek-Orthodox minorities, something like a million and a half Greeks from Asia Minor were settled in the islands and the mainland of Greece. This was an enormous addition to the population of a poor country whose total population was then only about 6½ million. The population of Greece in 1961 was about 8 million, much the same as greater London. It is scattered over a total land mass roughly equivalent to that of the United Kingdom. It is this relative "thinness" of population which gives Greece and the islands an added attraction for the visitor used to the cities and the urbanised countryside of the north. Only in Greece could one find a bay as beautiful as **Koukkounaries** in Skiathos relatively unencumbered with human beings. This "Bay of the Stone Pines," with one of the most perfect beaches anywhere in the Aegean, is best reached by caique, for it lies on the opposite side of the island to the port. This is the best way also to visit Castro, which is situated on a high peak of rock at the northern end of the island. Originally connected to the mainland by a drawbridge, **Castro** is even more of a castle than most of these old fortified townships. Robert Liddell mentions some "good eighteenth-century ikons" in the Church of the Saviour, but the only time that I visited Castro was in the early afternoon. The church was closed and the whole town seemed to have fallen into its siesta. It was here in the "Liberation Bar" that I first heard the story of Kaliarina of Skiathos.

During the last war, Skiathos was for a time one of the main staging posts for refugee Allied soldiers after the British, Australians and New Zealanders had withdrawn from Greece before the German advance. Soldiers were ferried across to the island from

Greece, and later taken by boat to Turkey, whence many of them managed to return to their units in Egypt. More New Zealanders than any others seem to have used the Skiathos escape route and it was in Castro that they were often concealed. Kaliarina was a key figure in the escape system, making the arrangements for the hiding of escapees until such time as a caique was ready to take them off. She is an old woman to-day, but still with the fire in her eyes that must have been there some twenty years ago when the Italians finally ran her to ground. It is some tribute to the Italians that they did not shoot her on the spot, for she managed to wound one of their soldiers before being forced to surrender. Kaliarina, together with fifteen New Zealanders whom she had been sheltering in her cottage, was sent to Italy as a prisoner of war. In the town hall of Skiathos they proudly display the framed letter of thanks from General Freyberg to the people of the island: ". . . We will never forget how our soldiers left behind in 1941 were dressed and fed and helped by a people who themselves had so little and who ran a great risk by so doing." The *Guide Bleu* describes Skiathos briefly as "peopled by seamen" and, one might add, by heroes and heroines.

It is no accident, perhaps, that the "Saint of Greek Literature," Alexander Papadiamandis was born here. The son of a priest, Papadiamandis spent most of his working life in Athens, but returned to Skiathos to die. One of the apostles of vernacular prose, Papadiamandis, like Karkavitzas and Drosinis, found his subject matter in the everyday life of nineteenth-century Greece, and treated it in the language of the people. What Solomos was to poetry, Papadiamandis, though to a lesser extent, was to prose.

Only five miles east of Skiathos lies the cutlet-shaped sister island, **Skopelos.** This is another island where the green of well-wooded slopes refreshes the eye, and where the roofs are tiled— but here with grey slates, as opposed to the red of Skiathos. The town and port lies on the northern coast and has some of the most delightful architecture in the northern Aegean. Of the port the *Admiralty Pilot* says: "In summer, it is reported, that winds from the north-east do not blow home." Unfortunately, I can confirm that on some occasions they certainly do, and this is not a good anchorage for small boats. The steamers usually drop anchor and discharge passengers just inside the northern breakwater. For those who travel in their own boat, I recommend **Staphilis** (Grape) **Bay** at the southern end of the island. This is well-sheltered from the Meltemi and is a delightful place in which to idle and swim. Eastward lies Skantzura and the other islets that lead to Skyros, and around the bay are scattered summer villas belonging to the richer farmers and merchants of Skopelos. From here it is a two-mile walk into the town, through a valley with pleasant scenery and conical hills on either side. Like Skiathos, the island is rich in figs, vines and olives, but the soil is even more fertile and almonds and quince abound in the sheltered valley. Grape Bay probably derives its name from the curious reddish rock which forms the headland sheltering it from the north-east, although scholars have suggested that it takes its name from one of the Argonauts, a legendary founder.

Like Hydra, the town clambers up round an amphitheatre of rock. The houses are not only whitewashed (and much though one loves this bleak cleanliness in the Cyclades, it can after a time become monotonous), but washed in pinks and blues and even rich terra-cotta reminiscent of some of the eastern Sicilian villages. Like Skiathos there is one small hotel, but unlike Skiathos, one finds comparatively few summer visitors. But the island does not have a sleepy air, for it is as prosperous as any Aegean island can be. Vines, olives, the almond, and the plum, all of which flourish in its rich soil, have given Skopelos a certain security and its earth can only be compared by an Englishman to the deep red to be seen in parts of Devon. Looking down the valley towards the town, as one approaches from the south, the red earth, the green fruit trees, the bare backs of the mountains, and the colourful houses make a picture almost unique in the eastern Mediterranean.

If one can ever make a comparison between island peoples— and it is bound to be unfair on a short acquaintance—I must admit that I did not find the inhabitants of Skopelos as pleasant as those of Skiathos. Perhaps because, and here I must confess to a prejudice, the Skopeliots are primarily peasant farmers, whereas the Skiathians are fishermen. In simple societies throughout the world I have always found that "sea people" are generous and "land people" grasping. No doubt a psychologist could make something out of this—pointing out that men who daily risk their lives on the water have a certain contempt for money and tend to spend it in a wasteful way, while peasants and farmers apply to their fellows the same hard attitude that has earned them a profit from their fields or their cattle.

A good road leads from Skopelos across the island to Agnonda on the southern coast. Agnonda is a fishing village at the head of a bay, dark with trees, and with a pleasant beach. It lies a mile or two to the west of Staphilis. Here, as if in proof of my theory, I found the people more welcoming to the stranger than at Skopelos or at Glossa, the other main village in the island. **Glossa,** which faces towards Skiathos, is the second port of the island—or rather Loutraki the village at its foot, for Glossa is yet another cliff-town. A number of Greek and Roman remains have been found in the land around Glossa, most of which are now in the museum at Volos on the mainland, but if I were in charge of any excavations on Skopelos, I would take a gamble on the rose-red spur of Staphilis. It is so typical of the type of semi-detached rock on which the early settlers liked to found their fortified cities that I feel sure, if there ever was a Minoan colony on Skopelos (as has been suggested) it is at Staphilis one would find it. A study of the cities of ancient maritime peoples (Tyre is a perfect example) shows that, wherever possible, they were built on small islets just separated from the coast. This was for the very obvious reason that, like the castles of the Middle Ages, they were protected by water. The inhabitants, presuming that they had command of the sea, could continue to reinforce their cities even when they were besieged from the landward side.

Skyros, unlike the other northern Sporades, is a bare and classical island. It is best reached by steamer or caique from Kumi Bay in Euboea, for it lies a good forty miles south-east of

Skopelos across a wind-swept sea. It is, above all, the island of Achilles, for here "what song the Sirens sang, or what name Achilles assumed when he hid himself among women, though puzzling questions, are not beyond all conjecture."

Skyros is the island where Achilles was hidden disguised as a girl by Lycomedes, King of Skyros, at the plea of Achilles' mother, Thetis. Thetis had learned from the Fates that her son was

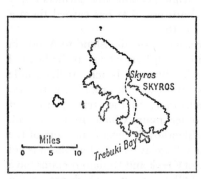

destined never to return from Troy if he went on the expedition, but that if he could be induced to stay at home, he would enjoy a long life—"a short life with eternal fame, or a long but inglorious existence." Thetis, being rational and life-loving like all women, decided that the latter would be best for her son. Unfortunately her concealment of Achilles was foiled by Odysseus, another reluctant hero who had himself unsuccessfully tried a rather similar piece of disguise artistry in Ithaca. Arriving in Skyros, Odysseus was given permission by King Lycomedes to search his palace for the supposedly hidden Achilles. The wily Odysseus had brought an armful of gifts for the ladies of the court, jewellery and dresses (he reckoned, perhaps, that even if he did not find Achilles, he might profit from his generosity). At a given moment, Odysseus retired from the palace and ordered his trumpeter to sound the alarm. The inevitable happened. While the ladies rushed to make certain of their clothes and gems, Achilles stripped himself to the waist and seized a sword and buckler—which Odysseus had thoughtfully placed among his gifts. Odysseus re-entered the palace in the midst of the panic and Achilles was forced to accept the glories of war and a brief life.

Skyros, the port and capital of the island, lies on the east coast, and boasts a modern hotel, the Thetis, as well as a number of houses where rooms can be found. It is a strange little town. Unlike the other nearby islands, Skyros follows the architectural pattern of the Cyclades with geometric houses, flat-roofed and brilliant with whitewash. It lies at the foot of **Castro**, which was built on the site of the ancient acropolis by the Naxian Dukes during their overlordship of the island. The acropolis, in its turn, was most probably built on the site of Lycomedes' palace. Theseus, who seems to have had ancestral estates in Skyros, is reputed to have been killed here by the same Lycomedes. Lycomedes, Plutarch relates, "cast him headlong from the top of the rocks." After the battle of Marathon, when Theseus was seen to appear in the Athenian ranks, the Athenians sent to Skyros and had his bones removed for burial in Attic earth. This was done by Cimon in 469 BC and his festival, the Theseia, was celebrated annually in Athens on 21st October.

Tris Boukes, or Trebuki Bay, is a large but uninspiring anchorage, with its mouth half-sealed by twin islets. It was here that Rupert Brooke died, on board a French hospital ship, on his way to Gallipoli. He is buried in an olive grove, about a mile from the shore. One reaches the grove by a walk from the deserted bay, crossing en route a dried-up stream bed. (The burial party with the poet's body took two hours to reach the grove in April, 1915). A white cross now surmounts the grove, and the small plot of ground is fenced off by iron railings. When I first saw it just after the last war, the railings were bent and broken, grass grew high over the mound, and the surrounding stone was deep-chiselled with the names of Greek visitors. My first reaction was one of indignation, but then I remembered Byron's name carved in the marble of Sunium—If Byron on Cape Sunium, why not "Anagnos" and others on Brooke at Skyros? Representations were made during the intervening years to the Greek Ministry of Tourism, but nothing was done about Brooke's grave—understandably enough, for Greece is the burial ground of far greater men than the English poet, and no man knows where most of the great dead lie buried.

It was not until 1960 that the Reverend John Garwell, a fleet chaplain from Malta, led a naval expedition to the grave and restored it. The railings were renovated, a blacksmith straightening them out over a fire of olive wood. The tomb was cleaned and re-whitewashed, and the initials R.B. were etched at the base of the cross. "The tomb stands again," the Reverend Garwell wrote in his report, "a worthy monument to the once popular poet." So indeed it does, but the irony lies in those words "the once popular poet. . . ." Literary fame is as treacherous as it is elusive but, whatever his successors in the chorus of the Muse may have said about him, I doubt if any of them will find so pleasant a resting place. "Well this side of Paradise! . . . There's little comfort in the wise." I do not think that Rupert Brooke was under half so many illusions as has been supposed by his detractors.

When I anchored in the great bay of Trebuki it was quite empty (it is easy to get to, incidentally, by motor boat from Skyros town). The eternal northerlies were blowing, and the islets at the bay's mouth were lipped with foam. There was only the sound of the sea, and the wind in the olive groves. Perhaps Brooke, even though he was writing about the faraway Pacific, had some foreknowledge of this:

> And there, on the Ideal Reef,
> Thunders the Everlasting Sea!

Curiously enough, Skyros itself has a somewhat Nordic quality about it. It is the only place I know in the Aegean where one finds woodcarving in the Victorian-Swiss style. The interiors of the houses are often quite un-Aegean, with rounded and arched fireplaces, plates hanging on the walls, or supported on special plate ledges, and even chairs with barley-twist legs. The sitting-room in the Hotel Thetis was rather on this pattern, and I can well imagine many purists finding it all very unattractive. Perhaps when I last visited Skyros (I had been away from England for over two years), I was in the mood to enjoy nostalgia.

Rupert Brooke, as is clear from many of his letters and poems, had a sense of humour. I think he would not have been unappreciative of the statue erected in his name, a bronze in the Greco-Germanic manner of a naked youth symbolising "Immortal Poetry." The poet who reverenced Webster, and whose favourite poet was Donne, would surely have been delighted to hear, as I did from the Mayor of Skyros, that "It is popularly considered rather indecent." In Greece the antique delight in the naked human body has not survived the disapproval of the Orthodox Church.

CHAPTER 15

Lemnos, Thasos, Samothrace

Few visitors go to **Lemnos**. It lies off most of the shipping routes, on the way to nowhere except the other islands of the Thracian Sea. But it is still possible to get here from Piraeus, although the steamer may make a long circuit, calling at Salonika, or even Alexandroupolis, on the way. Cruise boats sometimes call in, for the harbour is a fine one, and the island's association with the Gallipoli campaign makes it of interest to English travellers. Lemnos lies in the heart of the northern Aegean, almost half-way between Turkey and Greece, with the great harbour of Mudros like a mouth open to the south. Purnea Bay takes another bite out of the island from the north, so that Lemnos is almost cut in half, and indeed the characters of its two halves are quite different.

Larger than any of the northern Sporades, Lemnos is about twenty miles long by ten miles deep. **Castro,** the island capital, is on the western coast and it is here that the steamers call from Salonika. There are three small hotels, the Actaeon, the Ethnikon and the Alexandroupolis, several cafés, and a bustling waterfront. This was also the site of the ancient capital, Myrina. It is an excellent harbour, protected from the prevailing winds, and with a wonderful view over the sea. At sunset Mount Athos, thirty-five miles away, lifts its fantastic head out of the western sea. Although Lemnos to-day is almost barren, a pasturage country with fruit trees only in the eastern valleys, it is not difficult to see how, when it was well-wooded, it must have been one of the finest islands in the Aegean. It has form and contour, the magnificent bay of Mudros, and the fertility of its eastern side in contrast with the mountains of the north and west.

Dominating Castro is an old Genoese castle, built during the thirteenth century. Lemnos was for a time after the Fourth Crusade, a Genoese outpost. Ceded to the Turks in the late fifteenth century, it was re-occupied a century later by the Venetians, and then fell once more to the Turks. Until 1924, when the Greco-Turkish exchange of populations took place, Lemnos had quite a large Turkish population. They are all gone now, the mosques are closed and no Turkish *hodjas* divide the worship of God with their Orthodox brethren.

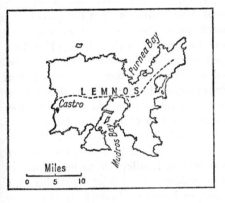

Although there is no volcanic activity to-day, ancient myth claims Lemnos as the home of Hephaestus, the patron of smiths, metalworkers and jewellers. The story goes that Hephaestus was rash enough one day to berate Zeus about the way in which he treated Hera—whereupon Zeus hurled Hephaestus out of Olympus. The smith-god fell upon Lemnos, breaking both his legs with the result that ever afterwards he could only walk with special leg-braces that he himself had made out of gold. It is probable that it was not only the volcanic nature of Lemnos which made the Greeks consider the island sacred to Hephaestus. Metal-working first reached continental Greece from the north, and it is more than likely that Lemnos had an early tradition of ironwork and metallurgy.

The "Lemnian deeds," which gave the island so ill a reputation in classical times referred to the occasion when all the men of Lemnos were massacred by their women. The women of the island, indignant at the way in which Aphrodite treated Hephaestus (she was notoriously unfaithful), refused to pay any more service to the goddess. Whereupon Aphrodite caused them to become singularly unattractive to their husbands, by a combination of what would seem to have been those friends of advertising copy writers, "body-odour and halitosis"! The husbands somewhat naturally neglected their wives, and the wives—illogically perhaps—thereupon murdered their husbands. But the good ladies of Lemnos, however much they have deserved it, were not destined to live in celibacy for the rest of their lives. The *Argo*, on her way north, dropped anchor off the island, and Jason and the Argonauts discovered a sailor's paradise—an island full of frustrated women. There is no record if the ladies had recovered from their affliction, but perhaps it was the old case of "sailors don't care." The Argonauts stayed for two years in Lemnos and successfully repopulated the island. A later visitor was Philoctetes during the Trojan War. The celebrated bowman, the smell of whose gangrenous leg had proved insufferable to his shipmates was put ashore here to convalesce. Sophocles based his play *Philoctetes* on the hero's stay in Lemnos. Philoctetes ultimately recovered, and killed Paris with an arrow shot in front of the walls of Troy.

It seems to me that there must be some connection between this legendary hero suffering from gangrene, and the famous Lemnian earth, the *terra sigillata* of antiquity. This "stamped earth" was impressed in classical times with the head of Artemis, and was considered an infallible cure for snake-bite and festering wounds. The earth was dug up by a priestess, on one day of each year, from a barren mound near the modern village of Kotchinos on the eastern side of the island. This Lemnian earth continued to have a wide sale throughout eastern Europe until quite recently, and it is still used in the island. One can buy it from the chemists in Kastro or Mudros, shaped into cubical blocks. Galen went to see the digging of the Lemnian earth, and recorded that, so valuable was it considered, only one wagon-load was allowed to be removed every year. This tradition is still observed. August 6th, the Feast of Christ the Saviour, is the elected day and the proceedings are carried out under the surveillance of a Greek priest. I imagine chemical analysis would show that the earth has, undoubtedly, some curative powers. (The fungus from a rock off Gozo in the Maltese archipelago was similarly esteemed during the Middle Ages.)

On the east coast also lies the site of ancient **Hephaestia** (Palaiokastro) a Pelasgian settlement, where there was once a fine harbour which had silted up even by classical times. Hephaestia has been associated with ancient Troy, and Schliemann came to the conclusion that it antedated Troy, and that Lemnos had for centuries been one of the principal trade-bridges between Asia and Europe. Before the Second World War the Italians had conducted carefully planned excavations at Hephaestia, but in recent years Lemnos has lain forgotten by the archaeologist. Now, in 1961, an Italian archaeological expedition has been busy here again, under Professor Luigi Brea of Sicily. When I visited the island, Marquis Piero Gargallo of the Italian Institute of Underwater Archaeology was at work with a team of aqualung divers, searching for the shrine of Chryseis. Chryseis was the daughter of a priest of Apollo, who was captured by the Greeks on their way to the siege of Troy, and whom Agamemnon later refused to return to her father. The Italian theory is that the shrine of Apollo, an important one as is made clear in the *Iliad*, lay on an islet just off the Lemnian coast, and that it was later overwhelmed in a volcanic disturbance.

The site of a bronze-age city has been uncovered at Hephaestia, as well as a necropolis dating from the Athenian period of the fifth century BC. There is little to be seen by the layman but it is worth making the expedition by car from Castro, for the eastern side of the island is more attractive than the barren western hills and lowlands. Unlike so many of the islands, Lemnos has a number of streams, and the eastern valleys are rich in fruit. Plums are grown and, as in Skopelos, prune-drying is one of the local industries. The true home-dried Aegean prune, with its delicate aroma and its lovely dark-blue colour, is a far call from those dark, withered things which are—or used to be—the bane of English schoolchildren.

Mudros Bay, familiar to all students of the Gallipoli campaign, is a magnificent natural harbour, about twice the size of Kalamitza in Skyros. It is curious to compare these empty acres of water to-day with old photographs which show hundreds of transports, battleships, cruisers, destroyers and submarines at anchor. The sea keeps no records, and only the Allied War Graves in Mudros and a few place-names such as "The pier of the Australians" serve as a reminder that it was from here that the vast and ill-fated expedition was launched. I found good shelter for a small boat on the western side of the bay opposite to Mudros town, protected by a small peninsula, with Alago island astern of me. Mudros although not attractive scenically is excellent for swimming and sailing, and there is good under-water-fishing off the rocks that fringe the western shore near Alago.

I have only once seen Mudros in a mood that reflected its Gallipoli days and that was in 1941, when I came here in a ship whose task was to evacuate troops who had been building an airstrip on the island. The Germans had by then broken through in Greece and the whole Allied forces were in retreat. That night the great bay was glimmering with lights as boats ferried stores backwards and forwards, and as tired unshaven men stumbled up the gangplank, cursing and swearing at "being evacuated again." (Many of them had been in Dunkirk the year before.) Dawn the next day found us slipping south for Crete and Alexandria through the outermost Cyclades.

To see the islands at dawn from the deck of a ship in the middle of a war at the age of nineteen, is one sure way of arousing a life-long passion. Those pale sleeping shapes, granitic humps, high white Castra, with here and there a fold of green, have stayed with me as a bright image ever since. During the sordid, and often frightening dreariness of the war, when the married men consulted their family snapshots for an image of happiness, I used to remember the Aegean islands at daybreak. Often though I have seen them since, from my own boat and in my own free time, that initial vision has never faded. Mudros harbour filled with frenzied activity, with cargo nets rising and falling against a dark sky, and with a group of sailors (who had been drinking *mastika* as if it was beer) singing, shouting and brawling on the quayside is something else that I have never forgotten.

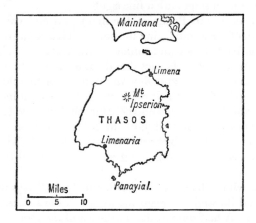

The northernmost of all Aegean islands, **Thasos,** that "mountain of marble and trees," is romantic and inspiring. It is a pity that relatively few visitors ever come so far north, for Thasos has a beauty that eclipses many of the better-known islands. There is no regular steamer service from the Piraeus and, although it is possible sometimes to find a ship out of Salonika bound for Thasos, the best way is to take train or bus to Kavalla which lies just across the strait on the mainland. From Kavalla there are daily steamer services throughout the summer, for Thasos is to the inhabitants of eastern Macedonia what Mykonos and Poros are to the Athenians.

The island takes its name from its legendary founder, Thasos, the son of Agenor, and grandson of Poseidon. There was a cult of Heracles on the island and a famous temple to the hero, the remains of which can still be seen. The island was colonised by

191

Ionians from Paros in the eighth century BC, and rapidly became
one of the most prosperous of the island-states on account of its
marble and the gold-mines on the island and on the mainland
opposite. Thasos was famous for its wine and nuts, and it still
produces a very drinkable red wine. Its chestnut trees and its
olives are important in the modern economy and its thickly-
wooded mountain slopes are a fine sight.

Limena, or Limin Panagias, the main port and capital, lies
on the north of the island facing the narrow Thasos Strait and the
plain of the Nestus, hot and humid in the distance. The great
charm of Limena lies in the fact that the town is built on the same
site as the ancient city, and that the remains of the old capital
co-exist happily side by side with the modern buildings. The
remains of the Heracleion and the triumphal arch of Caracalla
are only about two hundred yards from the waterfront. Behind
them, and encircling both the modern and ancient buildings, rise
the great walls which at one point embody a natural bastion of
rock.

"Persons who dislike steep and difficult climbs," says the *Guide
Bleu,* "would do well to forego the ascent of the ridges." I can
confirm this. A half-mile to the north-east of the modern village
there is a delightful Greco-Roman theatre in the usual magnificent situation, with a rocky ridge at its back and the ancient port
in front. Thasos has only one real drawback, it is rather humid in
summer, being out of the track of the Meltemi.

The island has other attractions for the visitor, fine beaches—
Makri Ammos is the best—and pretty inland villages. There is
a bus service to Panayia from the harbour, and the road goes
through grand and wooded country. Thasos with its trees, its
fertile valleys and its rugged coastline, has more in common
with the romantic Greek island of English poets than most. The
years of Turkish occupation, the Genoese fortress on the Acropolis,
the satyr over the gate of Silenus to the south of the modern port,
all seem to constitute an organic whole. Here one can live side
by side with the past and yet never have the sense of being in a
museum. The museum, in fact, is a little disappointing, although

An olive grove on Lesbos

Sigri, a fishing village on Lesbos

there are one or two attractive things—among them a head of Dionysus—but the more important finds (excavated by the French School) are in Paris.

Limenaria, the second largest village in the island, lies in the south and is best visited by boat. (The views of Thasos from the sea are particularly fine.) Limenaria has a comfortable hotel, the Alcyon, with a good restaurant and a delightful view. Here, as at Makri Ammos, there is a good beach and underwater-fishing off the rocks that fringe the bay. I had the unusual satisfaction here of spearing a good-sized crayfish and eating him on deck for supper. A little later the fishing boats put out for the night with their acetylene lamps hissing and the shine of them like so many moons in the still water. **Panayia** islet, just off the southernmost tip of Thasos, should be visited by those keen on underwater-fishing. One can hire a local boat from Limenaria, landing in a small bay on the southern coast. The island is deserted, but there are many fish off the rocks that fringe it to the south. Limenaria, although a dangerous anchorage if the wind gets into the south, is a good point of departure for yachts bound for Athos, or eastwards for Samothrace and Imbros.

Samothrace is the most mysterious island in this sea—mysterious perhaps only because it is almost inaccessible, and so has been preserved over thousands of years from the ships of the trader, and the war-galleys of the invader. One can reach it from Alexandroupolis on the mainland (but not many people ever go to Alexandroupolis), or sometimes by caique from Lemnos or Thasos. Other than that, the only way I know of reaching Samothrace is by yacht, and even then one's problems are only beginning—for there is no harbour and no really secure anchorage. In the winter I cannot imagine how one could find a safe anchorage for any length of time, but in the summer on the other hand it is possible to anchor on the north-western coast in Kamariotissa Bay, just to the east of Cape Akrotiri where the lighthouse stands. The ancient capital, **Palaiopolis,** lies a little farther to the east, and it is possible that the beach here was used as a summer harbour by the ancients. The *Admiralty Pilot* cautions the sailor accurately and ominously that "The coast is fringed in places by sunken rocks lying close inshore," and "at night or in thick weather . . . great caution must be exercised when in the vicinity of Akrotiri, as the proximity of the high land renders any judgment of distance doubtful."

Mount Fengari, over 5,000 feet high and the loftiest peak next to Athos in the Thracian Sea, dominates the island. Seen from

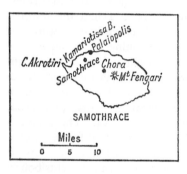

the south, if one is approaching from Lemnos, the island has a withdrawn and haunted look. It is without doubt one of the strangest places in this sea and the atmosphere of the Cabeiri surrounds it like a mist, even on days when the horizon is as sharp as a razor. Samothrace was the centre of a remarkable cult which still serves for a point of disputation among scholars. The Cabeiri were a group of deities of Phoenician or Phrygian origin. Their name in itself was not Greek, but has been conjectured by some scholars as coming from the Phoenician "Qabirim," meaning "The Mighty Ones." They were fertility gods, the phallus their symbol, and their rites kept strictly secret from all but initiates. In the classical period they were often called "The Samothracian Gods" and their cult reached its height in Hellenistic times, although it is mentioned much earlier than this. On account of the Cabeiri the island was always regarded as a sacred place and a sanctuary. Partially perhaps because of its inaccessibility, but also because of the Cabeiri, Samothrace managed to remain an independent and free state throughout all the Greek internecine struggles. Philip of Macedon and his queen Olympias both became initiates of the Cabeiri, and much later Queen Arsinoe, sister and wife of the Ptolemy Ceraunus, took refuge here. In gratitude for her preservation, she later erected a monument, which was excavated by Austrian archaeologists in the late nineteenth century.

The Cabeiri were considered propitious to all seafarers and initiation into their rites was supposed to preserve men from the dangers of shipwreck, a purple amulet being worn by initiates. Pilgrimages to the island continued late into the Roman period, for the Romans claimed the Cabeiri as a legacy from their Trojan ancestors. They identified them with the Penates Publici, who were represented by the images of two youths holding spears. The Greeks seem to have identified the Cabeiri with Castor and Pollux, but there is little doubt that their worship was long pre-Greek.

In recent years American archaeologists have continued the excavations begun by the Austrians, and a great deal of the ancient Sanctuary of the Great Gods has now been uncovered. The site of the shrine lies in a deep narrow valley at Palaiopolis. It can be reached either by foot from Kamariotissa Bay, or better still by landing at the small jetty used by caiques at Palaiopolis itself. It was here, in a niche near the fountain, that Champoiseau, in 1863, discovered the Winged Victory of Samothrace, which had been dedicated by Demetrius Poliorcetes after his naval victory over Ptolemy II in 305 BC. The remains of a theatre, the Arsinoeion, and the ramparts of the ancient city are the main features of the site. Above them, on what was almost certainly the acropolis, stand the ruins of a Genoese castle. This was built in the fifteenth century, when Samothrace like Thasos was part of the fief of the Gateluzzi family. Another Genoese fort protects the Chora of Samothrace, a typical fortified hill-town a little over a mile inland from Palaiopolis. There are no hotels in the island, but there is a hostel designed for the use of archaeologists, which I was told is also open to the casual visitor. It is next to the small museum at Palaiopolis. On the other hand anyone intending to make a stay in Samothrace would probably do better to make arrangements in advance, since the hostel is small and archaeologists naturally have first claim upon it.

Samothrace is not an island where the yachtsman can go hap-

pily ashore and feel confident that his boat is secure. Kamariotissa Bay is a tricky anchorage, and I think that if I went here
again I would anchor in the lee of Mount Fengari to the south-
west of Cape Akrotiri. It was from the peak of Mount Fengari
that Poseidon sat to watch the progress of the Trojan War. The
island appropriately enough is still a haunt of sailors and sponge-
fishers, the men crossing in open boats to Alexandroupolis, thirty
miles away, to sell their catch.

It was alongside the jetty at Palaiopolis that I met a rarity,
an ex-Brooklyn Greek skippering a caique. Usually the American-
Greek will be found running the local bar or taxi, but few have
much of a taste for the sea once they have been "dipped in the
waters" of the American Way of Life. We shared a bottle of Fix
beer together. It was lukewarm, for my ice-box (last stocked at
Castro in Lemnos) had long since run dry. I explained that I
had come there to have a look at the ruins.

"Ruins?" he laughed. "Jeez, that's all there is in Greece—
ruins!"

He was off that afternoon for Alexandroupolis—back to his
wife, his children, the cafés along the waterfront—Life! But it
was not as good as the old East River or the Hudson at night. I
told him how I had crossed with some friends in a yacht from
England a few years before, and what a sight Manhattan had
been after thirty-six days at sea—Manhattan on a bright morning with its great man-made cliffs of glass, steel and concrete.

"Here it's just cliffs," he said sadly.

But the cliffs and the landscape of Samothrace cannot be dismissed so lightly. The island is even more impressive than Paros
and Naxos. At one point on the south coast a waterfall drops
sheer into the sea out of a cliff face of granite, and there are white
sand beaches where one could bathe without sight or sound of
other human beings. Although there was no one left in Samothrace to initiate me into the rites of the Cabeiri, I hope that I am
entitled to wear the purple amulet and be spared the dangers of
shipwreck. I would like to return.

CHAPTER 16

Lesbos

Forty miles long by twenty-five miles wide, Mytilene is one of the largest islands in the Aegean. It is separated from Turkey by the narrow stretch of the Mytilene channel on the east, and the Muslem channel to the north, the latter no more than five miles at its widest point. Rich in olive and grape, the island has an economic balance rare in the Aegean, and because of its comparative prosperity Mytilene is easy for the traveller to reach. The authorities, I am glad to say, are trying to revive its classical name, so I shall call the island Lesbos and use the name Mytilene only to refer to its capital. Air flights link the island with Brindisi, Constantinople and Athens. By sea one can reach it from Piraeus, Salonika, Alexandroupolis, or almost any of the larger northern islands. In summer, regular ferry services run to Smyrna, while Chios and the neighbouring ports on the mainland can easily be reached by caique.

If one approaches the island from the south-west the deep gulf of Kallioni opens like a wound in the shore. The entrance to it is narrow but, once inside, there is a magnificent, land-locked bay nearly ten miles long. Still better, and scenically more attractive, is the Gulf of Yera at the south-eastern corner of the island. Like Kallioni it is almost land-locked, but the blue **Bay of Yera** is surrounded by olive trees and backed by mountains. Yera is a fine place for the yachtsman, while the visitor staying at Mytilene would do well to take a caique round here for a day's swimming. The olives of Lesbos seem to be richer, thicker and more luxuriant

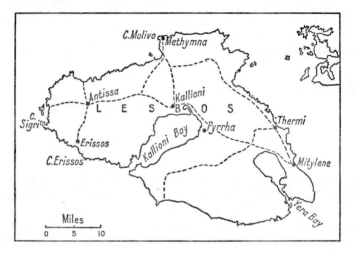

than in any other island. To lie at anchor in the Bay of Yera and watch the wind run through them like a wave of the sea, while westwards Mount Olympus stands up blue-grey against the sky-line, is to experience a dream-like impression of tranquillity. Lesbos is above all a peaceful island.

The modern capital, **Mytilene,** lies east from the Gulf of Yera across a narrow peninsula, and faces towards Turkey. It is a curious hodge-podge of a town, combining twentieth-century nondescript with nineteenth-century Ottoman and small herb-like bundles of Genoese that give a flavour to the whole. It spreads in an aimless sort of way, with mosques and churches, *ouzo* exporters' warehouses and olive refineries, around its bay and along the arm of the peninsula. No one could call it architectur-ally distinguished, but it is bustling and full of life. It is pleasant to come to Mytilene after the quietness and timelessness of the remoter islands. This, one feels, is the Levant—not the sculp-tured Greek silence of Delos, nor the "International set" flavour of Mykonos—but the chaffering Levant. Those who like Alex-andria, or Alexandria as it was in its cosmopolitan days, will find

198

a reflection of the polyglot city in Mytilene. There are several hotels, the Lesvion, and the Aighaion, both comfortable and clean. Food is better in Lesbos than in many other places, and not surprisingly there is a Turkish flavour to much of the cuisine. There are several restaurants and good cafés along the waterfront, and the *mezé* of Lesbos are more enterprising than the usual handful of olives and slices of goats' cheese.

Lawrence Durrell, writing about Corfu before the last war in *Prospero's Cell*, had the following to say about black olives: "The whole Mediterranean, the sculpture, the palms, the gold beads, the bearded heroes, the wine, the ideas, the ships, the moonlight, the winged gorgons, the bronze men, the philosophers—all of it seems to rise in the sour, pungent taste of these black olives between the teeth. A taste older than meat, older than wine. A taste as old as cold water." Often, wryly spitting a worm-eaten husk into the palm of my hand, I have thought harshly of poets, and understood why Plato would have banned them from his Republic. But the olives of Lesbos, whether green or black, go far towards justifying such a eulogy. So does the *ouzo*, as good as any to be had in the Aegean, and one of the island's exports. If you go to the Poseidon restaurant in Mytilene try some of the fresh sardines. Fresh sardines from Bay Kallioni are excellent, especially if boned, mashed flat, and fried—rather like fritters —in olive oil and a little garlic. Lesbos is good for fish and fruit. Its sweet chestnuts are famous, and there are drinkable local wines, quite apart from retsina.

The town itself has comparatively little to show in terms of antiquity, an ancient theatre on the hill behind, and a Genoese castle on an islet. This islet is now linked with the shore but was once, like so many others, approachable only by boat. It was almost certainly the site of the ancient city. The Castro, built by the Gateluzzis who also held Thasos and Samothrace, clings to the hill on the north side of the harbour. From here there is a fine view over Mytilene, over the island, and the hills of Turkey across the narrow strait. Sappho's name is on the lips of many misinformed guides as well as well-intentioned townsfolk. I was shown fragmentary Roman remains near the small church of St. Kyriaki: "The house of the poetess, captain!" But there is not even any certainty that Sappho lived in Mytilene. One account connects her with the ancient city of Erissos on the south-east coast near Cape Sigri.

Pentapolis was an early name for Lesbos, The Five Cities. These were Mytilene, Erissos, Methymna, Antissa and Pyrrha. There is a small village on the site of what may have been Sappho's home town, and a delightful cove next to Cape Erissos at its foot. Methymna, near Cape Molivo, is still the second city of the island. Antissa, also near the north coast, was destroyed by the Romans. Pyrrha, (Palaiokastro) lies just back from the north-east shore of Kallioni Bay, the remains of its ancient acropolis still dominating the anchorage from a small hill.

Lesbos was always a rich and important island. Pelasgian aboriginals and Ionian immigrants are supposed to have been the first settlers, but historically it was settled by Aeolians from Boeotia, probably about 1000 BC. In later days, the nobility liked to trace their descent from Agememnon who conquered the island at the time of the Trojan War. Lesbos' prosperity, then as now, was firmly based on its agriculture and its good harbours. Its geographical position off the Ionian coast, and linking the northern Aegean islands with Chios and the southern Aegean, must also have added to its importance. Pergamum lay just across the straits and Mytilene must have been able to enjoy a trade with the mainland even in winter—something denied to most other islanders in the Aegean.

The most prominent Aeolian settlement, with colonies in the Troad and in Thrace, Lesbos was at the height of its prosperity in the sixth century BC when Pittacus was elected dictator of the island. By settling the internal strife which had been dividing Lesbos, and by his wise laws and administration, Pittacus secured peace and prosperity for the island, and won for himself a place among the Seven Sages of Greece. Both Alcaeus and Sappho were contemporaries of Pittacus, but they were by no means founders of the Lesbian school of lyric poetry. Both Terpander and Arion had been active in the island a century before. The arts necessarily require a soil of culture and prosperity in which to flourish and one can easily understand how this gracious and rich island provided it.

There is, so far as I know, only one complete collection of all the known material of Sappho's text, E. Lobel's work published at Oxford in 1925. It is one of the greatest tragedies of antiquity that only comparative fragments of one of the world's greatest poets remain to us. Only Catullus ever caught something of her note, and in English only Swinburne ever had the ear to imitate —however imperfectly—the Sapphic metre:—

> Heard the flying feet of the Loves behind her
> Make a sudden thunder upon the waters,
> As the thunder flung from the strong unclasping
> Wings of a great wind.

The most dramatic moment in Mytilene's classical history occurred early in the Peloponnesian War, when the oligarchy of Mytilene forced a revolt against Athens. After a two-year siege, the islanders were compelled to submit, and Cleon swayed the Assembly at Athens to take a strong line—"Put every man in Lesbos to death, and sell all the women and children into slavery." A boat was accordingly dispatched to carry out these brutal orders. Next day a more sober and less vengeful mood prevailed in the Assembly, and a wise spokesman, Demodotus, son of Eucrates, managed to turn it to good account. Here are his words as reported by Thucydides: "I am not here to defend the Mytileneans, nor indeed to accuse anyone else. It is not a question of their guilt, but of our interest. . . . The death penalty has been enacted in many cities and for various offences, yet men still commit them, driven to do so by the hope of success. No city has ever rebelled except that it believed there was a fair chance of success. Men by their nature are disposed to act wrongly, both in their public and private affairs, yet penalties however severe have never checked them. . . . I do not, any more than Cleon, wish you to be guided only by pity and moderation, but I do ask you to give a fair trial to the ringleaders and let the others go unpunished. This policy is not only advantageous but it is also a strong one. For the party which deliberates wisely and carefully against its enemy is always more formidable than the one which acts with a reckless violence."

The speech is worth reading in its entirety, for it is one of the noble speeches of antiquity. When one reflects that Athens was engaged in a life or death struggle with Sparta, and that the defection of Lesbos had cost them a great deal, their subsequent action must redound to their credit. They immediately sent another ship after the first, with orders to try the ringleaders but spare the ordinary people of Lesbos. Thucydides tells us, "her crew ate and drank as they rowed and slept in turns . . . whereas the first ship did not make any haste being engaged on so distasteful an errand." Paches, the Athenian commander of the first galley, had actually read out the proclamation, decreeing death to all the men of the island, when the reprieve galley swept into the harbour of Mytilene. Looking out over the blue bay to-day, from the island-site of the old city, it requires little imagination to see that second ship coming into the bay. The sweat-stained oarsmen are half-fainting on their wooden benches as Paches folds away the decree of death, and turns to see what this new arrival portends. It is one of the great dramatic moments of history.

Lesbos subsequently became part of the Roman province of Asia, and then of the Byzantine Empire. Its prosperity under Byzantine rule was interrupted by successive invasions—Barbarians, Seljuk Turks, and Venetians. Recovered by the Byzantine emperors, it was made a fief of the Genoese Gateluzzis. This remarkable family, whose history is written all over the northern Aegean, maintained the island in prosperity for over a hundred years until, in 1462, it passed under Turkish control. Despite a number of attempts to restore Lesbos to Greece, it remained part of the Ottoman Empire until its annexation to Greece in 1912.

It is only quite recently that any attempt has been made to

attract tourism to Lesbos. In 1960 a privately financed programme for converting the island into a rival to Mykonos and
Poros got under way with the building of a new hotel at **Methymna**. There are plans to build other new hotels in Mytilene
and at Thermi (which already has one hotel, the Sarlitsa).
Methymna, the second town of Lesbos, is a delightful place to
stay. It is just beginning to become, as the new hotel sponsors had
hoped, something of an artists' resort. When I was there, there was
a good exhibition of paintings and drawings, while the Athens
School of Fine Arts had just started a painting and pottery-
making school in the village. The association of the arts with
Methymna is appropriate enough, for it was here that the head
of Orpheus is said to have been washed ashore after his dis-
memberment by the Thracian women—a warning, perhaps, to
modern poets. Arion, the lyric poet and musician, who was saved
from drowning by the music-loving dolphin, was a citizen of
Methymna.

Methymna is an attractive small town built on a headland
facing Cape Baba on the Turkish coast. The channel at this point
is only five miles wide, running blue and deep with white flecks
of broken water where the current swirls in towards the Gulf of
Adramyti. There is quite a good road from here to Mytilene and
the drive is pleasant, for the road dives inland after leaving the
capital, and then skirts the bays of Yera and Kallioni before
striking northwards to Methymna. All Lesbos, except for the
marshy area to the north of these two bays, enjoys a reputation for
good air and healthy conditions, but Methymna is the most
exhilarating place in the island. Land and sea breezes swirl back
and forth across the strait even in midsummer, when Mytilene
can be humid and relaxing. The Trojan mountains, with Mount
Ida some thirty miles away, lie to the right of Methymna and
another castle built during the time of the Gateluzzis surmounts
the town. There is good swimming in the long sandy bay just
below, and plenty of fishing. The roadstead at Methymna is,
unfortunately, of little use to yachtsmen, for it is open to the north
and a long swell sets into the bay. If by any chance the visitor

203

should still be awake at dawn—and Lesbos is a cheerful island where parties often last all night—then is the time to enjoy one of the great moments of the Aegean. The sky lightens behind Mount Ida and Asia Minor, as the sea begins to take on colour all the way from Adramyti down the gulf. The night fishing boats are coming in, and there is usually a caique or coastal trader engraving a deep scroll through the clear silver of the strait.

Before leaving Mytilene and sailing south for Chios and Samos, one other story in the island's long history deserves mention. It was here, during the storming of Mytilene by the Romans, that Julius Caesar first "won his spurs" as a soldier. As Suetonius recounts the tale, Caesar's first experience of warfare had been in Asia under Marcus Thermus. The latter was governor-general of the province and dispatched Julius Caesar to Bithynia to raise a fleet for the campaign. Caesar delayed a long time at King Nicomedes' court, and it was during this period that he incurred the reputation of having had a homosexual relationship with Nicomedes. This was the incident later celebrated in a Roman soldier's song, which Robert Graves has translated:

> *Gaul was brought to shame by Caesar;*
> *By King Nicomedes, he.*
> *Here comes Caesar, wreathed in triumph*
> *From his Gallic victory!*
> *Nicomedes wears no laurels,*
> *Though the greatest of the three.*

That this charge was widely believed during Caesar's lifetime is proved by a number of references to Caesar having been Nicomedes' catamite. It was just after this questionable period in Caesar's life that he came to Mytilene. During the attack on the citadel he distinguished himself by his bravery in saving a fellow-soldier's life, and was awarded an oak-leaf crown by Marcus Thermus.

The associations of Lesbos are mostly literary, and it may be because its archaeological interest is slight that it has featured so little in most books about the Aegean. As a place for a holiday, for a rest, or for quiet work, Lesbos is hard to better. It is big enough to permit that change of scene so necessary if one is to avoid "island claustrophobia." It has the further obvious advantage that it is easy from here to organise a visit to the site of Troy. Mytilene also makes a good base for excursions to the coastline of ancient Ionia.

CHAPTER 17

Chios and Samos

The town of **Chios** makes no great impression when first seen from the sea. It has for so long been of commercial importance that it has assumed the nondescript appearance—bland but unrevealing—which is the hallmark of the business man in any quarter of the globe. Delos and Byzantium are far away, and the Chiots one feels would not agree with Honorius of Augsburg that the economic life of man "is nothing but the struggle of wolves over carrion."

Chios is on the regular mail-boat route from Piraeus (Chios, Lesbos, Cavalla, Salonika, Piraeus). There is also a direct Piraeus-Chios steamer both in summer and winter. There are several hotels, the Actaeon, and the Pelinaeon (both C) and the Xenon (B). The latter is one of the new Tourist Board hotels and is undoubtedly the most modern (I had a bath here—something that is often difficult to find in the islands.) There are also one or two small hotels and pensions like the Philoxenia which are clean and cheap. As for food and drink, Chios is much like Lesbos—there is a little Turkish influence, fruit and fish are good, and so is some of the wine. Chios has its two specialities, it is renowned for its fruit preserves and it makes the best *mastika* in the islands.

The town lies on the east side of the island, facing the rugged peninsula of Karaburnu some ten miles away. In the middle of the strait Kumuthi shoals flash white in the sun when the north wind is blowing, and just to the north of them the islets of Goni and Spalmatori jut out of the sapphire waters. It is a pleasant

206

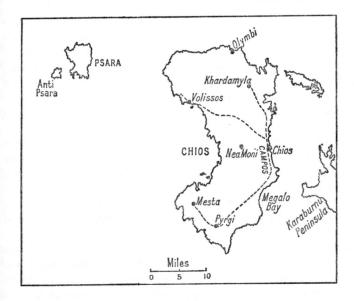

prospect and the activity in the harbour can be welcome after the silence of an island like Samothrace.

Vounaki Square, the town centre, lies a little back from the waterfront, distinguished by a mosque which has been turned into the local museum. Like the square itself the museum has not a great deal to offer, except for its collection of vases. But if one comes here expecting or hoping to see many remains of the sculpture which once made Chios famous, then one is likely to be disappointed. The flavour of Chios is best appreciated by a walk across the bridge by the harbour, into the Castro. This ancient citadel of Chios is a fine example of the sea-surrounded fort, and bears the arms of the Giustiniani family.

Chios passed into the hands of the Genoese in the mid-fourteenth century, and the Giustiniani family had a monopoly of the mastic trade for nearly two hundred years. This was one of the most prosperous and settled periods in the history of Chios, the memory of which is preserved by these ancient walls and by the

207

remains of the Genoese settlement on the Castro. The Genoese rule ended with the coming of Piali Pasha, Admiral of the Grande Porte, in 1566. Worsted in the siege of Malta the previous year, Piali regained his reputation by the capture of prosperous Chios, and the mastic trade now passed into Turkish hands. The centre of Castro is still reminiscent of an old Turkish village and has a charm that is lacking in modern commercial Chios. It reminds me in miniature of parts of Rhodes.

A car can be hired in Chios for the drive to the southern end of the island, where the villages of the mastic-makers are to be found. On the way one passes through **Campos,** the long fertile plain which is the main source of the island's wealth. Here the houses of the rich Chiots abound, and there is a certain "*lacrimae rerum*" about these evidences of the island's past prosperity—not that Chios is impoverished to-day, but its trade has considerably declined since the boom days of the nineteenth century. Osbert Lancaster in his *Classical Landscape with Figures* has caught the atmosphere very accurately: "If one steps aside through any of the ornamental but crumbling gateways which impose an ineffective barrier of rusty wrought iron between the urban squalor of the street and the discernible greenery beyond, one enters an Eden-like region of terraced but neglected gardens, long perspectives of olives and thick groves of lemon stretching away up the gentle slope until they merge imperceptibly into the open mountainside . . . these shuttered stone-built mansions that loom up here and there through the green shade are almost all empty and deserted, as silent and abandoned as the shipyards in the harbour, and their owners a thousand miles away in the air-conditioned comfort of the Dorchester or the rhododendron-shrouded cosiness of some half-timbered Surrey mansion, far beyond the reach of the lemon blossom which is here so strong as to be discernible, so it is said, when the wind is offshore, five or six miles out to sea."

The houses are not so desolate as when this was written, in 1946, and nowadays one would do better to inquire at the Tourist office in the town and get permission to visit one of the gardens. I can confirm that one can smell the citrus groves of Chios from the sea, especially if one arrives in the early morning and there has been a dew-fall overnight. The fertile islands like Samos, Corfu and Rhodes, to mention but three, all have a definable scent. After a fourteen-hour crossing from Andros to Chios arriving at dawn on a July morning, I noted: "We could smell the land now, damp after the night, a blend of earth and pine-trees, lemons perhaps, and something indefinable, like the memory of a herb garden."

Pyrgi, Mesta and Olymbi in the south of the island are the best-known mastic-villages. Mesta is an almost perfect example of a fortified township, with fine old ramparts and winding streets. It was formerly the main centre of the mastic industry. Mastic was, to the odalisques of the Sultan's seraglio, an essential delicacy—a combination, as it were, of chewing-gum, breath-sweetener, and tranquilliser. It is a product of the *Pistacia Lentiscus*, an evergreen shrub indigenous to the Mediterranean coastline but only, as far as I know, grown with a view to its gum product in the island of Chios. The *Encyclopaedia Britannica* says that, "The production of the substance has been, since the time of Dioscorides, almost exclusively confined to the island of Chios." I have no idea why this should be so, for one finds mastic shrubs growing in many other parts of the Mediterranean, but it is true that only in Chios are the shrubs specially tended, growing to a height of six feet or more. The resin is collected from incisions made in the bark and looks rather like crystal tears. The chewing-gum manufacturers of America and the inventors of synthetic varnishes have deprived the mastic grower of his former sources of prosperity. Only the drink *mastika* remains, that and a curious concoction which every visitor to Greece is certain to come across sooner or later—the "submarine." The "submarine" is a jelly-like mastic jam, served on a spoon at the bottom of a glass of water—hence its name. You eat the mastic jam and afterwards drink the water. " Children," as my uncle Nigel Bruce used to say, putting on his "Dr. Watson" voice and face, "would consume any *quantity* of it." Personally I prefer my mastic in the drink

The Companion Guide to the Greek Islands

which, as I have said before, is akin to *ouzo* or arak, and very good if taken in moderation.

Like Mesta, Pyrgi and Olymbi are both examples of the fortified townships which once protected the island (there were fifteen of them all told). Olymbi is rather like Mesta, but it is to Pyrgi that the visitor is more often taken, for the women of the village still wear traditional costume, though nowadays rather self-consciously. It is interesting to note that, so important to the Grande Porte was the mastic trade, the inhabitants of these southern villages were all spared at the time of the great massacre of 1822. The massacre, which was sparked off largely by the Samians who had occupied the island and were trying to get the inhabitants to join them against Turkish rule, brought disaster to Chios. The event was commemorated by Delacroix in his famous picture (a copy of which is in the Chios museum). Like Guernica which Picasso celebrated, the massacre of Chios and Delacroix's image of it shocked the conscience of the Christian world and led indirectly to the French expedition of 1827. Fought over, devastated by the earthquake of 1881, Chios recovered slowly and recovered only because its natural fertility made this inevitable.

Shortly after the massacre at Chios, the neighbouring island of **Psara,** which lies ten miles to the west, was similarly attacked and devastated by the Turks. This tragic episode inspired the poet Solomos to the short but famous poem which Professor J. N. Mavrogordato has translated:

> On the island's blackened stone
> Glory paces all alone,
> Thinking on the shining dead,
> Wears a garland on her head
> Of the little that is found
> Green upon the wasted ground.

Seven cities claimed to have been Homer's birthplace— Smyrna, Chios, Colophon, Salamis, Rhodes, Argos and Athenae. **Chios** has perhaps the best claim of them all, and there is the well-known line in one of the Homeric hymns which refers to "the blind old man of rocky Chios." I think that most scholars

210

are nowadays agreed that the author of the *Iliad* (whatever may be one's conclusions about the *Odyssey*) came from ancient Ionia, and from that part of Ionia which was originally Aeolic. The village of Khardamyla in the north of the island is traditionally supposed to have been Homer's birthplace. "Homer's Stone," which lies just outside the town of Chios to the north, is as inaccurately named as "Sappho's house" in Mytilene, being in fact an ancient shrine. Near "the Stone" is the Pasha's Fountain, Pasavrysi, one of the many natural springs which render Chios so pleasant after the barren islands. The beach nearby is a popular summer resort, and there are one or two small restaurants, but the swimming can be rather tricky since the northerlies send a swell down into the bay. There is better bathing to be found in Megalo Bay and small boats can find quite a good anchorage at the north of Megalo Bay, sheltered by the cape, and almost in line with Paspargo islet.

The Monastery of **Nea Moni** can be reached quite easily by a new road, with the usual indifferent surface. Formerly the only way to get to the monastery was by mule, but taxis are now obtainable from the town, and Nea Moni in any case was always worth even the discomforts of mule-back. The monastery lies just below the peak of Mount Provatium in a magnificent situation, one which unfortunately did not protect it during the great earthquake of 1881 when the monastery, like the nearby villages, was badly damaged. Nea Moni possesses a tremendous grandeur, a grandeur that is explicit in the cycle of mosaics that depict the life of Christ. The monastery is an eleventh-century foundation and the mosaics are of the same period, most probably the work of artists brought down especially from Constantinople. Unfortunately, the great head of Christ in the dome was destroyed during the earthquake, but the remaining mosaics are outstanding. They have none of the stiffness of the more famous mosaic cycle of St. Luke at Stiris, and scenes like the "Descent of Christ into Limbo" are moving in their colour and semi-realism. Few monks are left to maintain this monastery which once housed many hundreds. The abbot (who gave me a "submarine") seemed to reflect in his stained clothes and generally unkempt appearance the neglect which has fallen upon Nea Moni ever since 1881.

If Chios may lay claim to having been the birthplace of Homer, **Samos,** its neighbour twenty miles to the south, has the distinction of having been the birthplace of Aristarchus. If his name

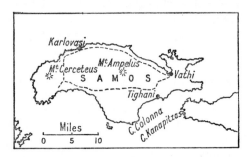

is considerably less well-known than Homer's, then that is probably because Sir Charles Snow is right and that our "Two Cultures" have never been equally disseminated. Aristarchus worked mostly in Alexandria, between 280 and 264 BC, but I like to think that it was in Samos, under the clear night sky of this part of the Aegean which was called the Sea of Icarus, that he first began to speculate on the nature of the universe. Aristarchus, as Professor Hoyle has written in *The Nature of the Universe*, was "as far as we know, the first man to perceive that a far simpler description [of our Solar System] could be achieved by taking the Sun as the centre of the system. . . . He found it possible to explain the observations by supposing that all the planets, the Earth included, move around the Sun in essentially circular orbits of various radii. If sufficiently detailed historical records were available it would be an interesting study in prejudice to see why Aristarchus' views were ignored by his fellow Greeks. At all events they were forgotten until revived by Copernicus nearly 2,000 years later." I think, in fact, one would find that they were not ignored by his fellow Greeks, but that they were con veniently forgotten or suppressed by the early Church, unwilling to have its Judaic cosmogony queried.

Approaching the island by the channel between Ikaria and Furni, Samos presents a grandeur unequalled in the Aegean. A great mountain chain runs right along the island from east to west, rising into two main peaks. Mount Cerceteus at the western end, nearly 5,000 feet high, spins up out of the sea like a fantastic top, while away to the east the head of Mount Ampelus dominates the fertile plains. Regular steamer services link the island with Mykonos, Syra and Piraeus, although—short of taking a caique or having one's own boat—there seems to be no way of reaching Samos from Chios. The Aegean traveller must be prepared for such strange anomalies in the shipping routes, whereby an island twenty miles away will prove more difficult to reach by steamer than one at least a hundred miles distant. This is one reason why the yacht-chartering agencies are beginning to flourish in Piraeus. High though their rates are, I think that if the cost can be divided between enough people, they are—short of having one's own boat—the best way of travelling in the Aegean.

Ships call at the modern port and capital, **Vathi**, in the north-east corner of the island. It is a sheltered harbour at the head of a long narrow inlet, with red-tiled houses banked up around the slopes in a manner reminiscent of Skopelos. But Port Vathi has definitely a Levantine feel, even if the upper town, which over-hangs the bay in colourful terraces, has more of a Northern Greek atmosphere. There are two hotels, the Xenon (B) recently built by the Tourist Board, and the small Poleos. Other than these there is the Pythagorion at Tighani, the ancient capital in the south, and the Aktaion and the Samion Palace at Karlovasi. The latter is an attractive village twenty miles to the west, along the coast from Vathi.

Pleasant though Port Vathi is, it has the big drawback, at any rate in midsummer, that the northerly winds do not "blow home," but lift up over the port into the hills. Except for Port Livadhi in Seriphos I cannot recall anywhere where I have lost more weight in the short space of a day or so. At the far end of the gulf the heat can be stifling and, short of finding accommodation in the upper town of Vathi, I would recommend **Tighani** as the better place to stay. Apart from being healthier and more exhilarating, Tighani is more interesting and is in a lovely site. The view of the Turkish mountains where they run down to Cape Kanapitza less than five miles away, is—if anything justifies the descripion—"sublime." Tighani is on a circular harbour, its name meaning "frying pan" is self-explantory, and the mole to which the caiques secure rests on the foundations of the famous mole built by Polycrates. Further remains of the ancient mole were being investigated by aqualung divers from the school of archaeology when I lay here at anchor. The harbour is safe, well-sheltered, and a boat can lie comfortably stern to the mole except if the wind is strong from the south. I would recommend yacht-charterers to see that they are taken to Tighani rather than Vathi (yacht skippers—for reasons best known to themselves, the customs, the bars and their girl friends—always make straight for the largest port in any island). Tighani is easy to reach by bus from Vathi and, wherever one stays in Samos, it should be visited not only for its situation and view, but for its historical associations.

It is built on the site of the old capital of the island, with the ancient citadel dominating it from the south. This was the city of the tyrant Polycrates, under whom about 535 BC Samos became the "ruler of the seas." Here is Herodotus' pen-picture of Polycrates in the translation of Aubrey de Sélincourt: ". . . the rapid increase of his [Polycrates'] power became the talk of Ionia and the rest of Greece. All his campaigns were victorious, his every venture a success. He had a fleet of a hundred fifty oared galleys and a force of a thousand bowmen. His plundering raids were widespread and indiscriminate—he used to say that a friend would be more grateful if he gave him back what he had taken, than if he left him alone and never took anything at all. He captured many of the islands and a number of towns on the mainland as well. Amongst other successes, he defeated at sea the

Lesbians, who had sent their whole fleet to the help of Miletus; the prisoners he took were forced to dig, in chains, the moat which surrounds the stronghold in the capital city of Samos." The story of Polycrates, and of the emerald ring which he threw into the sea in order to escape the jealousy of the gods, is one of Herodotus' small masterpieces. After a few days, a fisherman turned up at the tyrant's palace with a huge fish as a present, and the ring was found inside—a sure sign that "Polycrates, whose luck held even to the point of finding again what he had deliberately thrown away, would one day die a miserable death." Polycrates was later lured to the mainland of Ionia, arrested, and crucified.

It was under Polycrates that what Herodotus describes as "three of the greatest building and engineering feats in the Greek world" were carried out. The first of these was the great mole which protected the harbour, the second was a tunnel through the hill of Astypalaea to the north of the town, and the third was the temple of Hera, "the largest temple in Greece." The tunnel through the hillside was a fantastic feat of engineering for the time, being about a mile long, eight feet wide and eight high, driven from north and south through the hill, and carrying a pipeline to feed water to Polycrates' capital. It is still possible to explore the tunnel, the mouth of it lies only about fifteen minutes' walk from the harbour, but one can no longer pass right through the hill for the diggings have collapsed in the middle. There are, I am told, the remains of a Byzantine chapel inside the tunnel but I leave it to bolder explorers than myself to investigate them. After a few minutes, the dank smell, the slippery passage, and the feeling that someone was creeping up behind me, drove me out into the fresh air again.

The temple of Hera, one of the wonders of the ancient world, lies just south of Port Tighani at Cape Colonna. Here, as the name suggests (as at Cape Colonna on the site of Croton in Southern Italy), only one column survives. It is a lonely and rather desolate spot, a place to remember one's Shelley: "My name is Ozymandias king of kings. . . ." But it would be unfair to Polycrates to think of him only as a pirate chief and tyrant. Like so many old princelings and *condottieri*, he was a man of taste, a patron of the arts, and the friend and admirer of Anacreon. "The most eminent artists and poets," it is said, "found a welcome at his court."

There is a small museum at Tighani, as well as at Vathi (mostly small objects from the temple of Hera). At Tighani there are several archaic statues, as well as a number of statues and other finds from the Hellenistic period. The ruins of the theatre just outside the town, near the grotto of the Virgin, are of no great interest but from the ancient ramparts to the north there is a wonderful view of the bay, and of the peak of Mycale on the mainland. It was somewhere in this strait that, during the War of Independence, Kanaris blew up a Turkish frigate right under the eyes of the Turkish army assembled for the invasion of Samos. The sight apparently daunted the Turkish commanders. They abandoned the attack, and the island managed to hold out until the end of the war.

The island's early history was stormy. Falling first to Sparta and then to Athens, Samos ultimately became part of the Roman Province of Asia. Augustus spent the winter here after his victory at Actium. Earlier, Anthony and Cleopatra had stayed here, "giving themselves up," as Plutarch states, "to feasting and ease." Its proximity to the Roman province, and its fame as an artistic and intellectual centre, seemed to ensure that Samos would play an important part in the Empire. But, by the second century AD, possibly due to the incursions of pirates, the island had sunk into insignificance. It revived under Byzantine rule, becoming the head of the Aegean theme, or military district, but with the fall of Byzantium Samos again fell prey to pirates. The inhabitants were forced to flee, either up into the mountains or, leaving the island altogether, across to Chios and Lesbos. In the thirteenth century, like Chios, it became a possession of the Genoese trading firm of the Giustinianis, being captured by the Turks under Piali Pasha in 1566. For the second time the island was almost completely depopulated. The birthplace of Aristarchus, the sculptor Pythagoras, and the home of many famous architects, poets, sculptors and potters, became no more than a grazing ground for goats and sheep.

In the seventeenth century it was largely repopulated by immigrants from Lesbos, Asia Minor, and Albania, with the result that it is unlikely that many of the present Samians are indigenous. A possible exception are some of the inhabitants of the Cerceteus region who may, like the Cretans under similar conditions, have managed to survive in their mountains throughout those hard centuries of rapine and devastation. The island remained a tributary of the Turkish Empire (with a Greek governor nominated by the Grande Porte) until its union with Greece in 1912.

For so beautiful an island it has had one of the most tragic histories. It was not even spared in the last war, for it was occupied by the Germans, and then shelled by the Royal Navy during the Dodecanese campaign. It is surprising that the people of Tighani and Port Vathi do not have a more impoverished air, but fortunately the island's fertility, its vines, olives and tobacco, have managed to restore its economy in a comparatively short space of time. The Samian wine—though whether it bears any relation to its famous classical ancestor I cannot say—is good but hard to find. That is to say, the dry Samian wine is rare, although there is plenty of the sweet *moschato* which is rather like the red wine of Santorin.

There are a number of excursions to be made in Samos and the roads are a good deal better than in many of the islands. **Karlovasi,** the second most important town in the island, is nothing much in itself, but Upper Karlovasi, the small village just inland, is attractive. The pine forests and the drive back to Vathi through vineyards and olive groves make it a pleasant day's outing. Samos has a happy landscape, despite the affliction which the island has suffered. I know of few other places where one can pass from magnificent mountain scenery like that around Ampelos into fertile plains which are not tedious—as flatlands so often are—for each section is different and self-contained. Samos has as many varieties of scenery as are to be found in some of the

English counties, but without that "salad-bowl" effect which so depressed Norman Douglas. The grandeur of its mountains serves as a reminder that, geographically, Samos belongs to the same great Asiatic spur as Mount Mycale on the Turkish mainland.

CHAPTER 18

Patmos, Leros, Calymnos and Cos

The Dodecanese, the Twelve Islands, lie down the western coast of Turkey like a cable linking Samos to Rhodes. The Turks always referred to them as "The Privileged Islands," since they enjoyed special privileges and tax exemptions granted them at the time of Sultan Suleiman the Magnificent. These privileges they retained right up to 1908, when the twelve islands united against Turkish rule. They were liberated in 1912, and a promise was given by the Allies that they would be restored to Greece at the end of the war. This promise was conveniently forgotten at the Treaty of Sèvres, when they were awarded to Italy for her share in the Allied victory, and they did not finally become united to Greece until 1948. Despite these centuries of foreign occupation, the islands are as distinctively Greek as anywhere else in the Aegean. Although the term Dodecanese was not officially applied to them until 1908, Theophanes, a Byzantine chronicler, writing between AD 810-185 refers to them in his Chronography as the "Dodeka Neesoi," the Twelve Islands.

Most of them can be reached from Piraeus by the regular mailship, which does the circuit of the islands about three times a week, while the southerly islands like Symi and Khalki can be reached by caique from Rhodes. They, too, are visited once a week by a steamer from Piraeus.

Most northerly of all is **Patmos** where the steamer calls at least three time a week in summer, and which has an excellent harbour in Port Scala for those who travel in their own boat. Patmos is also visited by many of the cruise liners.

"At last I near the port of Patmos," wrote W. E. Gell, whose Aegean travels were published in Philadelphia in 1897, "Patmos —Island of the 7 hills! Island of the 7 letters! Island of the 7 golden candlesticks! Island of the 7 stars! Island of the 7 lamps of fire! Island of the 7 spirits! Island of the 7 trumpets! Island of the 7 seals! Island of the 7 angels! Island of the 7 vials! . . .'

A little more soberly, he continues, "Patmos to-day is a wild and desolate island, of which the prevailing colour is brown, and which does not only arise from the lava character of the rocks, but also from the heather and shrub arbutus."

Patmos, in fact, is a barren island, formed by three large volcanic masses, the central mass being joined to the northern and southern sections by a narrow isthmus. **Port Scala** is a fiord-like channel that almost cuts the island in two. The first thing I noticed, coming here after Samos and Chios, was the predominantly Cycladic quality of the buildings. Scala, but more particularly Chora, the upper town, is a blinding surgical white. Gone are the red tiles and the Levantine muddle of Chios or Mytilene and in their place one finds once more the cubist pattern of light and shade, the flat-roofed square houses, and the patches of green vineyards vivid against a predominantly bare landscape.

Patmos is mentioned only two or three times in antiquity. An Ionian settlement, it was chosen as a place of exile for political prisoners during the Roman period, and the old town was built on the isthmus at the head of the gulf. **Chora,** the modern capital, lies on a ridge just south of the port. There is a small hotel in Scala which seemed clean and reasonable, but if I were staying here, I think I would try and find accommodation in Chora. Scala can be rather airless in midsummer, and Chora is a charming small town where it would be pleasant to spend a few days.

"I John, who am also your brother, and companion in tribulation, and in the kingdom and patience of Jesus Christ, was in the isle that is called Patmos, for the word of God, and for the testimony of Jesus Christ. I was in the Spirit on the Lord's day, and heard behind me a great voice, as of a trumpet, Saying, I am Alpha and Omega, the first and the last: and, What thou seest, write in a book, and send it to the seven churches which are in Asia. . . ." Thus St. John the Divine in the opening passages in the Book of Revelation, a book, incidentally, that has never been officially accepted by the Syriac-speaking Church.

There is a poetry to be found in the Apocalypse that can be found nowhere else in the Old and New Testaments—though, to one of my temperament, less sense than in Ecclesiastes. But no one who has ever read the Book of Revelation could willingly pass by the island where it was supposedly written, I say supposedly because St. John's exile in Patmos falls into the region of conjecture. Traditionally, he was exiled here during the reign of the Emperor Domitian in AD 95, but there is no certainty that the Apocalypse was written in Patmos. The Acts of St. John, written by his disciple Prochorus, which describes the miracles wrought by the Saint while he was in Patmos makes no mention of the Book of Revelation having been written here.

"Beloved," runs the First Epistle General of John, "believe not every spirit, but try the spirits whether they are of God: because many false prophets are gone out into the world." Certainly, the Revelation was not considered acceptable by all the early Christian Church. The Alexandrians made an attempt to interpret the book in allegorical terms, although some of them rejected the book altogether. There seems nowadays little doubt that it was meant to interpret the immediate future—and as such, time and time alone has proved us wiser than our forefathers. "Be that as it may the power and attractiveness of the Book of Revelation are undeniable" wrote F. C. Burkitt, D.D. "There is in it a personal note that differentiates it from the other Apocalypses. . . . So the Christian Apocalypse renews its youth in the hearts of fresh generations of readers, notwithstanding that the clearly taught thousand-year Reign of Christ on earth was rejected by the Church of the third century, and that we in our Copernican world are not expecting 'the holy city of Jerusalem coming down out of heaven '."

Above Chora, and dominating the town, the bay and indeed the whole island, stands the great monastery, an imposing building and a true fortress of God. Half-way between Scala and Chora on the left-hand side of the road is the chapel of St. Anne, and the church of the Apocalypse. It was here, so legend has it, that St. John received the words of God which his disciple Prochorus wrote out at his dictation. The church is cut out from the hillside so that the inner aisle is roofed by rock and there, as one of the monks pointed out to me, is the crack in the rock made by the voice of God. Part of the rock wall served Prochorus for a desk, and a silver halo on the wall nearby shows where the Apostle laid his head to rest. The site was neglected for centuries, and it was not until 1088 that the Emperor Alexis Comnenus granted the island to St. Christodulos for the purpose of founding a monastery. The golden bull of the Emperor is still preserved in the monastery. In the ikonostasis of the church of the Apocalypse and Chapel of St. Anne there is a delicate ikon of St. Anne, the mother of Mary.

The monastery itself is awe-inspiring rather than beautiful. It was built during those centuries when the waters of the Icarian sea were infested by pirates, and one feels that its thick, frowning walls were designed to repel sea-rovers like Torghoud or Suleiman of the Islands, just as much as to repel the legions of the Evil One. Inside, in a silver shrine, lies the body of the founder, St. Christodulos. There is also some extremely rich Byzantine jewellery in the sacristy. I regretted that I had had no time to make special arrangements to be able to view it at leisure, and undisturbed. The monk who showed me round was naturally reluctant to open

he cupboard and let me examine the pieces—a pity for I thought
detected more than one example of *plique-à-jour* enamelling in
roziers and crosses. There are also a number of presentation
pieces from the Russian Imperial Family, lavish and ostentatious
pieces in a style that foreshadows the Edwardian vulgarity of
Fabergé. If I should come here again I hope to be able to examine the jewellery thoroughly. There is nothing finer that Byzan-
ine cloisonné work, the restrictions of the medium being so suited
o the hieratic quality of Byzantine art.

The library is still the chief glory of the monastery, even if
more than half the original manuscripts have been dispersed.
Six hundred manuscripts are recorded as having at one time been
preserved in the monastery. Now only two hundred and forty are
eft, the most valuable of which is the *Codex Porphyrius*, a fifth-
century work of great delicacy, the major part of which is in
Russia. A few of the leaves can be seen in the British Museum,
while a number of manuscripts formerly in Patmos are in the
Bodleian. Edward Daniel Clarke, the English mineralogist and
raveller, was responsible for securing these manuscripts during a
our of Europe and the Near East which he made from 1799-
-803. He published his *Travels in Various Countries of Europe, Asia
and Africa* (1810-19), and presented a "Colossal Statue of the
Eleusinian Ceres" to Cambridge University.

From the monastery one gets a magnificent view of the whole
island, the church of the Panayia with its surrounding village to
he north, and the bay of Merika cutting into the land from the
west. One can see on how narrow a peninsula the ancient town
was built—no doubt an excellent site, with its two anchorages of
Merika and Scala which between them would give shelter at all
imes of the year. In 1664 it was recorded by the French
raveller Thévenot that the harbour of Patmos was much
avoured by the corsairs, who used it as a place to lie up and refit
heir vessels. It is still a good anchorage, dangerous only during
outh-easterly winds, but subject to strong squalls which whip
down from the surrounding slopes when the northerlies are
blowing hard. The Lipso islets and Leros lie east and south, and

223

to the north the trident-head of Mount Cerceteus is white against the wind-washed Aegean sky.

Legend has it that at certain times of the year a strange light can be seen on the peak of Cerceteus and the people of Patmo connect it in some way with St. John. Clarke was sceptical "It is probably one of those exhalations of ignited hydrogen gas found in many parts of the world, which are always most conspicuous in hazy or rainy weather." I have seen a summer thunderstorm browsing over the peak of Cerceteus, and it is possible that, if there are deposits of natural gas on the mountain they may sometimes get touched off by lightning flashes. But if one cannot let sleeping legends lie in the Aegean, then it were better not to go there. A Chair of Applied Chemistry in the red brick university of some northern industrial town is no doubt reserved for sceptical spirits in the world to come.

Leros lies only ten miles south from Port Scala, a pleasant sail with rocky islets on all sides but not one I would like to attempt at night. All this area holds ominous memories for me for which reason I find it impossible to view Leros in an impartial light. It was during the "Leros-Cos party," as it was bitterly known, that about one third of the Mediterranean fleet was sunk or crippled in 1943. As the navigator of an escort destroyer grew to know the narrow channels between these islands with the vivid memory of nightmare. There were no lights in those days on any of the islands, islets, and rocks that scatter the sea from Leros in the north to Symi in the south. It was a far from pleasant experience navigating at some twenty knots by what seamen call "dead reckoning" in an area where the error of a knot, or the miscalculation of a current, would have you aground in a matter of minutes.

Port Lakki, capital and main harbour of the island, lies in the south-west. It is a fine harbour, but I cannot say much for the town itself which is sad and unattractive. Revisiting it, I found little more to enthuse about than I did on that first occasion when we put ashore here a tough and blood-thirsty group of the Greek Sacred Brigade. Never have I seen a unit of soldiers look

Islanders. *Above left*, a monk at Poros; *right*, a street in Mykonos. *Below left*, a Samian shepherd; *right*, an itinerant two-man band in Crete

A gateway in the ramparts at Rhodes, built by the Knights of St. John

less sacred, nor one so encumbered with every weapon of death—hand-grenades slung all over them, knuckle-duster knives, sub-machine-guns, automatic pistols and even butchers' cleavers. They landed and went up into the hills, and I never heard of them again. Two days later Leros fell.

I did not recapture that heady compound of fear and excitement when revisiting Lakki, but found only a sad village still, so it seemed, exhausted by war. Yet Leros has an interesting history, and is probably one of the few islands left where field research into customs and habits might produce some findings of real value. I say this, because a fisherman, who gave me a hand with my lines and later accompanied me into the town, pointed out his house and referred to it as "My wife's house." It struck me as a curious expression to hear in Greece where, even more than in Sicily or Southern Italy, one feels oneself in a heavily masculine world. I discovered then that much of the property in Leros, houses in particular, is inherited through the female line.

Robert Graves in a study called "The Fifth Column at Troy" has described the customs of the people of Bagnarotte in Calabria and traced their descent from the "Western" Locrians, a matriarchal society which emigrated to Bagnarotte in the sixth century AD. He goes on: "Such a system seems to have been common in Europe before the arrival, late in the third millenium BC, of the barbarous Greeks, Latins and Teutons, who worshipped a Father-God, rather than a Mother-Goddess; but by Classical times matriarchy survived only in distant Galicia, Majorca, Libya, Pictish Scotland, Wild Wales—and among the Locrians. Traces of it also lingered among certain Aegean islands. . . ."

I think that Leros may well have been one of these islands, for the good reason that it was the centre of a curious old cult of Artemis—a cult considered strange and conservative even in classical days. Legend had it that the daughters of Oeneus, inconsolable for the death of their brother Meleager, aroused the pity of the virgin Artemis, who turned them into guinea-fowls and set them on Leros. Artemis was certainly worshipped in the guise of a guinea-hen in Leros, and guinea-fowl were specially bred on the marshy ground near the Lerian temple to Artemis (the remains of which can still be seen). Graves has a footnote in his *Greek Myths* on the subject of Artemis of Leros: "The Lerians' reputation for evil-living may have been due to their religious conservatism. . . ." I suspect that this was so, and that this reputation for evil-living was the same one which pursued the "Western" Locrians—namely that they maintained a matriarchal society in a world where the Father-God had everywhere else assumed control. The Lerians, incidentally, are still unpopular with their neighbours and I was told in other islands that they were liars, thieves and cheats.

After spending several hours with my limited books of reference, I sailed up the western coast of Leros and then turned east, leaving the Pharios Islands to the north of me. Sheltered from the north by the Pharios group, a deep bay winds into the northern coast of Leros. It is known as **Ormos Partheni,** the Bay of the Virgin, but its name without any doubt derives not from the Virgin Mother, but from the Lerian Artemis. In the marshland, at the head of this bay, lie the ruins of her temple. On the eastern side there is a small village, Ayia Matrona, and the sheltered basin here is known locally as the "Little Harbour of the Holy Mother"—but again I feel confident that its name comes from Artemis and not the Christian Virgin. This basin was almost certainly the ancient disembarkation point for pilgrims to the shrine. It is a fine and lonely place in which to anchor, and is sheltered from all winds. Yachtsmen who like the lonely life could easily spend a winter here and there would be good shooting in the marshes. I saw no guinea-fowl, but I was told that they are still to be found. Guinea-fowl, which are African by origin, have made their home in many parts of the Mediterranean. The Lerian guinea-fowl of antiquity, which had blue plumage, was most probably introduced from Somaliland where the breed still flourishes. On the site of the old temple are the remains of a Byzantine church; the place is known as Partheni.

No doubt, nestling away in some obscure and scholarly

quarterly lie the answers to the questions which Leros provoked in me. If not, then here is fresh and fertile ground for some original research "On Artemis Meleagris and the Survival of Matrilineal Customs in the Island of Leros." Lakki, with its one

small hotel, would not be an attractive place to stay, but the island abounds in fine coves and bays where it would be a pleasure to camp out: it has the best natural harbours anywhere in the eastern Aegean. There is a regular steamer to Lakki from Piraeus three times a week.

Calymnos, which lies just to the south, with the one-mile-wide Leros channel dividing the two islands, is mountainous and imposing. Approached from the north, the islands seem to blend into one another and they were, in fact, known collectively in the past as Lero-Calymnos. Ovid described Calymnos in the *Ars Amatoria* as "shaded with woods and fruitful in honey." Now, as in so many other places, the woods have all gone. Calymnos is as bare as Astypalia in midsummer, with which island, incidentally, it shares a bishop. The port and the capital of the island is

227

Pothia, facing towards Cos at the head of a wide bay in the south.

It is a pleasant situation but architecturally the town is undistinguished, for this is another of those island capitals which is only about a century old. **Chora,** the old capital, lies two miles inland at the head of a valley that is protected on both sides by ancient forts perched on rocky tumuli. The Knights of St. John of Jerusalem, during the two centuries that they were based on Rhodes, maintained a garrison force on Calymnos, the harbour serving them as a summer base during their eternal warfare against the Turk. In Chora there seems to me a distinctive Rhodian influence in the architecture. Robert Liddell in his *Aegean Greece* also comments on this: "Over many doors and windows there is a semi-circular blind lunette; this I have also frequently noticed in Rhodes." He mentions also "the two small windows, divided only by a column or thickness of brick. . . ." Both of these features are to be found in Rhodes and Malta and are, I suspect, Norman inheritances. In Malta, the semi-circular lunette is not blind but open. It originated as a simple way of keeping a cool draught flowing through a house even in midsummer, and it could be boarded up in winter.

The Calymniots are a proud and cheerful people. They still depend largely upon sponge fishing for their livelihood. Symi, Calymnos, Chalki, and Astypalia used to be the islands of the sponge fishers. Astypalia, which the chronicler Stephanos of Byzantium says was once called "the Table of the Gods," because it was so fertile and rich in flowers, remains the best area in the Aegean for sponges. In general, however, the modern sponge fishermen have to go farther afield—Egypt, Cyprus and the coast of Tripoli—since the Aegean beds have been largely worked out. Theirs is perhaps the hardest life in a part of the world where life is never easy, yet it still attracts young men because it is one of the few ways in which an adequate living can be made. It is a dying industry, for world demand for real sponges has declined rapidly since the invention of rubber and synthetic substitutes.

The history of sponge fishing is as old as the history of civilisation in this sea. In the *Odyssey* we find the servants of Odysseus using sponges to wash down the tables in the dining-hall on Ithaca, while in the *Iliad* there is a reference to Hephaestus cleaning himself from the dirt of his smithy with a sponge. Sponges were also used as padding inside classical armour. This "very fine, very dense and very strong" sponge, as Aristotle describes it, was known as *Achilleion* and was almost certainly the shallow, cup-like sponge nowadays called "Elephant's Ear." The honeycomb and the cup are the two main types which still find a market, the honeycomb being the familiar Mediterranean bath sponge, while the cup has a harsher surface and is used in industry. During the Middle Ages the Venetians gained a monopoly of the sponge traffic, to such an extent that a sponge became known as a "Venetia" (the honeycomb sponge is still called a "Venise" in France).

Before the discovery of the diving suit, all sponges were fished from shallow waters, a method still used and one which has not changed over the centuries. The sponge-fisher wears a face mask and carries a trident with which he scoops the sponge off the bottom. He is secured to a rope and dives by holding a heavy stone to his chest. In the Bay of Maltezana, off Astypalia, I have seen sponge fishers from Calymnos still using this age-old method. But sponge diving such as is carried out in the deeper waters off North Africa requires a diving suit, a diving boat with air pump, and all the conventional apparatus. Some of it is terrifyingly antiquated, and in **Pothia,** the capital of Calymnos, I saw old German, Italian and ex-Royal Navy suits and gear which would be condemned at once in any more prosperous society. It is not surprising that one sometimes sees "old men" (who are perhaps no more than forty) with all the symptoms of diver's palsy, or with the swollen joints that come from nitrogen saturation. Yet, despite the dangers and hardships of their lives—or perhaps because of them—the Calymnians are a cheerful and spirited breed of men. I was told, and I can well imagine it to be true, that— rather like the old square-rigger sailors—their return from the sponge fishing grounds is marked by wild parties in the tavernas around the port. I am afraid that few of them manage to save much of their so hard-earned money.

Pothia is architecturally rather crude, and dirtier than most ports in the Cyclades or the northern Sporades. There are two small hotels, inns with beds would be a more accurate description, of which the Acropolis is perhaps the best. From Pothia I went out to Telendos Bay for the sake of the view, and for the swimming. On this western side of Calymnos there are a number of villas, the summer houses of the richer citizens of Pothia. But it is not necessary in the islands to be rich to have more than one house, and I have met fishermen and peasants who owned "a summer house," as distinct from their winter quarters in the village. In the indulgent climate of the southern Aegean one needs little in the summer months: four walls and a roof, a charcoal or paraffin stove, a bed, a table, and one or two chairs.

At **Damos,** the site of the ancient capital, near the point where the valley road winds down to the sea, there are a number of rock tombs, and a Mycenaean tomb which is known as the "Monolith of Damos." The English traveller and archaeologist Sir Charles Newton came here in 1852 and again in 1855. He made a number of important excavations in this area, some of his finds now being in the British Museum.

Somewhere near Damos, I was told, lies the Cavern of the Seven Virgins, but it—or they—escaped me. The story goes that they were seven Calymnian ladies who fled from pirates and took shelter in a cave, from which they never re-emerged. One suspects that it is a cavern which was once sacred to the nymphs or the muses, particularly in view of the mystical number "seven."

Calymnos's history during the classical period is somewhat obscure, but it would seem to have been a dependency of Cos until its incorporation into the Roman Empire along with the other Dodecanese islands. After 1310, when the Knights of the Order of St. John emigrated to Rhodes from Cyprus, Calymnos, like the other nearby islands, came within the sphere of this last of the great militant Orders of Christendom. When the Knights were driven from Rhodes by Sultan Suleiman the Magnificent in 1522, all the Dodecanese group gradually became incorporated into the Ottoman Empire.

The olives of Calymnos are good, the wine less so, but I was given an excellent *mezé* in a taverna at Pothia which is, I suspect, of Arabic origin. It probably reached the island through sponge fishermen who had encountered it in Egypt or Tripoli. Haricot beans, parsley, garlic, and green coriander are left to soak and are then put through a mincing machine. The result is a kind of dough to which is added a spoonful of bicarbonate. After the mixture has set, it is cut up into small cakes and fried in deep fat. It may sound peculiar, but it is a very good appetiser.

One can reach **Cos** from Piraeus on the boat bound for Rhodes or, better still, if you have been staying in Calymnos, go down by caique through the Calymnos channel. The land- and sea-scapes here are very fine—Calymnos mountainous to the north, colourful rocks and islets fringing the Turkish coast, and the green sides of Cos. The channel sweeps round into the wide bay where the town and port are situated. Guarding the harbour is another reminder of the Knights of St. John, a fifteenth-century castle. On the peaks of the hills are old look-out stations which were also built by the Knights to keep the Cos and Calymnos channels under observation. It was in these narrow waters that their armed galleys carried on "the eternal war against the Moslem," that organised piracy of Ottoman merchant shipping which had the blessing of the Pope and Christendom.

"There is no pleasanter land under the Heavens than Cos," wrote the French traveller Pourqueville, "and viewing its lovely scented gardens you would say that it is a terrestrial paradise." The island's natural beauty and fertility, the views of the distant hills east of ancient Halicarnassus, and the pleasantness of its climate (even on the hottest days a breeze is always moving on or off the island) have attracted a number of visitors and summer residents in recent years. It seems to me preferable in many ways to such well-known beauties as Mykonos and Hydra. Not that Cos is entirely unsophisticated, and there are half-a-dozen hotels ranging from the Zephyros (B) to the little Avra and Aktaeon (C). There are good beaches, a delightful boulevard, cheerful tavernas, the fruit, fish and wine are good, and living is cheap.

The ancient capital, Astypalaia, was built on the southern coast about four miles from Krokelo Point. It was sacked and destroyed by the Spartans during the Peloponnesian War. The Coans thereupon moved to the present site, where they founded their new city in 366 BC. Diodorus, describing the removal of the inhabitants, wrote: "The people of Cos at that time settled themselves in the town they now enjoy and gave it the garden it now has. For it became very populous, and a costly wall was drawn round it, and they provided it with an excellent harbour. From this time forward it grew more and more, both in its public revenues and in the private wealth of its inhabitants, and in general it rivalled the most conspicuous cities of the world."

If the same cannot be said of the **Chora** of modern Cos, at any rate the situation, the oleanders, and the vines, still maintain the Theocritean mood. Theocritus was not a Coan by birth, he was a native of Syracuse, and would seem to have come to Cos as a pupil of Philetas. The painter Apelles also worked in Cos, and its most famous citizen was the physician Hippocrates. One of the most delightful parts of the town is the small square where the so-called "plane of Hippocrates" leans its tired forearms on old marble columns, and shadows a delightful small mosque. There is something wrong with legend, however, for according to Soranus, a Greek physician of the first century AD who wrote a Life of Hippocrates, the "Father of Medicine" was born in Cos in 460 BC, nearly a century before the Coans transferred their capital to this side of the island. Be that as it may, the plane of Hippocrates is a magnificent old tree, one of the largest trees in Europe—even if it is only four or five hundred years old. The plane tree, nevertheless, is native to Greece and Western Asia and was popular with the Greeks and Romans as a shade-tree, the Romans introducing it into south-western Europe. It is not impossible that this plane is a descendant of some Hippocratic tree.

The three-terraced **Asclepion** of Cos which lies about two miles outside the town, originally contained temples, a medicinal spring, and the famous Aphrodite of Apelles. Parts of the site have been reconstructed from the Hellenistic Asclepion which was remodelled on the ancient site by Xenophon, that physician who—oblivious of his Hippocratic oath—is supposed to have poisoned the Emperor Claudius. The famous Oath, although the version of it which has come down to us is much later than Hippocrates, reflects a nobility that one would like to ascribe to these priest-physicians of the Asclepion: "I will look upon him who shall have taught me this Art even as one of my parents. I will share my substance with him, and I will supply his necessities, if he be in need. I will regard his offspring even as my own brethren, and I will teach them this Art, if they would learn it, without fee or covenant. I will impart this Art by precept, by lecture and by every mode of teaching, not only to my own sons but to the sons of him who has taught me, and to disciples bound by covenant and oath, according to the Law of Medicine. The regimen I adopt shall be for the benefit of my patients according to my ability and judgment, and not for their hurt or for any wrong. I will give no deadly drug to any, though it be asked of me, nor will I counsel such, and especially I will not aid a woman to procure abortion. Whatsoever house I enter, there will I go for the benefit of the sick refraining from all wrongdoing or corruption, and especially from any act of seduction, of male or female, of bond or free. Whatsoever things I see or hear concerning the life of men, in my attendance on the sick or even apart therefrom, which ought not to be noised abroad, I will keep silence thereon, counting such things to be as sacred secrets."

It is still a subject for dispute as to how many of the Bucolics and Mimes of Theocritus can be said to have owed their setting to the island of Cos. The Seventh Idyll, *The Harvest Feast*, is definitely set in Cos, and Theocritus makes a point of praising his teacher Philetas. Herondas, another poet of the Coan school and a contemporary of Theocritus, describes in one of his mimes three women going to the Asclepion to make an offering. Herondas and Theocritus may well have known one another. Scholars have pointed out similarities in their language and phraseology, but which poet borrowed from which is likely to remain a matter of dispute. Certainly, Theocritus—like any intelligent poet—was not above making use of his predecessors, Sophron, Alcaeus and Aratus among others.

There is a small museum in Cos containing a good statue of Hippocrates, the castle of the Knights is the best medieval building in this part of the Aegean apart from the town of Rhodes itself, and Dhikaios, the main peak of the island, is a noble mountain. There are some delightful villages on the mountain slopes, the countryside is pleasant, hand te Cos melons are better than the celebrated lettuces. Strabo rightly praised the island's fertility, its wines and grapes. If I have one regret it is that the famous "*Coae vestes*," those Coan dresses of light transparent silk— so highly prized in the ancient world—are no longer worn. In the town one sees a few graceless Egyptian cottons, but elsewhere I saw only that ubiquitous and dusty black, which turns almost every Greek peasant woman into an image of Niobe.

CHAPTER 19

Rhodes

"Nothing in the world was ever so well lost as was Rhodes!"
The remark was made by the Emperor Charles V of Spain, on
hearing the story of the great siege of 1522 when the Knights of
the Order of St. John of Jerusalem were finally driven from their
fortress island by Sultan Suleiman the Magnificent. The Siege of
Rhodes remains one of the epics of war, and it is the shadow of
the Knights which still falls across this island. The Knights of St.
John have left their imprint so firmly on the town that their
armoured feet still seem to ring down the alleys. The sandalled
shuffle of the ancient Rhodians has become no more than a faint
lisp.

Rhodes is without doubt the easiest island to get to in the
Aegean, even though it is a long way from Piraeus. Nearly all
cruise ships call at Rhodes, it is on a regular air service with
Athens, and it is also linked by air with Heraklion in Crete, and
with Cyprus, and Alexandria. There are regular steamer
services from Piraeus, Corfu, Brindisi and Venice, and there are
also five-day summer excursions to Rhodes by boat from Piraeus,
as well as three-day air trips from Hellenikon Airport, Athens.
But, as so often in the eastern and southern Mediterranean, the
summer is not the best time for a visit. The best months in which
to see Rhodes are April, May, September and October. In summer the island can be hot and humid. Although most of the
year its climate is maintained at a pleasant temperature by either
the west or north winds—which blow almost like trade-winds—

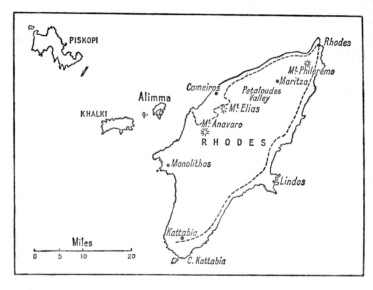

in midsummer a hot breath off Asia Minor can bring an oven-like heat reminiscent of the North African *khamsin*.

Lamartine in his *Voyage en Orient* (1835) wrote of Rhodes: "I do not know in the whole world a more excellent strategic position, nor a more beautiful sky, nor a more smiling and fecund soil." Every one of his statements might be questioned: Malta (as the Knights were later to find out) is in a better strategic position; the sky above the Cyclades is more beautiful; and there are other islands with just as good a soil. Taken altogether, though, the virtues of Rhodes are practically unique. One might add that it has some of the finest military architecture in the world, a lovely town, fine beaches, grand mountains and gracious valleys, and—for the relaxation of the modern traveller—some first-class hotels. Outside of Athens, it is one of the only places in the Aegean where there is a selection of luxury hotels, comfortable "family" hotels, attractive small hotels, and pleasant pensions. Even the Swiss hotelier has in recent years noted the potentialities of Rhodes, and in 1961 the owner of the famous Schweizerhof in Berne took over the Miramare beach hotel in Rhodes (as well as the Miramare and the Palace Hotel in Corfu). The Miramare in Rhodes has its own swimming pool, and *de luxe* chalets for those who like hotel comforts combined with privacy. The Hotel des Roses is another luxury hotel on the north-east beach where—a rarity in the Aegean—every bedroom has its private bathroom, and where there is also a private beach for the residents. There are three Class A hotels, the Cairo Palace, Thermai, and the Elafos and Elafina (out of town on Mount Elias overlooking the plains). There are two or three Class B hotels, at least six Class C, including the pleasant little Lindos and the Acropole, and several small Class D hotels for those who want no more than a bed for the night. In addition, there are a number of private houses where furnished rooms or flatlets can be rented. Prices, as might be expected, are higher than in most other Aegean islands but then the standard of comfort is higher as well. It would be unwise to arrive in midsummer and expect to be able to find a room in the hotel of your choice, without booking in advance. Rhodes, without intending any comparison between the two, is rapidly becoming the Mallorca of the Aegean. Those who knew either, or both, of these islands before they became popular, may regret this. At the same time it is wrong to be sentimental about a prosperity which has inevitably improved the lot of the ordinary inhabitant.

Ships, if they are small, anchor in Mandraki, larger vessels in the central or commercial port to the south. This is, incidentally, one of the few harbours in the Aegean where the traveller is spared the discomfort of having to disembark by caique or open boat. Immediately on entering the harbour you are within the fortifications built by the Knights. On your left, at the head of the outer mole of the central port, is the Tower of France with its windmills. On the other hand lies the Tower of St. George. The old city with its battlements and fortifications is all around, and it is only a few hundred yards from the customs office to the museum, the Street of the Knights, and the winding alleys of the Turkish quarter.

"These armoured dedicated men," as I wrote in *The Great Siege*, "who move across the history of Malta and Rhodes like visitors from another planet, represented the last active element of the three great military orders which had sprung out of the Crusades. The most powerful of the three, the Templars, was suppressed in the early fourteenth century. The second, the Teutonic order, never really recovered from the defeat inflicted upon it at Tannenberg in 1410. . . ." The Knights of the Order of St. John, who survived into the nineteenth century, were different from the two other bodies in that they were primarily a nursing brotherhood.

The Order stemmed from a Benedictine hospital for pilgrims (dedicated to St. John the Baptist) which was established in Jerusalem in the eleventh century. In 1113, in gratitude for the services which the hospital had rendered to the crusaders, Pope Paschal II took the Order and its possessions under his protection. In 1291, after the fall of the last Christian strongholds in Palestine, the Knights of St. John emigrated to Cyprus. At that time, Rhodes was under the control of the Genoese admiral of the Byzantine Empire, who had fortified the port to some extent, but who felt incapable of holding the island against the depredations of Turkish corsairs. In 1309 at the instigation of the Pope, and with the connivance of the Genoese, the Knights of St. John took over Rhodes together with the neighbouring islands of Leros and Cos. The whole transaction was marked by much bad faith on both sides, and the Knights were finally compelled to capture Rhodes at the point of the sword. The Pope had two good reasons for wanting to see the Order established in this former outpost of the Byzantine Empire. The first was practical—to have a militant body of Christians in a place where they could do the maximum damage to the Moslem enemy. The second was political—in Rhodes the Order could be of little trouble to Catholic Christendom. The Genoese had a third reason for wanting to see the Knights established in Rhodes, which then, as always when one investigates Genoese behaviour, was simply commercial.

For over two centuries, the Knights of St. John held the island of Rhodes against the Turks. From being hospitallers first, and fighting soldiers second, they became seamen first and hospitallers second. Unable to prosecute the Holy War against the Moslem by land, they now turned themselves into Christian corsairs. They became the finest fighting seamen the Mediterranean had ever seen, and Rhodes, leaning against the coast of Turkey like a spear, was the ideal base from which to harry and sink the shipping of the Grande Porte. It is to these two centuries that we owe the harbour and the defences of Rhodes. It was here too that they perfected the form of their Order—"the most remarkable body of religious warriors that the world has ever seen," as W. H. Prescott described them.

Divided into eight national languages or "tongues," Auvergne, Provence, France, Aragon, Castile, England, Germany and Italy, they were an aristocratic foreign legion of militant Christians. United by their vows of chastity and obedience (vows that were often taken lightly) they were divided into five groups: Military Knights, Conventual Chaplains, Serving Brothers, Magistral Knights and Knights of Grace. The last two were honorary knights who had been nominated by the Grand Master. He himself was a knight who had been elected by the Grand Council after he had served in all the major positions in the Order. The Serving Brothers were soldiers, required to be of "respectable birth," while the Chaplains, apart from their religious duties, were mostly employed in the Great Hospital of the Order. It was the Military Knights who gave the Order its distinctive characteristics, and from whom its Grand Masters were drawn. The sons of the great houses of Europe, they were required to prove noble birth on both sides of their families for at least four generations before they could be admitted to the Order. In the case of the German Langue, entry was made even more difficult, since the Germans required a proof of eight generations of nobility. That these proofs of nobility were no light matter can be judged from the records of the Order (which still survive in Malta). In these early days, at any rate, no taint of illegitimacy or suspicion of common blood was accepted. It was not surprising that, with such a constitution, the Knights of St. John should have been both aristocratic and arrogant. They were also brave and ruthless against their hereditary foe. Gibbon remarked of them with some accuracy: "The Knights neglected to live, but were prepared to die, in the service of Christ."

The Knights lived inside the **Collachium** or citadel, which is at the north of the city. Here were the Auberges of the national Langues, the great Hospital (now the museum), the Palace of the Grand Master, and the arsenal. In the Street of the Knights one finds the finest Gothic in Rhodes and, familiar though it is from a thousand photographs and indifferent paintings, it is still one of the grandest sights of the Mediterranean. The Grand Master's palace was entirely rebuilt in 1940 by the Italian Governor, who has come in for some harsh criticism from architects and others, for what has been described as "Hollywood Baronial" and "Mussolini Gothic." Pompous the building certainly is, but time is tempering the vulgarity. At night it blends with the true Gothic and is a moving and imposing silhouette. Conducted tours round the Collachium and the battlements are organised by the museum and are well arranged. I would advise anyone without previous acquaintance with Rhodes to go on one of the tours first of all, and then make his own explorations at leisure.

Just to the north of the Collachium and the old gardens lies the small port of **Mandraki,** nowadays used by caiques, small trading vessels, and visiting yachts. In the days of the Knights this was the Port of the Galleys and here they kept those long lean war-craft which proved so ill-omened to the masters of Turkish ships. Mandraki is guarded by two breakwater arms, on the northernmost of which is the old Lazaretto, and on the other, the fort of St. Nicholas. In the Turkish siege of 1480, when the Knights under their Grand Master Pierre d'Aubusson held out successfully for over three months, it was against the fort of St. Nicholas that the Turkish attack was mainly directed.

As well as the galleys of the Knights, their flagship the Great Carrack of Rhodes was moored in Mandraki. She was one of the largest and most extraordinary vessels of the Middle Ages. I can never look at Mandraki without seeing the Great Carrack at rest there, with the tower of St. Nicholas behind her, and the wolfish galleys idling in her shadow. The Great Carrack was described by J. Taafe in his *History of the Order:* "It had eight decks or floors, and such space for warehouses and stores that it could keep at sea for six months without once having occasion to touch land for any sort of provisions, not even water; for it had a monstrous supply for all that time of water, the freshest and most limpid; nor did the crew eat biscuit, but excellent white bread, baked every day, the corn being ground by a multitude of hand-mills, and an oven so capacious, that it baked two thousand loaves at a time. The ship was sheathed with six several sheathings of metal, two of which underwater, were lead with bronze screws (which do not consume the lead like iron screws), and with such consummate art was it built, that it could never sink, no human power could submerge it. Magnificent rooms, an armoury for five hundred men; but of the quantity of cannon of every kind, no need to say anything, save that fifty of them were of extraordinary dimensions; but what crowned all is that the enormous vessel was of incomparable swiftness and agility, and that its sails were astonishingly manageable; that it required little toil to reef or veer, and to perform all nautical evolutions; not to speak of fighting people, but the mere mariners amounted to three hundred; as likewise two galleys of fifteen benches each, one galley lying in tow off the stern, and the other galley drawn aboard; not to mention various boats of divers sizes, also drawn aboard; and truly of such strength her sides, that though she had often been in action, and perforated by many cannon balls, not one of them ever went directly through her, or even passed her deadworks."

Such a prodigy of strength and size would have been remarkable even among the sailing ships of the nineteenth century, but that the Knights of Rhodes had a vessel of these dimensions and strength in the fifteenth century is clear enough evidence of the grandeur of the Order. She was the "*Mighty Hood*" of her time.

For the student of military and fortress architecture Rhodes is eternally interesting. Here one can see curtain walls defended by towers, some of the curtains being as much as forty feet thick— proof in itself that, when they were reconstructed under the direction of Pierre d'Aubusson, the age of the cannon had begun. Prior to this, a thickness of about twelve feet was considered adequate against the rams and siege engines which had changed little since Roman times.

"In the siege of Rhodes in 1480," writes Sidney Toy in his *History of Fortification*, "the most vulnerable part of the walls was that stretch, called the Jews' wall because the Jews' quarters were behind it, running eastwards from the Koskino gate to the sea." Behind it to-day lies the Turkish quarter. Its delightful small streets are crossed by flying buttresses, to protect them against the earthquakes to which Rhodes is subject like almost everywhere else in the Aegean. Despite the beauty of other Aegean islands and citadel towns, and despite the austere attractions of the Collachium, it is here that I would like to live. The **Chora,** the old town or Turkish quarter of Rhodes, has the agreeable distinction that it is not just fossilised in time, held in a drugged amber. Life still circulates and—if one did fall into a dream here—it would be pleasant enough.

The Turkish quarter is a reminder that the island of the knights could not hold out for ever. It had been too great an irritant to be borne, these Christian seamen plying in the Sultan's seas. "They have sown the wind, let them reap the whirlwind!" In 1522, Sultan Suleiman I, Suleiman the Magnificent, invested the island with a force of about 200,000 men. The siege lasted for some six months, and ended in the capitulation of the Order. Yet, so valiantly had they fought that the Sultan agreed to honourable terms being accorded to them. (Some authorities reckon that out of his initial invasion force he had lost nearly 90,000 men.) On a cold December day, the seventy-year-old Villiers de l'Isle Adam, the Grand Master of the Order, together with his remaining Knights, servants-at-arms, and followers (including some native Rhodians loathe to stay behind), embarked aboard their galleys and the Great Carrack of Rhodes. It is said that the Sultan, contemplating the departure of the Grand Master, remarked to his staff; "It is not without some pain that I oblige this Christian at his age to leave his home."

The island now became part of the Ottoman Empire, and such it remained until its occupation by the Italians in 1912. The churches were converted into mosques, but apart from that little happened to change the character of Rhodes. It decayed a little, and the Latin city took on something of an Oriental appearance. It was saved, however, from the devastation which overtook Moslem cities whenever the Christians happened to capture them. In this connection it is worth bearing in mind Moritz Brosch's comment: [1]"The exaction of a tithe of their boys from the defeated Christians [to form the corps of Janissaries] was an act of cruelty, but apart from this no one was persecuted in Soleyman's time, when the Inquisition was carrying on its deadly work in Spain and in the Netherlands. In view of all this, it cannot be said that in the wars of Soleyman barbarity was to be found only on the side of the Turks."

For myself, I can never walk through the old streets of the Turkish town without hearing the titles of Suleiman the Magnificent resound in my ears: "Sultan of the Ottomans, Allah's deputy on Earth, Lord of the Lords of this World, Possessor of Men's Necks, King of Believers and Unbelievers, Emperor of the Chakans of Great Authority, Prince and Lord of the most happy Constellation, Majestic Caesar, Seal of Victory, Refuge of all the People in the whole World, the Shadow of the Almighty dispensing Quiet in the Earth." Rhodes is a place in which such sonorous appellations, such assumptions of dignity, do not seem out of place.

If you have the time, stay here for several months and read everything that you can about the island, the Knights of St. John, and about its classical history. For Rhodes was distin-

---

[1] *The Cambridge Modern History* (The Wars of Religion)

guished in more ways than one during its classical period. The great Colossus alone singled out the island as a place that had to be visited by any cultivated Greek making the Grand Tour in the third century BC. The classical city was on the same site as the modern city and the city of the Knights, on this crescent bay looking north-eastward towards Asia Minor. Mandraki was also the classical port, and it was here most probably that the Colossus of Rhodes was erected. The Colossus itself was indirectly the product of yet another siege, when Demetrius Poliorcetes attempted to conquer the island.

Demetrius Poliorcetes was so impressed by the Rhodians' bravery that, on withdrawing, he presented them with the vast siege engines which he had used against the city. The Rhodians, in their turn, sold them to defray the cost of a vast statue to the Sun God, their protector. "The colossus, which was 105 ft. high, stood for 56 years, till an earthquake prostrated it in 224 BC. Its enormous fragments continued to excite wonder in the time of Pliny, and were not removed till AD 656 when Rhodes was conquered by the Saracens, who sold the remains for old metal to a dealer, who employed 900 camels to carry them away. The notion that the colossus once stood astride over the entrance to the harbour is a mediaeval fiction."[1] I can see no reason at all why this should be so. Mandraki harbour, the ancient harbour of Rhodes, is only about sixteen feet deep to-day and has an entrance no more than 100 feet wide. It is a small-boat harbour, and one must bear in mind that the ships of the ancients were, by modern standards, only small boats. Most of them, no doubt, lowered their masts when entering harbour under oars—just as the galleys did in the time of the Knights. In any case, a statue with a total height of 105 feet would have given plenty of clearance between its legs. What is really interesting to anyone who has studied the subject of bronze casting, or who has read Cellini's *Treatises* (which describe the difficulties of large-scale casting during the Renaissance) is that so large a statue could have been cast at so early a date. Chares of Lindos, who was the

[1] The 14th Edition of the *Encyclopaedia Britannica*

artist responsible for the Colossus, must have been a superb technician. I presume that the figure was cast in a number of plates, supported on an armature of iron, and with the legs possibly of stone or marble blocks, covered with bronze plates.

There is much about modern Rhodes, particularly its suburbs, which is reminiscent of many other resorts in the world—that international villa architecture which is a sad proof that the Trimalchio of all ages remains unchanged. Nevertheless, the restorations inside the city, even including the Palace of the Grand Master, are mostly excellent. The sunsets here are deservedly famous, for there is something about Gothic architecture and battlemented walls which belongs to the sunset. I can well imagine that the Kaiser—had travel been easier in his days—might well have picked Rhodes instead of Corfu for his summer palace. On the battlements of Rhodes at sunset, one might do worse than remember Matthew Arnold:

> *Charge once more, then, and be dumb!*
> *Let the victors, when they come,*
> *When the forts of folly fall,*
> *Find thy body by the wall!*

Rhodes has a greatest breadth of twenty miles and is about forty-five miles long. A mountain range runs from north-east to south-west, reaching its highest point in the centre at Mount Anavaro, close on 4,000 feet. On either side of the main ridge lie the fertile plains and valleys. Olives and carobs, juniper and fruit trees abound, as well as innumerable aromatic plants and shrubs. I think it was these which the ancient mariners could smell at sea rather than the rock-rose from which the island takes its name. On a hot day the scent of the maquis-like scrub on the foothills of Mount Elias is as heady as wine. The celebrated Rhodian wine of the ancients is alas! no more, and the modern Rhodian wine seems to me inferior to that of Samos or Santorin. But we have so little idea of what the ancients considered a good wine—or whether they even had any. The Romans who thought that the comparatively coarse silk of Cos was the height of luxury and degeneracy (Caligula got roundly abused for wearing a Coan silk cloak), may well have had rather crude ideas about wine.

Rhodes is one of the only places in the Aegean where there is a good road system, regular bus services, and even organised coach tours. One of the best of these goes down the west side of the island to **Petaloudes,** the Valley of the Butterflies. Petaloudes is Coleridge's "deep romantic chasm," not "savage," but certainly "holy and enchanted." Streams pound through a narrow gorge, the air is scented with thyme and myrtle, and galaxies of red and gold butterflies quiver among the plane trees and above the rocks. From here one goes on by the same road to Mount Elias where the scenery is Alpine, more reminiscent of parts of the Troodos range in Cyprus than of the Aegean. Looking down from the slopes of Elias, one sees the islands to the north, Alimma and Khalkia, only a few miles off the coast. Beyond them lies Piskopi, the ancient Telos. **Khalkia** was once famous for its schooner-building. Theophrastus wrote about Khalkia in his work *On Plants:* "They say that there is a spot there which is so exceedingly fertile that crops mature very early, and as soon as one crop has been reaped another can be sown, and one or two more harvests are thus gathered in one year." This is more than likely, and in many islands of the Mediterranean to-day double crops are regularly harvested. This is only achieved nowadays with the use of intensive fertilisers. The barren soil of many Greek islands cannot only be attributed to their deforestation but to the indiscriminate working of the soil, leaving it to blow away in powder under the winds of midsummer.

The present capital, built on the small harbour of Khalkia, is a typical Dodecanese fishing village. Both Khalkia and Piskopi were owned by the Knights of Rhodes and the name **Piskopi,** which means "Look-out," was accurate enough. The Knights maintained watch-posts here, from which they could signal to Rhodes whenever Turkish shipping was sighted in the Nisero-Piskopi channel. Pliny mentions that this island was famous for its unguents and the islanders still make a scent which has a sage base.

The eastern coastal excursion is the finest in Rhodes for it goes to **Lindos,** one of the most dramatic places in the Aegean, and the only city surviving from pre-classical Rhodes. Rhodes was a Dorian settlement, and the three Homeric cities were Lindos, Cameiros and Ialysos. The island's fertility and its geographical position made it prosperous, and soon the Rhodians themselves were sending out colonists—to the south coast of Asia Minor, to Sicily where they founded Gela, to the Lipari Islands, and even as far afield as Rhoda in north-east Spain. It was not until 408 BC that the three cities decided to pool their resources and found a new capital on the site of the present Rhodes, the architect of which was the famous Hippodamus of Miletus.

Of the three ancient cities, Ialysos on the peak of Phileremo (on the north-west coast) has practically disappeared. Cameiros lies in a delightful valley on the west coast but has little to show except the remains of a restored colonnade on the hill above. Lindos, on the other hand, is one of the great monuments of ancient Greece. If you come to it by road, you have the pleasure of one of the best drives in the island, along a wild and craggy coastline and passing through several attractive villages. Lindos stands on a steep promontory, the land falling sheer into the sea where two islets guard the approach to the harbour. This, one feels, is what a fortress-town should look like—white and powerful, on inaccessible heights, with a small port lying in a fold of land beneath it.

In Lindos one finds a microcosm of the island's history. There is the acropolis poised some four hundred feet above the water, the remains of the theatre, and the sanctuary of the Athena of Lindos. In the Greek Anthology one finds:

> *On the summit of the citadel of Lindos thou art,*
> *O Athena, the glory of this ancient city . . .*

Among much else to be seen here is a carving of an ancient ship, showing the poop, keel and pilot's seat, even more interesting to students of antique vessels than a rather similar carving in ancient Corinth. Of Dorian Lindos there is an abundance. But there is also the Lindos of the Knights, who were naturally un-

247

able to resist so perfect a site for a castle. A connecting link between the classical world and the Middle Ages is the ruined Byzantine church, while evidence of the Turkish occupation can be found in the small town itself.

Another building dating from the Knights of St. John is the delightful Church of Our Lady of Lindos in the harbour town. Here, the fifteenth-century houses dating from the last years of the rule of the Knights abut seventeenth- and eighteenth-century buildings, whose courtyards are pebbled in the same way as is the floor in the nave of the church. Few things in this world are pleasanter than to come on deck in Lindos harbour, on a bright, dew-smelling morning, and see the white village across the water. The acropolis catches fire from the early sun as it streams across the sea from Asia Minor.

Perhaps in Rhodes, where tourism and a comparatively prosperous agriculture combine with scenic beauty and a delightful climate, one comes as near as possible to the ideal life. Tiberius, that island-lover and much-maligned Emperor, clearly thought so. Suetonius described his visit to the island: "As Tiberius sailed past Campania news reached him that Augustus was ill. He cast anchor for a while but when gossip began to circulate, accusing him of standing by in the hope of seizing the throne, he at once set off for Rhodes, even though the wind was almost dead against him. He had happy memories of that beautiful and healthy island, since he had first set foot there, during his voyage from Armenia, many years before. He settled down in a town house with a country villa near-by, neither of which were on a grand scale. Tiberius behaved most unassumingly: after he dismissed his lictors and runners he would stroll about the gymnasium, talking and chatting to ordinary Greeks as if they were his equals. . . ." Unfortunate Tiberius! I think there is little doubt he would have been content to stay in Rhodes living his simple life for the rest of his days. Even Suetonius, who had a mind that would have fitted him for the post of gossip writer in our daily press, was unable to find any reason for Tiberius's self-imposed exile in Rhodes—except, presumably, that he liked it.

It would be difficult not to like Rhodes, even though the countryside may not have the grandeur of some other parts of the Aegean. There is plenty to do—visit the Aquarium near Mandraki, see the Aphrodite of Rhodes in the museum (dredged out of the sea, she has a soft, wave-worn beauty that seems as if she was made of smoke rather than marble), or spend a cheery, retsina-filled evening in one of the tavernas at Kouva. Herpetologists can find an excuse for staying here by tracking down the so-called "Dragons of Rhodes," lizards even bigger than the ones on Delos. Floriculturalists have equally valid excuses for staying in the island. Students of architecture probably profit most out of Rhodes, for it is the city which makes the island unique.

The Knights of St. John, after eight years in exile, were finally given the islands of Malta and Gozo by Charles V of Spain as a new home for their Order. It is said that, when they sailed across from Sicily in the autumn of 1530 and saw the barren limestone islands of the Maltese archipelago, they wept, remembering Rhodes. It is not difficult to understand their feelings.

CHAPTER 20

Symi and Carpathos

Only twenty miles from the harbour of Rhodes, so close to the shores of Asia Minor that at first sight it does not look like an island but a peninsula running out from the Dorian isthmus, lies Symi. One can reach it either by boat from Piraeus, by caique from Rhodes, or from one of the other nearby Dodecanese. The capital and harbour town is at the north-eastern end, at the head of a deep gulf. Like Calymnos, this is an island of fishermen and sponge-divers. It was in the small port here, eager to practise his almost forgotten English, that I met Nikos, a former petty officer in the Greek Navy. He had sailed in the caiques out of Alexandria in the bad years of 1941 and 1942. Like myself he had been in Tobruk in its garrison days. He recalled Alexandria with nostalgia.

"So many years ago. And now I cannot even go diving any more." He pointed to the stump of his right arm. Missing fingers, hands, and even arms, are not all that rare in the Aegean. Like many another, Nikos had fallen foul of a fast-burning fuse while dynamiting fish.

It has been said that the sponge-fishers of Calymnos are as different from those of Symi as are the lines and the rig of their boats. I could not see any difference between the fishermen, but even to-day, when the boats are all motor-powered, the lines of those coming from Symi are certainly finer and more graceful. The island, one of the most rocky and bare in the Dodecanese, was once well-wooded, and the boat-builders of **Symi** were famous. Along with the Rhodians, they manned the galleys of

250

the Knights. Their *skaphai*, light, fast sailing galleys, were as active as hawks along the trading routes of the Ottoman Empire. With the fall of Rhodes, they and the other nearby islanders became subject to the Grande Porte.

The Symiots later distinguished themselves by being the first to revolt against the Turks, at the time of the battle of Psinthos in

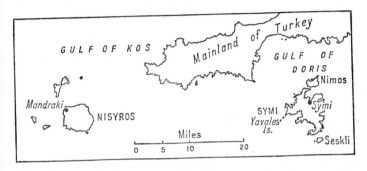

1912. Michael Volonakis, in *The Island of Roses and her Eleven Sisters*, describes them as being "worthy of their earliest ancestors, the best divers and the boldest seamen in the Aegean. . . ." Unfortunately, Symi suffered badly in the last war and the decline of the sponge-fishing industry has hit the island even harder. As in so many other islands, local boat-building is a declining trade, since most owners prefer to build larger vessels than the traditional caiques, in the yards of Athens.

Small though the island is, only about eight miles at its longest point, it is studded with delightful bays and coves, with bright sand beaches at the heads of many of them. There were no hotels when I was here, but it would be easy enough to get a room in the upper town. The islet of Nimos, which guards Symi harbour from the north, is worth visiting and there is good under-water fishing to be had. Symi is remarkable for the number of rocks and grassy little islets which lie scattered all round its coast—from the Yavales islets on the west, to Seskli with its lighthouse at the southern end.

251

Symi would seem to have been undistinguished in classical times, being always overshadowed by its prosperous large neighbour, Rhodes. Buondelmonti has the following amusing, but almost certainly inaccurate, conjecture as to the origin of the island's name: "Prometheus, the son of Iapetos, was forced to come to this island, where he revealed many means for the preservation of human life. He, being powerful in genius, created man from clay. On account of which, when Zeus heard of it, he transformed Prometheus into a *simia* (monkey) and maintained him there to his death."

Nisyros, like Pholegandros, seems to be one of those islands I am never destined to reach. Perhaps I have missed nothing, and certainly Robert Liddell in his *Aegean Greece* does not make it sound very attractive. The capital, Mandraki, lies on the northwestern corner, but the only time I closed the island it was blowing so hard that I dared not try and make the entrance. "... Rich in sulphurous earth and hot springs of various qualities," Nisyros is clearly the peak of an ancient volcano. Legend has it that Poseidon broke it off from the side of Cos with his trident when he was pursuing the giant Polybotes and hurled it at the giant, imprisoning him underneath it. (It is the same story which one finds in one way or another associated with all volcanic islands.) Viewed from the sea it is impressive and green, rather reminiscent of Stromboli and no doubt the volcanic earth is fertile and good for the vine. I shall get there one day, but on this occasion I was in a hurry to get down to Carpathos and the north-easter was too good a wind to miss. It gave me a clear run to Carpathos, the long fish-like island which lies between Rhodes and Crete, and which gave its name to this southern stretch of water, the Carpathian Sea.

One of the largest of the Dodecanese, **Carpathos** is also one of the least visited. The Piraeus steamer calls here once a week, and it would not be difficult to find a caique out of Lindos going this way. Pighadia, the capital, is on the east coast at the head of a large bay. It is a modern town, that is to say it was only founded in 1894 and it has, therefore, little architectural interest. There

are no hotels, but one or two clean cafés where one can find a room. That same North Wind of which Horace remarked ". . . *Notus invido/Flatu Carpathi trans maris sequora,*" blew all night long as I lay at anchor. I watched the bright shine of lights around the harbour. It is curious, when one reflects on it, how many a poor Aegean island shines like a diamond with electric light. The Dodecanese, whatever their inhabitants may say on the subject, did benefit a little from the Italian occupation. Determined to make them something of a showpiece in their short-lived empire, the Italians improved many of the public services. It is a pity, though, that their occupation of the islands coincided architecturally with the inflation of Fascist pomposity. Wherever one sees ugly concrete halls in the Dodecanese, or a post office bigger even than the village church, one senses that megalo-

253

mania which produced charts of the Mediterranean showing it as
"*Mare Nostrum.*"

Certainly the Carpathian Sea is not Mare Nostrum, nor is it
anybody else's. Renowned since classical times as an area hostile
to sailors, it is here that the Meltemi, with the full fetch of the
Aegean behind it, rolls the sea foaming through the straits between
Carpathos and Crete. A steamer which came into Pighadia
while I was staying there had aboard a more woe-begotten
group of travellers than I have seen anywhere else in the Aegean.
Clutching lemons, that old wives' antidote, to faces that were the
same colour as the fruit, they were assisted ashore and seated in
café chairs. I can never understand why the Greeks, most astute
of all merchants, do not seem to have profited from some of the
seasick remedies that are now on the market. I imagine that the
more sophisticated travellers may have done so, but perhaps
the peasant—having paid for the price of his ticket—is unwilling,
or unable, to spend more on pills.

They make a good quince jelly in Carpathos, and the south of
the island is dense with quince and orange trees. This is the
fertile land, the part of the island which accounts for the business
and prosperity of the small port. The northern part—where the
women still wear traditional costume—is rocky and bare, a narrow ridge running up to the islet of Saria which is divided from
Carpathos by the narrowest of channels. There is a pleasant cove
here where I have anchored, but it is no place to remain for any
length of time. The current between Saria and Carpathos runs
fast and dangerous if the wind gets anywhere towards the west.

The costumes themselves are reminiscent of Crete and are remarkable only in that they are still worn without affectation—
not, I mean, as at Rhodes, where "traditional" dress is put on for
the benefit of the foreigner, and put off again the minute his back
is turned. White trousers of typical Oriental style are tucked
into high boots, the skirts are hitched up to the waist, and a dark
blue cloak covers body and shoulders.

Rugged and austere though the northern half of Carpathos is,
it has more quality than the south, and the hills which run up to

he main peak in the centre are quite well wooded. This is unusual enough in the Southern Aegean, and proof perhaps that a sensible re-afforestation programme could do the same for many other islands. This is an area to explore on foot or mule, or the island bus service, which runs to Aperei and other villages in the south, does not cover northern Carpathos.

"What is the book?" asked the harbour-master at Pighadia. He was intrigued to hear that I was reading a Greek writer, who wrote poetry in English. "Trypanis? In English? But then we have no poets in Greece any more."

He was wrong of course, for the Greek contribution to poetry in the last fifty years has been remarkable. But he set me wondering which, of all the many poets in English have captured anything of the Aegean flavour. Trypanis certainly does in the *Cocks of Hades* and so does Lawrence Durrell, whose two travel books on Corfu and Rhodes—*Prospero's Cell* and *Reflections on a Marine Venus*—ought to be familiar to anyone intending to visit either of these islands. Few other English poets have ever got the Aegean clearly in their sights. Perhaps there is something a little too sharp and hard, a little too astringent about the Aegean world, to be taken in the net of the English language.

In the necessarily limited library of a small boat I have found that Baudelaire and Lorca seemed best to catch its mood. One finds that violence in Lorca, that harsh distillation of the sun which is almost as much part of Greece as it is of Spain. As for Baudelaire—although Cythera is not as dismal as he conceived it —yet there is something about his poetry which seems to catch the sweet-and-sour bite of the islands.

> *Le navire roulait sous un ciel sans nuages,*
> *Comme un ange enivré d'un soleil radieux*

But I would have found it difficult to explain to the harbourmaster of Pighadia, that I thought a Spaniard and a Frenchman —neither of whom had ever seen the Aegean—had best caught its mood.

Visitors to Pighadia should try and visit **Arcassa** on the west coast, the most attractive village in the island, and one which still shows the signs of the long Venetian occupation of Carpathos. When Carpathos was a fief of the Cornari family, Arcassa was the principal town, and it still has some Venetian architecture and fortifications. The Cornari exercised suzerainty over Carpathos from 1306 to 1540. Linguistic experts have told me that more Venetian dialect-words survive in Carpathos than anywhere else in the Aegean. This I cannot tell, but one thing I did remark in Arcassa was some fine coral and silver jewellery worn by the local women. This may well be of Rhodian origin, where filigree work has long been practised, but I wondered whether the silver itself might be Carpathian. The silver and iron mines of the island were famous in classical times, and were still being worked when the Knights of St. John were occupying Rhodes. The coral from Carpathos has long been famous. One brooch which I saw, made in filigree silver, had the eight-pointed cross as its motif— that cross which has since become known as "The Maltese Cross," but which the Knights of St. John had borne as their emblem for many centuries before they were driven from the Eastern Aegean. It is on record that, when the Knights finally reached Malta, there were with them a number of Rhodians and other Greeks who had elected to follow them into exile. A similar type of filigree work in gold and silver is practised in Malta to this day (as in Rhodes), and I suspect that it was brought to the Maltese islands by Rhodian silversmiths — possibly, too, by silversmiths from Carpathos.

It would have been pleasant to investigate the history of Carpathian jewellery more thoroughly, but I had a boat to worry about. The harbour-master of Pighadia had assured me that, now the Meltemi had dropped, the wind was almost certain to go round and blow from the south. Pighadia is no place to lie at anchor in a Sirocco. There are many advantages to travelling the Aegean in your own, or a chartered, boat, but it is easy to list the disadvantages. One of them is that you see less of any island's hinterland than the traveller who comes ashore and finds for himself a hotel, or a room in a local house. Another disadvantage is that only too often, when you think you are on

The Temple of Lindos on Rhodes

Knossos, Crete. *Above*, the throne of Minos; *below*, Minoan amphorae, showing rope patterns

he verge of discovering something quite new, some shift of wind
ompels you to change your plans and move on.

Next night I anchored in Castello Bay with Casos a dark
hadow to the west. The wind, contrary to the harbour-master's
expectations, stayed firm in the north. There is nothing to say
bout Castello Bay, except what I wrote at the time: "The moon
s up now and the whole inlet is shadowed with blue and silver.
The smell of the island: earth breathing under the night sky,
blives twisting their roots yet deeper in search of water, the herbs
ind grasses crystallised with dew. Finally there comes the taste
of the pale straw-like Greek cigarettes as their smoke curls
bout us in the light that spirals up from the small cabin."
Carpathos, no doubt, holds many treasures which I neither ex-
blored, nor even saw. It holds for me, in memory, the essence of
many island nights, and that is enough.

CHAPTER 21

Crete. The End and the Beginning

Across the narrow strait from Casos, spiky with waves, lies Crete, the "sixth continent." This is not an island which lies at the foot of the narrow sea, shutting off the Greek Aegean from North Africa and Egypt. Technically, of course, it is:—"Kriti," says the *Pilot*, "formerly called Crete, is from its position, fertility and population the most important island in the Levant. It is traversed throughout its length by a mountain range. . . ." and so on. But to write of Crete in the same terms as any other Aegean island is to court disaster.

"Crete," said Michael, "is either a book or a scholarly monograph. It cannot be a chapter."

We were drinking some of the sharp red Cretan wine at anchor in the port of Heraklion. Michael had flown down from Athens the day before, to come sailing along that iron-bound northern coast of Crete—a coast where every rock and cape reminds one of a thousand shipwrecks. While it had taken me many weeks to make my way this far south, Michael had reached Heraklion in little over an hour from the airport at Athens. He still wore the surprised look of one who misses the roar of traffic, the clack of typewriters, and the jangle of the office telephone. I, for my part, had not used a telephone for weeks—the last occasion being an unsuccessful attempt in Rhodes to track down a friend who was reputedly staying in the island. If, as the Arabs maintain, the soul can only travel at the pace of a trotting camel, it would be several days before Michael became integrated again.

Two or three flights reach **Heraklion** daily from Athens, with a flying time of one hour and a quarter. In summer, there are also two-day air excursions—you leave Athens airport in the morning, arrive at Heraklion, visit the museum and go to Knossos in the afternoon. Next morning, you fly back to Athens. There are also flights from Athens to Khania at the western end

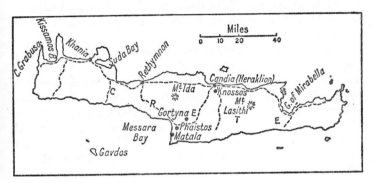

of Crete, once or twice every day. Khania, Rethymnon and Heraklion are all served by regular passenger boats—five or six sailings a week, the voyage from Athens lasting twelve to fourteen hours. In summer there are two-day excursions by boat to Crete, the ship leaving Athens about 6 p.m. and arriving at Heraklion the next day. The same afternoon there is a visit to Knossos, to the museum at Heraklion and you return overnight by ship, reaching Piraeus next morning. It seems a longish sea voyage for only a few hours in Crete, with the added disadvantage that the traveller is presumably asleep on both occasions while sailing through the archipelago.

If one is allergic to air travel, or wishes to travel more cheaply by boat, then I think that the answer is to take one of the many ships to Heraklion and make certain of having several days to spare at the other end. I must confess to being the type of traveller who is rather unfashionable to-day: I would prefer to spend several days in one place and get something of the feel of it, than spend my time rushing about an island, or a country,

259

intent on "doing it all." If your time for Crete is limited, go to Heraklion, put up in a hotel, and make two expeditions—one to Knossos and the other to Phaistos. Knossos is under five miles from Heraklion and is easily reached either by bus or taxi. Phaistos, although it is over twenty miles away on the southern side of the island, can also be visited in a day. There is a bus which leaves Heraklion at about 7 a.m. and comes back the same evening.

Even if you have plenty of time at your disposal, Heraklion is probably the best base for exploring Crete. For one thing, there are plenty of hotels, at all ranges of price and comfort—or lack of it. The Astir is the largest (bathrooms, central heating, restaurant and Class A), then there are two Class B hotels, the Candia and the Cosmopolit. There are a number of restaurants. The Limenikon Peropteron is Class A, good but undistinguished, and I have had a pleasant meal at the little Vigla on the old Venetian wall, memorable more for the situation than anything else. The Florida, Hellas, Palladion and Knossos are Class C hotels, and there are a number of pensions and Class D hotels— the latter are nearly always what the Greeks call "Hotels of Sleep." That is to say that your bed and your room will usually be clean, but, apart from telling you where the nearest café is, the hotel will do nothing more for you. I prefer it that way, but Class D hotels are definitely not for people who require a certain amount of service and comfort. If you get out of the main stream of tourist traffic in Crete, the memory of even a Class D hotel is rather like the sailor's dream of a night at the Ritz.

There is not a great deal to be said for Heraklion itself. It is hot and dusty in the summer when the north wind, which else- where sweeps away lethargy, seems more occupied in driving scraps of paper around one's ankles and the dust of centuries into one's eyes and nostrils. Architecturally, except for its fortifica- tions, there is little to the city, but the streets of the old Turkish town have a lively atmosphere. It is the fortifications and the berths for the Venetian galleys inside the harbour which lend a distinction to Heraklion.

The city was once known by the more attractive name of Kandia, and was the scene of the most prolonged siege in history. Kandia, the Arabic *Khandax*, was also the name given to the whole island. It is recalled in the English "candy," and derives from the Arabic word for the crystallised juice of the sugar cane. It was, incidentally, with sugar canes and vines especially brought from Crete that Henry the Navigator started the wine and sugar industry in newly-discovered Madeira in 1425. The hardy stock of the Cretan grape was found ideal for the soil of the Atlantic island. Good, unresinated wine is to be had in many parts of Crete, but a word of warning about the Cretan gin, *tsikudia*. This is an excellent gin, but every bit as strong as *mastika*—and should not be confused with what passes for gin in England.

Founded in the ninth century by the Saracens, Kandia rapidly became the capital and the administrative centre of the island. After the capture of Constantinople in 1204, when all the Aegean was parcelled out among the Latin conquerors, Crete was allotted to Bonifacio, Marquis of Montferrat. He, in his turn, sold the island to the Venetians.

Despite numerous revolutions against their Venetian overlords, Crete remained in Venetian hands for over four centuries. Whatever the Cretans felt about their Latin masters, this was probably the most prosperous period in the island's history. In 1645, however, the Turks landed an army of 50,000 men and reduced Khania and Retimo. Three years later they invested Kandia and thus began a siege that lasted twenty-one years. When Kandia ultimately fell, in September, 1669, the whole of Crete, with the exception of Grabusa, Suda and Spinalonga, passed into Turkish hands. The last three garrisons fell within the next twenty-five years and Crete remained a Turkish possession until it was finally ceded to Greece at the Treaty of London in 1913.

It is impossible to understand the modern Cretan unless one realises that he has lived in a state of revolt for centuries—revolt against Saracens, against Venetians, and finally, for two and a half centuries, against the Turks. In the last war, after the evacuation of the island by British forces in 1941, the Cretans together with a number of British, New Zealanders and other Allied troops took to the mountains in guerrilla warfare against the Germans. The Cretans, for their part, were going back to the kind of life that was native to them. So much has been written about these years that it only remains to say that the Cretans proved themselves, yet again, to be among the most hardy guerrilla fighters in the world. I remember being present in a naval craft when we put ashore a small group of Cretan and British irregulars in the south of the island. There was snow up in the mountains that night and I was glad to be going back to the fleshpots of Alexandria. I was almost sorry for any German sentries who happened to run into the men who were paddling ashore. I remember thinking: "Thank God, I am on the same side!"

There is a curious hiatus in Cretan psychology to-day—for almost the first time in history there is no one to fight against. Talking to Cretans, one senses this vacuum in their lives, and one senses that here—as in Sicily, where the hatred is kept for north Italians and the politicians of Rome—it is the administrators and the politicians of Athens who are likely to become the enemy. But I must immediately make one distinction between the Cretan and the Sicilian, or the Cypriot. Although Crete has had a reputation for banditry over the ages, it has nothing akin to the corruption of the Mafia, or the Levantine treachery of Cyprus. I am happy to disagree with the Apostle Paul, who, quoting the expatriate Cretan poet Epimenides, refers to them as "always liars, evil beasts, slow bellies." I was in the harbour at Khania, at the time when the recent troubles in Cyprus were at their height, and when the wife of a British sergeant had been shot in the back in Nicosia. It was a difficult time to be in Greece at all, for I felt that the British were behaving as badly as the politicians in Athens were behaving stupidly. That evening, as I was sitting in a café, a local schoolmaster came up and sat at the table with me. He said nothing for a few moments and then:

"You must not be bitter. You must remember that they are

not Cretans. They are Cypriots. As you know, we shot many Germans here during the war—but we would not have shot their women."

I assume that anyone who is going to spend some time in Crete will have read one of the many books on the island, or will be familiar with more of the detailed literature. The amateur who dares to intervene in Minoan affairs is treated not to a single shot in the back, but to a volley. When I was last in the island, the thunder of English scholars—though with a dying fall— echoed in the drawing-rooms of Heraklion. Old copies of archaeological and literary journals were eagerly passed from hand to hand. The body of Sir Arthur Evans was as hotly disputed over as that of any of the heroes on the windy plains of Troy.

The first thing that any visitor to Heraklion will want to see is the Archaeological Museum. Students of ceramics will find here the finest display of early European work in the world— from the simplicity of stone or terra-cotta vases, to the vases from Knossos and Phaistos in the so-called eggshell style. The latter seems to anticipate the work of the Chinese, and to rival in delicacy—but far surpass in design—the Belleek of the nineteenth century. There are some magnificent examples of Minoan goldsmith's work, with a delicacy of filigree and sophistication that has been equalled but never surpassed. There are also the restored frescoes from Knossos. These, more than anything else, seem to contain the essence of the Minoan world. They have an elegance that never perhaps existed, any more than did "the world" of Watteau or Fragonard. Curiously enough, of all European artists it is Gauguin of whom I have been most reminded by these frescoes. El Greco, with his Byzantine ancestors, is far away, but Gauguin came very close to the flat surfaces, the sensual styling, and the golden colours of these Knossos frescoes.

Schliemann, that genius whose flashes of insight seem to have derived more from psychic apprehension than logic, was the first to divine that the mound at **Knossos** might hold a secret greater even than Hissarlik. If it had not been for Turkish opposition, Schliemann's name would have been associated with the discovery of Knossos, rather than Evans. But whatever one may feel on visiting Knossos about the much-disputed reconstructions carried out by Evans (and paid for out of his own fortune), I can only see the modern scholars' disputations in the same terms as Ezra Pound's modern poets—"jackals fighting over a dried-up well."

Both at Knossos and Phaistos, one is acutely aware of the debt that is owed to Sir Arthur Evans. Without the reconstructions, it would be difficult, if not impossible, for the visitor of average intelligence, education and aesthetic sensibility to have any conception of the Minoan achievement in architecture. **Phaistos** I find infinitely more moving than Knossos, undoubtedly because of the site. The palace, built on tiers, overlooks the beautiful plain. Beyond it lies the gracious Bay of Messara—a good anchorage in summer and one of the only places on the southern coast where a small boat can lie in any security.

In Crete, even more than in many other parts of the Aegean, one senses the continuity of Mediterranean life. In the museum at Heraklion I had noticed the large pottery jars brought from Knossoswhich, like the later and more familiar *amphorae*, served as the general receptacles of the period. Incised into the clay, and serving only as decoration, were the vestigial patterns of rope handles. Later, lying at anchor in Port Matala below Phaistos, I saw almost identical jars being loaded aboard a caique. Not only had their shape remained unchanged over 3,000 years but there, incised in the rough clay sides, were the same looped patterns of rope.

The long backbone of Crete, a range of mountains stretching almost unbroken over the island's total length of 140 miles, is divided at the point where the road runs through from Heraklion to Phaistos and Messara Bay. It is in the White Mountains at the western end that the old Cretan spirit has been preserved more than anywhere else. Here one finds the heroic "*levendia*"—an attitude which can only be summed up by saying that it is a combination of the Spanish *pudonor* and the Sicilian *omertà*. That does not get us very far in English, but it is a stoic attitude, somewhat akin to what literary critics have liked to call the "Hemingway code," but instinct with a cheerful gallantry. It is conveyed a little in one of the *mandinathas*, those rhymed couplets which Cretans can sing almost inexhaustibly:—

> *Man's courage is the only true wealth;*
> *Eat, drink and make the best of the world.*

Almost dead in the centre of the island rises the high peak of **Mount Ida,** birthplace of Zeus—an honour which is disputed by the other major mountain of Crete, Mount Lasithi, in the east. Both mountains boast deep caverns which legend maintains were the cradle of the god. But Crete is full of caves. There is one in the mountains just behind Gortyna, the Roman capital of Crete, which served, I believe, as a hideout during the last war. The Reverend Tozer, writing in 1875 in *The Islands of the Aegean,* described how he was taken to this cave, which was known throughout the area as "The Labyrinth": "Our host, Captain George, undertook to be our guide; and accordingly next morning we started in his company and, fording the stream close under the Acropolis of Gortyna, ascended the hills towards the north-west and in an hour's time reached the place. . . . It is entered by an aperture of no great size in the mountain side, where the rocks are of clayey limestone, forming horizontal layers; and inside we found what looks almost like a flat roof, while chambers and passages run off from the entrance in various directions. . . . We were furnished each with a taper, and descended by a passage, on both sides of which the fallen stones had been piled up; the roof above us varied from four to sixteen feet in height. Winding about, we came to an upright stone, the work of a modern Ariadne, set there to show the way, for at intervals other passages branched off from the main one, and anyone who entered without a light would be hopelessly lost. Captain George described to us how for three years during the late war [1867-1869] the Christian inhabitants of the neighbouring villages, to the number of five hundred, and he among them, had lived there, as their predecessors had done during the former insurrection, to escape the Turks, who had burned their homes and carried off their flocks and herds, and all other property they could lay hands on. . . ."

The general insurrection to which Tozer refers was put down with the utmost barbarity. It had been preceded by two other major revolts during the century, and was followed by two more, culminating in the great revolt of 1897. Such is the Cretan background. Although it is to Knossos and Phaistos that the foreign visitor immediately turns, it would be a mistake to assume that Crete is one of these islands which ceased to play any part in world affairs two thousand years ago or more.

If one expects to find evidences of his Minoan ancestry in the modern Cretan, it is not all that difficult. W. A. Wigram confirms this in his *Hellenic Travel* (1947): "However many immigrants there may have been in the last three thousand years, the land has taken them in and made them its own. English lady anthropologists bear this out. They made a habit of measuring skulls in all villages, which excited some suspicion till it became a game and any unmeasured head had to be brought in and put under the tape. While there has been so much Venetian immigration that about one name in six in the isle is of that derivation, the proportion of broad Italian skulls is negligible. The Italian immigrants—and other types too—have become Cretan." But this is not so surprising. I can think of Englishmen who were in the island during the last war, who—even if they were not there long enough for their skulls to assume a Cretan contour—at least acquired a Cretan cast of thought.

I was reminded that the Minoans were the masters of these seas at a time when the Indo-Europeans had no word even for a boat, by a seal stone found at Knossos by Sir Arthur Evans, and showing one of the Minoan ships (one-masted and propelled by oarsmen seated beneath an awning). This Cretan thalassocracy, with its unique and attractive culture, has a curious appeal for the sailor. When I regret that I do not know the interior of Crete as well as I should like to, I tell myself that the Minoans most probably had no great affection for those grim mountains.

Compared with many a smaller island, it is still a difficult place for those who come here in their own boats. There is Kissamo, Khania, and Suda Bay (of evil memory) to the west, then there is little between Retimo and Heraklion. To the east, in the Gulf of Mirabella, there is the anchorage of **Spinalonga**, where a friend of mine spent a whole winter repairing his boat. I have not been to Spinalonga myself but, if solitude and primitive conditions, coupled with a good anchorage, appeal to any yachtsmen, then I have been told that Spinalonga is a fine place to stay. On the south coast I know only Port Matala, ideal for visiting Phaistos, which has a sandy beach at the head of the bay and a small landing place. As always, along the southern coast of Crete, one must keep an eye out for clouds gathering on the mountain peaks. Squalls, white or black, bursting down from the islands, are a regular feature of the Aegean. But the Cretan squalls are something that no one who has experienced them is ever likely to forget.

It was off this southern coast of Crete that, as St. Paul tells us in the Acts, the vessel carrying him to Rome ran into trouble: "And when the south wind blew softly, supposing that they had obtained their purpose, loosing thence, they sailed close by Crete. But not long after there arose against it a tempestuous wind, called Euroclydon. And when the ship was caught, and could not bear up into the wind, we let her drive. And running under a certain island which is called Clauda, we had much work to come by the boat. . . ."

Clauda is the modern **Gavdo,** a small island about thirty miles south-west from Port Matala (where St. Paul's ship hoped to winter). It is clear from the narrative that "Euroclydon" was the north-easter, known nowadays in the Mediterranean as the Gregale or Grego—the Greek Wind. It was with this "Greek Wind" astern of his ship that the Apostle was driven westwards across the sea, finally to run aground in the island of Malta. For St.

Paul, as for so many others, Crete was both an end and a beginning.

I, too, shall leave the islands with the sound of the Greek Wind in my ears. I shall leave them aware of many omissions—of Kithera and of Monemvasia unmentioned—and of many other things, places and people which I have either excusably forgotten, or inexcusably omitted. I have not gone into the legend and lore of the dolphins. I cannot thank (for I have lost both his name and address) the fisherman who helped me lay out another anchor, and thus saved my boat from dragging ashore on the west coast of Syra.

I shall have to fall back upon the excuse made by Benvenuto Cellini. It is true that he was writing about the art of the goldsmith, but it might equally well apply to the subject of Aegean travel:—"O thou discreetest of readers, marvel not that I have given so much time in writing about all this, but know that I have not even said half of what is needed in this same art, the which in very truth would engage a man's whole energies, and make him practise no other art at all."

One may travel about the Aegean nowadays by cruise liner, passenger or cargo boat, caique or yacht, without knowing a word of Greek. It is—to say the least—preferable to know a little, and there is one sentence, at any rate, which it would be most unwise not to commit to memory. If ever, on a stormy night in these seas, a beautiful woman rises from the waves alongside your vessel and calls out:

ποῦ ἔιναι ὁ Μεγαλέξανδρος;;

(Where is Alexander the Great?)
Be sure that you reply:

ὁ Μεγαλέξανδρος ζῆ καὶ βασιλένει

(Alexander the Great lives and reigns!)

If she receives the wrong reply, or no reply at all, your vessel is doomed. But answer her correctly, and the wind will drop, the seas subside, and the moon will break through the clouds to reveal a calm Aegean. I think that this mysterious storm-nymph is most probably Olympias, the witch mother of Alexander the

Great, still eager to be reassured that her son lives and reigns, and keeps the world at peace.

It is at any rate a wise precaution to be well rehearsed in your answer. A caique skipper out of Mytilene told me that it was only by his presence of mind—putting his head out of the wheel-house and shouting the reply—that his boat was preserved during a violent storm between Lesbos and Tenedos. I do not disbelieve him. When sailing these seas, it is only prudent to pay some small observance to the old gods. How else could I have sailed one dark, wet, and windy night, right through the middle of the Lagosa rocks and islets south of Salamis, without coming to any harm? I was spared, I think, because at sunset a few hours earlier I had tilted a glass of wine into the boat's wake in honour of Poseidon.

These islands and these waters constitute a land- and sea-scape which remain in the memory. They do not fade, as do other famous beauties of this world. In retrospect, it seems to me that one finds in the archipelago the Platonic essence of all natural shapes and forms. Watching a light mist pearling the English Channel the other day, I was reminded of an autumn morning south of Siphnos, and of how I sailed through a gossamer cloud in the centre of which the rising sun formed an opal rainbow. Just as Mount Cynthus seems to contain the quintessence of all mountains, so the battlements of Rhodes hold the dream of the Middle Ages. I have seen olives growing in many countries, but when I hear or read the words "olive grove," I think at once of the rocky slopes behind Port Gayo in Paxos. I see the leaves turning silver as they twist under the Grecian wind. The islands of Greece are more than a geographical entity. They are a climate of the heart.

Hotels and Accommodation in the Greek Islands

(Compiled from information supplied by the National Tourist Organisation of Greece, 1962)

List of Hotels

Island	Hotel	Class	
AEGINA	*Aegina*		
	Nafsika	B	restaurant
	Aktaion	C	
	Brown	C	restaurant
	Miranda	C	restaurant
	Olympic	C	restaurant
	Danai	C	restaurant
	Agia Marina		
	Afea	C	restaurant
	Galini	C	restaurant
	Moynti		
	Moondy Bay	B	restaurant
AMORGOS	Mice	C	restaurant
ANDROS	*Andros Town*		
	Paradissos	B	restaurant
	Xenia	B	restaurant
	Aigli	C	
	Apikia		
	Panorama	D	
	Sariza	D	restaurant
	Batsi		
	Lykion	B	restaurant
	Avra	C	restaurant
	Krinos	D	
	Korthion		
	Korthion	C	restaurant

CALYMNOS	Thermai	C	
	Plaza	C	
CHIOS	Xenia	B	restaurant
	Aktaion	C	
	Kima	C	
	Pelinaion	D	
CORFU	Corfu Palace	AA	restaurant
	Astir	A	restaurant
	Cavalieri	B	restaurant
	King Alkinoos	B	restaurant
	Olympic	B	restaurant
	Xenia	B	restaurant
	Achillion	C	restaurant
	Arkadion	C	restaurant
	Hermes	C	
	Ilios	C	
	Ionian	C	restaurant
	Kalypso	C	restaurant
	Splendid	C	
	Suisse	C	
	Gastouri (North)		
	Argo	C	restaurant
	Gouvies		
	Corcyra Beach	A	restaurant
	Hypso		
	Castello I	A	restaurant
	Castello II	A	
	Moraitica		
	Miramare Beach	AA	restaurant
	Delfinia	A	restaurant
	Palaio Castrizza		
	Peripteron Tourismou	B	
	Perama		
	Akti	B	restaurant
	Aigli	C	restaurant
	Oassis	C	restaurant
	Pyrgi		
	Bogdanos	B	restaurant
COS	Xenia	B	restaurant
	Zephyros	B	
	Acropole	C	
	Christina	C	
	Kos	C	restaurant

List of Hotels

Aghios Nikolaos

Minos Beach	A	restaurant
Dulac	C	
Lato	C	

Arcadi

Xenia	B	restaurant

Archanai

Dias	B	restaurant

Khania

Lisos	B	
Minoa	B	
Xenia	B	restaurant
Aptera Beach	C	restaurant
Canea	C	
Cyprous	C	
Elyros	C	
Plaza	C	

Heraklion

Astir	A	restaurant
Astoria	A	restaurant
Xenia	A	restaurant
Ariane	B	
Atlantis	B	restaurant
Blue Sea Hotel (bungalows)	B	
Cosmopolite	B	
Hellas	C	
Gallini	C	
Knossos	C	
Palladion	C	
Park Hotel	C	

Ierapetra

Creta	C	restaurant
Livikon	D	

Kartero (Heraklion)

Amnissos	B	restaurant

Kasteli

Castelli	C	

Mallia

Grammatikaki	B	restaurant

Neapolis

Vassilikon	C	

Omalos (Khania)

Xenia	B	restaurant

List of Hotels

	Phaestos		
	Xenia	D	restaurant
	Rethymnon		
	Xenia	B	restaurant
	Acropole	C	
	Valari	C	
	Minoa	D	
	Sitia		
	Crystal	C	
	Souda		
	Knossos	D	restaurant
	Stalis (Heraklion)		
	Blue Sea	B	restaurant
DELOS	Xenia	B	restaurant
EUBOEA	*Aidipsos*		
	Aigli	A	restaurant
	Avra	A	restaurant
	Peti Palais	A	
	Thermai Sylla	A	restaurant
	Akti	B	restaurant
	Heraklion	B	restaurant
	Hermis	B	restaurant
	Kentrikon	B	
	Anessis	C	
	Artemission	C	
	Ethnikon	C	
	Histiaia	C	
	Liouzi	C	
	Khalkis		
	Lucie	AA	restaurant
	Ethnikon	C	
	Palliria	C	
	Karystos		
	Louloudis	C	
	Karystion	C	restaurant
	Kymi		
	Aktaion	D	
	Lefkanti		
	Avra	D	restaurant
	Limni Evias		
	Avra	C	
	Nea Artaki		
	Tilemachos	C	restaurant

List of Hotels

	Nea Styra		
	Aigilion	C	restaurant
	Delfini	C	
	Aktaion	D	restaurant
	Steni		
	Dirfys	D	restaurant
HYDRA	Alkion	A	restaurant
	Miramare	A	restaurant
	Miranda	A	
	Hydra	B	
	Xenia	B	restaurant
	Lito	C	
KYTHNOS	*Thermia*		
	Anayennissis	C	restaurant
LEMNOS	*Myrini*		
	Akti Myrinis	A	restaurant
	Lemnos	C	
LESBOS	*Eressos*		
	Delphinia II	C	restaurant
	Boumna		
	Delphinia I	B	restaurant
	Mytilene		
	Lesvion	B	
	Xenia	B	restaurant
	Rex	C	
	Sapfo	C	
	Sigrion		
	Delphinia III	B	restaurant
	Thermi		
	Votsala	B	restaurant
MYKONOS	Lito	A	restaurant
	Afroditi	B	restaurant
	Alkistis	B	
	Rinia	B	
	Xenia	B	restaurant
	Delos	C	restaurant
	Apollon	D	

NAXOS	Ariadni	B	restaurant
	Apollon	C	
	Hermis	C	
	Dionyssos	D	
	Neon	D	
PAROS	*Paros*		
	Naoussa	B	restaurant
	Xenia	B	restaurant
	Pandrossos	C	restaurant
	Kontes	D	
	Kypraiou	D	
	Oassis	D	
	Dryos		
	Dryos	B	restaurant
	Marpissa		
	Xenon Marpissis	B	restaurant
POROS	Aigli	B	restaurant
	Latsi	B	restaurant
	Manessi	B	restaurant
	Saron	B	
	Xenia	B	restaurant
	Aktaion	C	
	Chryssi Argi	C	restaurant
	Galatia	C	restaurant
	Saronis	C	
RHODES	*Profitis Elias*		
	Elafos	A	restaurant
	Elafina	A	
	Rhodes		
	Akti Miramare	AA	restaurant
	Grand Hotel—		
	Summer Palace	AA	restaurant
	Hotel des Roses	AA	restaurant
	Golden Beach	AA	restaurant
	Belvedere	A	restaurant
	Cairon Palace	A	restaurant
	Ibiscus	A	restaurant
	Mediterranean	A	restaurant
	Oceanis	A	restaurant
	Park Hotel	A	restaurant
	Riviera	A	restaurant

List of Hotels

Thermai	A	restaurant
Alexia	B	
Delphini	B	restaurant
Europa	B	restaurant
Korali	B	
Olympic	B	
Palm Hotel	B	restaurant
Pindos	B	
Possidon	B	
Soleil	B	restaurant
Spartalis	B	restaurant
Achillion	C	
Acropole	C	
Aigli	C	
Afrika	C	restaurant
Aphroditi	C	
Als	C	
Arion	C	
Astron	C	
Angela	C	
Atlantis	C	
Château Fleuri	C	
Colossos	C	
Diana	C	
Diethnes	C	
El Greco	C	
Esperia	C	
Bel Mar	C	
Gloria	C	
Hermis	C	
Ikaros	C	
Irene	C	
Kentrikon	C	
Laokoon	C	
Lindos	C	
Mimosa	C	
Moschos	C	
Neon Ethnikon	C	
Noufara	C	
Pantheon	C	
Rodiakon	C	
Royal	C	restaurant
Savoy	C	

	Scandinavikon	C	restaurant
	Tilos	C	
	Ton Ippoton	C	
	Victoria	C	
	Zellois	C	
	Ideal	C	
SAMOS	*Karlovassi*		
	Samion	D	
	Vathy		
	Xenia	B	restaurant
SAMOTHRACE	Xenia	B	restaurant
SANTORIN	*Thera*		
	Atlantis	B	restaurant
SKIATHOS	Xenia	B	restaurant
	Akti	C	
	Koukounaries	C	
	Skiathos	D	
	Avra	D	
SKYROS	Xenia	B	restaurant
SPETSAI	Possidonion	A	restaurant
	Xenia	A	restaurant
	Roumanis	B	
	Acropole	C	
	Star	D	restaurant
SYRA	*Ermoupolis*		
	Hermis	B	restaurant
	Cycladikon	C	
	Possidonia		
	Delagratsia	B	restaurant
	Possidonion	C	restaurant
THASOS	*Limin*		
	Xenia	B	restaurant
	Timoleon	B	
	Lido	C	
	Theano	C	
	Palladion	D	restaurant

List of Hotels

	Limenaria		
	Panellinion	D	
	Makriammos		
	Makriammos	B	restaurant
TINOS	Theoxenia	B	restaurant
	Tinion	B	
	Avra	C	
	Flisvos	C	
	Galini	C	
	Possidonion	C	
ZANTE	Strada Marina	B	restaurant
(Zacynthos)	Xenia	B	restaurant
	Phoenix	C	restaurant
	Diethnes	D	
	Kentrikon	D	
	Alykai		
	Alykai	D	

Index

Achilleion (Corfu), 36
Achilles, 182
Actium, Battle of, 44-5
Adam, Sir Frederick, 29
Adamos Bay (Milos), 135-6
Aeacus, 72
Aegean Sea, 15-16, 18-23, 27-8, 177
Aegeus, King, 16, 19-20
Aegina, 66-73, 81, 88; temple of, 66, 73
Aegina (town), 67, 68
Aeolians, 200
Aeschylus, 65
Aetos, Mount (Ithaca), 48, 52
Agamemnon, 200
Aghios Stephanos (Mykonos), 119
Agnonda (Skopelos), 181
Air services, 16, 26, 197, 235, 258-9
Akrotiri, Cape (Samothrace), 193, 196
Albanians, 90
Alcaeus, 200
Alcinous, 36, 37
Alexandroupolis, 186, 193, 196
Alimma, 246
Ameinocles, 175
Amorgos, 148, 155-9
Amorgos (town), 158
Ampelos, Mount (Samos), 213, 217
Anavaro, Mount (Rhodes), 245
Andreas, Port (Ithaca), 51-2
Andros, 98-104
Andros, Port (Andros), 98, 99, 102, 103
Anidro, 159
Anoi, Mount (Ithaca), 48
Anti-Paros, 138
Antipater, 83
Antipaxos, 25, 42-3
Antissa (Lesbos), 200
Antony, Mark, 44-5, 216

Apeirantos (Naxos), 146
Apelles, 232
Aphalais Bay (Ithaca), 50
Aphrodite, 86, 143, 188
Apollo, 47, 121, 127-8, 135, 171, 189; Sanctuary of (Delos), 123; temple of (Santorin), 170-1
Apollona Bay (Naxos), 147
Apollonia (Siphnos), 134, 151
Arcassa (Carpathos), 255-6
Archias, 83
Archilochus, 141-2
Architecture, 25, 60, 89, 117, 134, 144-5, 149, 151, 164-5, 166, 180, 183, 198, 220, 228, 242, 245, 249
Arethusa's Fountain (Ithaca), 51
Argonauts, 160, 180, 198
Argos, 210
Argostolion (Cephalonia), 53-5, 56, 57
Ariadne, 143-4
Arion, 15, 201, 203
Aristaios, 171
Aristarchus, 212, 216
Arsinoe, Queen, 194
Art, 61-2, 141, 203
Arta, 44
Artemis, 121, 123, 128; cult of, 225-6
Artemona (Siphnos), 134, 151
Aspronisi, 160
Asteris, 52
Astypalaea, hill of (Samos), 215
Astypalia, 227, 228
Astypalæa (Cos), 232
Athenae, 210
Athens, 56, 61, 68, 71-2, 74-5, 183, 201-2, 216
Aubusson, Pierre d', 240, 242
Augustus, Emperor, 45, 216
Aulis, Bay of (Euboea), 74
Ayia Matrona (Leros), 226

279

Index

Bathing, 32, 66, 95, 107, 119, 141, 152, 197, 203, 211, 230

Batsi (Andros), 98, 103

Beaches, 32, 50, 103, 107, 112, 117, 119, 152, 170, 178, 192, 193, 211, 267

Benitsa (Corfu), 32, 38

Bent, James Theodore, 154-5

Benzina (motor boat), 38, 95

Bianco, Cape (Corfu), 38

Boat services, 25-6, 66, 73, 80-1, 87, 94, 98-9, 103, 111, 112, 114, 120, 132, 135, 148, 155, 156, 161, 173-4, 186, 191, 197, 206, 213, 219, 227, 235, 252, 259

Boccaccio, 40

Boeotia, 74-5

Books:

    Aegean Greece (Liddell), 145, 228, 252

    Classical Landscape with Figures (Lancaster), 208

    Cocks of Hades (Trypanis), 255

    Colossus of Maroussi, The (Miller), 84

    Cyclades, The (Bent), 154-5

    Greek Myths, The (Graves), 19, 39, 226

    History of the Order of St. John (Taffe), 241

    Iliad, 229

    Odyssey, 45, 47, 49, 50, 51, 52, 56, 229

    Prospero's Cell (Durrell), 199, 255

    Reflections on a Marine Venus (Durrell), 255

    The Island of Roses and her Eleven Sisters (Volonakis), 251

    Views in the Seven Ionian Islands (Lear), 59

Borgo (Tinos), 106

Botzaris, Marco, 45

Brooke, Rupert, 183-5

Brosch, Moritz, 243

Burkitt, F. C., 222

"Burnt Islands," 161, 172

Byron, Lord, 55, 62, 70, 79, 91, 128, 147, 183

Byzantine Empire, 202, 216, 238

Cabeiri, gods, 194-5

Caesar, Julius, 204

Caiques, 100, 176

Calavria, 83-4

Callimachus, 47, 159

Calymnos, 227-31

Cameiros (Rhodes), 247

Campos (Chios), 208

Capo d'Istria, President, 68, 69

Carpathian Sea, 252, 254

Carpathos, 252-7

Castello Bay (Carpathos), 257

Castro (Lemnos), 186-7

Castro (Siphnos), 134-5

Castro (Skiathos), 178, 179

Castro (Skyros), 183

Castro Nereido (Corfu), 38

Catapontismus (Sea Dive), 47

Caves, 119, 265-6

Cellini, Benvenuto, 244, 268

Cephalonia, 25, 50, 53-9

Ceramics, 67-8, 263, 264

Cerceteus, Mount (Samos), 213, 217, 224

Cerigotto, 25

Chares of Lindos, 244

Charles V of Spain, 235, 249

Chios, 111, 197, 206-12, 216; massacre (1822), 92, 210

Chios (town), 206-8

Chora (Amorgos), 158

Chora (Calymnos), 228

Chora (Patmos), 220-1, 222

Chora (Samothrace), 195

Christodulos, St., 222

Chryseis, 189

Cigarettes, 37

Citron (drink), 146

Clarke, Edward Daniel, 223, 224

Cleon, 201

Cleopatra, 216

Climate, 17-18, 20-22, 29, 58, 113, 131-2, 174, 192, 203, 213-14, 231, 235

Cloth, peasant-weave, 119-20, 163

Codex Porphyrius, 223
Codrington, Admiral Sir Edward, 69, 70
Colonna, Cape (Samos), 215
Colophon, 210
Colossus of Rhodes, 244-5
Corfu, 15, 16, 17, 25-40, 56, 61, 112-13, 209, 255
Corfu (town), 28-9, 30-36; Esplanade, 32; Kanoni (Cannon Promenade), 35-6; Old Fortress, 32-3; Palaeo-polis, 35-6; Royal Palace, 28-9; St. Spiridion church, 34-5
Corinth, 19, 56
Corinth Canal, 18-19
Cos, 230, 231-4, 238
Council of the Greeks, 69
Cranioi (former Cranaea, Cephal-onia), 53, 56
Crete, 22, 28, 137, 152, 258-68
Cricket, 34
Crusade, Fourth (1202), 27-8, 75, 142, 160, 187
Cyclades, 28, 111, 129, 160, 173
Cynthus, Mount (Delos), 120, 126, 127, 128, 172, 269
Cyrene, 169, 171

Dalmatia, 27-8
Damos (Calymnos), 230
Dandolo, Doge, 27
Daskalio, 52
Delacroix, Eugène, 210
Delia, festival of, 122-3
Della Grazia (Syra), 112
Delos, 104, 110, 118, 119, 120-8, 147, 159, 172; Apollo, Sanctuary of, 123; Dionysus, Shrine of, 124; museum, 124; Sacred Cavern, 128; Sacred Lake, 123; Sacred Way, 126, 127; theatre, 125
Demetrius Poliorcetes, 195, 244
Demodotus, 201-2
Demosthenes, 83
Dhassia (Corfu), 32
Dhikaios (Cos), 234

Dhokos, 95, 96
Diodorus, 232
Dionysus, 143-4; Shrine of (Delos), 124; temple of (Thera), 171
Dodecanese, 219 *et seq.*
Dorians, 72, 73, 170
Doro Channel, 98
Dörpfeld, Wilhelm, 46
Drapani (Troezen), 85
Dress, 78, 94, 234, 254
Drink, 30, 33, 41, 42, 44, 63, 72, 78-80, 108, 113, 136, 139, 146, 163, 168, 192, 199, 206, 209, 217, 245, 261
Ducato, Cape (Levkas), 47
Durrell, Lawrence, 27, 199, 255

Earth, Lemnian, 188-9
Earthquakes, 44, 53, 58, 59, 60, 88, 160-1, 210, 211
Echinosa, 156
Elato, Mount (Cephalonia), 58
Elgin, Lord, 34
Elias, Mount (Aegina), 72
Elias, Mount (Hydra), 95, 97
Elias, Mount (Milos), 136
Elias, Mount (Mykonos), 119
Elias, Mount (Rhodes), 245, 246
Elias, Mount (Santorin), 172
Elli (cruiser), 106
Epidavro (Methana), 81
Episkopeion (Syra), 112
Ere, Mount (Hydra), 90, 95
Erissos (Lesbos), 200
Ermones river (Corfu), 37-8
Etesian winds, 20-22, 73, 98, 171
Euboea, 73-6, 102, 173, 174
Eumaeus, 51, 110
Euripus Channel, 74, 75, 173
Euroclydon wind, 18, 267
Evans, Sir Arthur, 263, 264, 266
Exoborgo (Tinos), 106

Faneromeni monastery (Salamis), 66
Fano, 17
Fartax, El Louck Ali, 177

Index

Fengari, Mount (Samothrace), 194, 196

Fish, 18, 23-4, 41, 42, 95, 139, 193, 199, 206

Flag, Greek, 70

Flaubert, Gustave, 80

Food, 33-4, 42, 49, 77-8, 95, 108, 120, 145-6, 168-9, 199, 206

Foscolo, Ugo, 61

Frazer, Sir James, 82

Freyberg, General, 179

Frogs, 126, 127

Fruit, 30, 63, 113, 136, 180, 189, 199, 206, 234, 245

Galata, 82, 84, 86

Gallipoli campaign (1915-16), 190

Gargallo, Marquis Piero, 189

Garlic, 31

Gartringen, Hiller von, 170

Garwell, Rev. John, 184

Gateluzzi family, 202, 203

Gavdo (Crete), 267

Gavrion, Port (Andros), 98-100

Gayo, Port (Paxos), 29, 40-1, 43, 269

Gell, Sir William, 49, 220

Ghika (painter), 89-90

Gibbon, Edward, 240

Ginger beer, 33

Giustiniani family, 207, 216

Gladstone, W. E., 41-2

Glossa (Skopelos), 181

Goats' milk, 79

Goni, 206

Gortyna (Crete), 265

Grabusa (Crete), 261

Graves, Robert, 19, 39, 121, 204, 225, 226

Greco-Turkish war (1921), 178

Greek War of Independence, 62, 69-70, 88, 91-2, 111, 216

Gregalé wind, 17-18, 267

Grotto of the Nymphs (Ithaca), 48, 50-51

Guinea-fowl, 226

Hamilton, Captain G. W., 85

Hecate Island, 126, 128

Helena, St., 140

Hephaestia (Lemnos), 189

Hephaestus, 187, 229

Hera, 16, 121, 187; temple of (Samos), 215

Heracles, 191

Heraklia, 156

Heraklion (Crete), 258, 259, 260-1, 263, 264

Hermoupolis (Syra), 111

Herodotus, 63, 65, 142, 174-5, 214-15

Herondas, 233

Hippocrates, 232, 234

Hippocratic Oath, 233

Hippodamus of Miletus, 247

Hippolytus, 80, 86

Homer, 45, 50, 51, 148, 210-11

Hotels, 31-2, 49, 54, 60, 75, 82, 93, 96, 103, 104-5, 111, 115, 139, 146, 156, 161, 183, 184, 186, 193, 199, 203, 206, 213, 230, 231-2, 236-7, 260, 273-8

Housman, A. E., 40, 171

Hydra, 85, 87, 88-96

Hydra (town), 88, 92-3, 94

Hypso (Corfu), 31

Ialysos (Rhodes), 247

Icara, Jean François, 137

Ida, Mount (Crete), 265

Io, 16-17

Ionia, 205, 211

Ionian Sea, 15-18, 22

Ios, 148-53

Ios, Port, 22, 148-51, 152; St. Irene Church, 148, 149

Iphigenia, 74

Irene, Port (Kythnos), 108, 109, 110

Irene, St., 160

Iron mining, 130-1, 256

Ischia, 136

Ithaca, 18, 25, 27, 46-7, 48-52, 53, 55, 56, 229

Jason, 188
Jewellery, 157, 223, 256
John, St., 221-2, 224
Jura, 107

Kaliarina of Skiathos, 178-9
Kalikiopoulo (Corfu), 36
Kallioni Bay (Lesbos), 197, 200, 203
Kalotari, Cape (Amorgos), 159
Kalvos, Andreas, 61
Kamares Bay (Siphnos), 132-4
Kamariotissa Bay (Samothrace), 193, 195, 196
Kamini (Hydra), 95
Kanaris, Konstantinos, 216
Kandia (now Heraklion), 261
Karaburnu Peninsula, 206
Karavostasi (Pholegandros), 155
Karlovasi (Samos), 213, 217
Karos, 156
Kastrades (Corfu), 36
Katapola (Amorgos), 156, 158
Kavalla, 191
Keats, John, 24
Kerenyi, Carl, 171
Keri (Zante), 63
Khair-ed-din (Barbarossa), 71
Khalki, 219
Khalkia, 246
Khalkis (Euboea), 74, 75, 173
Khania (Crete), 259, 261, 262, 267
Khardamyla (Chios), 211
Khelidhromi, 174
Khitho Bay (Naxos), 147
Kinara (Tinos), 106
Kini (Syra), 112
Kioni (Ithaca), 50
Kirkwall, Viscount, 30-1, 41-2, 58
Kissamo (Crete), 267
Kitto, Professor H. D. F., 64
Knights of St. John of Jerusalem, 228, 230, 231, 235, 237-43, 248, 249, 251, 256
Knights Templars, 238
Knossos (Crete), 160, 259, 260, 263-4, 266

Kolokotrones, Theodoros, 95
Korthion Bay (Andros), 103
Kotchinos (Lemnos), 188
Koukkounaries Bay (Skiathos), 178
Kouva (Rhodes), 249
Kovari, Mount (Andros), 98, 101
Kriezes, Antonios, 88
Kumi Bay, 173, 181
Kupho, 156
Kutusi (painter), 61
Kythnos (or Thermia), 103, 108-10, 111

Lakki (Leros), 224-5, 227
Lamartine, Alphonse de, 236
Lancaster, Osbert, 208
Lasithi, Mount (Crete), 152, 265
Latinadika (merchant ship), 90
Lear, Edward, 59
Lemnian earth, 188-9
Lemnos, 186-91
Leros, 224-7, 238
Lesbos, 16, 197-205, 206
Leto, 121
Leucimna (Cape Bianco), 38
Levkas, 25, 44-8, 58
Liddell, Robert, 145, 178, 228, 252
Limena (Thasos), 192
Limenaria (Thasos), 193
Lindos (Rhodes), 247-8
Literature, 61-2, 141, 157, 179, 200-1, 210, 233-4
Livadhi (Seriphos), 94, 130, 131-2, 213
Livadhi, Gulf of (Cephalonia), 53
Livy, 57
Lixourion (Cephalonia), 53, 56
Lizards, 127-8, 249
Lobsters, 18, 23, 41
Louis XIII, 111
Loukoumi (Turkish delight), 113
Louza (smoked meat), 120
Lutra (Tinos), 106
Lycomedes, King, 182, 183
Lysander of Sparta, 72

Index

Madonna islet (Paxos), 40, 41
Magnesia, 174-5
Maitland, Sir Thomas, 32, 34
Makri Ammos (Thasos), 192
Malta, Cape (Sikinos), 154
Mandraki (Hydra), 92
Mandraki (Nisyros), 252
Mandraki (Rhodes), 237, 240-1, 244
Manolas (Santorin), 162
Marathia (Ithaca), 51
Marathon, Battle of, 142, 183
Marble, Parian, 142
Marcus Fulvius, 57
Mark of Argos, 66
Marmarospaelia (Grotto of the Nymphs, Ithaca), 48, 50-1
Mastic trade, 207, 209
Mastika (drink), 80, 206, 209
Matala, Port (Crete), 267
Matapan, Cape, 18, 19
Mazarata (Cephalonia), 56
Mediterranean Sea, 15-16, 17, 20, 23
Meen (boat), 100-101
Megalo Bay (Chios), 211
Meltemi winds, 21-2, 107, 115, 137, 138, 152, 174, 180, 254, 256
Merika Bay (Patmos), 223
Merovigli (Santorin), 162, 164, 167-8, 172
Messara Bay (Crete), 264
Messaria valley (Andros), 101
Mesta (Chios), 209
Metal-working, 187
Metaxata (Cephalonia), 55, 56
Methana, 67, 80-1
Methymna (Lesbos), 200, 203
Miaoulis, Andreas, 91, 92
Mikra Kaumene (Santorin), 161
Milk, goats', 79
Miller, Henry, 84
Milokotos Bay (Ios), 152
Milos, 136-7
Miltiades, 142
Minoan culture, 137, 263, 264, 266-7
Minos (Amorgos), 158
Missolonghi, 79, 86, 91, 92

Mohammed II, 75
Molo (Hydra), 92
Molo, Gulf of (Ithaca), 48
Moschato (wine), 217
Motor boats, 38, 95
Mouse Island, 27, 35, 36
Mudros Bay (Lemnos), 186, 187, 190-1
Museums, 50, 68, 118, 124, 142, 169, 192, 207, 216, 234, 249, 263
Mycenaeans, 22, 56
Mykonos, 104, 114-20, 134, 213
Mykonos (town), 114-20, 125, 139; museum, 118; Paraportiani, 118; pelican of, 115-17
Myrina (Lemnos), 186
Mytilene (Lesbos), 198-200, 203, 211

Naoussa Bay (Paros), 141
Napier, Admiral Sir Charles, 54-5
Nauplia, 96, 97
Navarino, Battle of (1827), 69
Navigation, 20-1, 28, 67, 88, 90-2, 95-6, 120-1, 132, 193-4, 223-4
Naxia (Naxos), 144-6
Naxos, 111, 122, 138, 142, 143-7, 183
Nea Kaumene (Santorin), 161
Nea Moni monastery (Chios), 211-12
Nero, 19
Newton, Sir Charles, 230
Nicholas, St., 68
Nicomedes, King, 204
Nicopolis, 45
Nikaria, 157
Nimos, 251
Nisyros, 252

Odysseus—*see* Ulysses
Oenone, 72
Oia (Santorin), 161-2
Olives, 29-30, 199
Olympi, 209, 210
Olympias, Queen, 194, 268
Ormos Partheni (Leros), 226
Orpheus, 203
Ortygia, 121

Ottoman Empire, 29, 35, 75, 142, 202, 216, 231, 242-3, 251. *See also* Turkey, Turks
Ouzo (drink), 80, 199
Ovid, 47, 227

Palaeis (Cephalonia), 53
Palaeopolis (Andros), 101-3
Palaia Kaumene (Santorin), 161
Palaio Castrizza (Corfu), 37
Palaiochora (Aegina), 71
Palaiopolis (Samothrace), 193 195,
Pan, 39
Panagia (Hydra), 92
Panayia, feasts of, 104-5
Panayia islet, 193
Panayia of the Presentation, Monastery of (Amorgos), 158
Pandocrator, Mount (Corfu), 33
Panormos Bay (Mykonos), 117
Panormos Bay (Tinos), 106
Papadiamandis, Alexander, 179
Parian Chronicle, 142-3
Parian marble, 142
Paroikia (Paros), 139-41; Katapoliani church, 140-1; museum, 142
Paros, 138-43
Partheni (Leros), 226
Pasavrysi (Chios), 211
Paschal II, Pope, 238
Patmos, 219-24; monastery of St. John, 222-3
Patras, Gulf of, 53, 59
Paul, St., 18, 262, 267-8
Paxos, 25, 29, 39-42, 269
Pelican, of Mykonos, 115-17
Pelikata (Ithaca), 50
Peloponnesian War, 38, 72, 201, 232
Perachoron, Mount (Ithaca), 48
Perapigadi Bay (Ithaca), 51
Pericles, 69
Persian wars, 64-6, 72, 122, 142
Petaloudes (Rhodes), 246
Phaeaceans, 27, 37, 39
Phaedra, 80, 86
Phaistos (Crete), 260, 264

Phaleron Bay, 65
Pherecides, 110
Philacopi (Milos), 137
Philetas, 232, 233
Philip of Macedon, 61, 194
Philoctetes, 188
Pholegandros, 148, 154-5
Phrikes, Port (Ithaca), 50
Piali Pasha, 208
Pighadia (Carpathos), 252-3, 256
Piracy, 25, 69-70, 85, 92, 157, 177, 216, 222, 223
Piraeus, 64, 66, 173, 176, 186, 213, 219
Pisistratus, 122
Piskopi, 246
Pitch wells, 63
Pittacus, 200
Plaka (Milos), 136
Pliny, 246
Plutarch, 39
Poetry, 141, 157, 200-1, 210, 233-4, 255
Polis (Ithaca), 49, 50
Polycrates, 214-15
Pondikonisi (Mouse Island), 27
Poros, 80, 81-5, 88, 95, 96
Porpoises, 24
Poseidon, 27, 105, 121, 196, 252; temple of (Calavria), 83
Pothia (Calymnos), 228, 229-30
Pottery, 67-8, 263, 264
Preveza, 44
Prochorus, 221, 222
Prodroms (winds), 98
Prometheus, 252
Pronnaioi (Cephalonia), 53
Psara, 91, 97, 111, 210
Psathura, 174
Psittalia, 64
Ptolemy II, 195
Pumice, 161, 162
Pyrgi (Chios), 209, 210
Pyrgos (Santorin), 161, 170
Pyrgos (Tinos), 106
Pyrrha (Lesbos), 200

Index

Pythagoras, 216

Quail, 121

Rainfall, 29
Raven's Rock (Ithaca), 51
Religion, 104, 106, 112, 113, 146, 194-5
Restaurants and cafés, 32, 68, 82, 199, 260
Rethymnon (Crete), 259
Retimo (Crete), 261
Retsina (wine), 79
Revelation, Book of, 221-2
Rheneia, 104, 119, 121, 126, 128
Rhodes, 16, 208, 209, 210, 228, 230, 235-49, 251, 252, 254, 255, 256, 269; Colossus of, 244-5; Great Carrack of, 241-2, 243; Siege of (1480), 240, 242, (1522) 235, 242-3
Rhodes (city), 237-8; Chora, 242; Collachium, 240; Turkish quarter, 242-3
Rock doves, 42
Rodd, Rennell, 67

Saddle, mule, 164
Sailing, 95-6, 120-1, 132, 193-4
St. Angelo, castle of (Corfu), 37
St. Elias, Mount (Paros), 138
St. Nicholas (Zea), 107
St. Nicholas Bay (Tinos), 107
St. Nicholas convent (Salamis), 66
Saktouris, Commander, 92
Sakturia (sailing ship), 90, 92
Salamis, 64-6, 210; battle of (480 B.C.), 64-6, 72
Salonika, 174, 186
Sami (Cephalonia), 53, 55, 57
Samos, 209, 213-18
Samothrace, 193-6
Santa Euphemia (Cephalonia), 55
Santa Marina Bay (Aegina), 66, 73
Santorin, 23, 159, 160-72, 217
Sanudo, Marco, 144

Sappho, 47, 199-200, 201, 211
Saracens, 261
Sardines, 199
Saria, 254
Scala, Port (Patmos), 219, 220-1, 223
Scheriae, 37
Schliemann, Heinrich, 49, 189, 263-4
Sea routes—see Boat services
Seamanship, 20-1, 28, 67, 88, 90-2
Second World War, 19, 23, 178-9, 217, 224-5, 261-2
Sepias, Cape, 174, 175
Seriphos, 94, 95, 129, 130-2, 213
Seskli, 251
Ships and shipbuilding, 90, 92, 94, 97, 100-1, 176-7, 251
Shirley, Antony, 40
Sidero, Cape (Corfu), 32
Sikinos, 148, 153-4
Silver mines, 256
Simonides, 157
Siphnos, 95, 129, 132-5, 151
Sirocco wind, 17
Skala Bay (Sikinos), 153-4
Skaros (Santorin), 164, 166, 167, 172
Skiathos, 173, 175-9, 181
Skopelos, 173, 174, 179-81
Skopos, Mount (Zante), 60, 61
Skyli, 95
Skyros, 173, 181-5
Smyrna, 210
Solomos, Dionysios, 61-2, 210
Spalmatori, 206
Spartans, 61, 216, 232
Spetsai, 91, 96-7
Spinalonga (Crete), 261, 267
Spiridion, St., 34-5
Sponge fishing, 228-9, 250, 251
Sporades, 28, 160, 173-4
Stamps, 63
Staphilis Bay (Skopelos), 180, 181
Stavros (Ithaca), 49
Steamers, 87
Steno Strait, 104
Stenón Ídhras, 96

Stiris, 211
Strabo, 234
"Submarine," 209
Suda Bay (Crete), 267
Suetonius, 248
Suleiman the Magnificent, 219, 231, 235, 242, 243
Sweetmeats, 113, 120, 209, 231
Swimming, 32, 66, 95, 107, 119, 141, 152, 197, 203, 211, 230
Symi, 219, 228, 250-2
Syra, 78, 91, 92, 104, 107, 110-13, 213

Taafe, J., 241
Talanta Channel, 76
Tamelos, Cape (Zea), 108
Telemachus, 47, 52
Telendos Bay (Calymnos), 230
Terpander, 200
Teutonic Knights, 238
Thamus (pilot), 39-40
Thasos, 191-3
Themistocles, 142
Theocritus, 232, 233-4
Theophanes, 219
Theophrastus, 136
Thera (Santorin), 161-2, 163-5, 168-70
Thera, ancient, 170-1
Theras, 169
Therasia, 160, 161, 172
Thermia (or Kythnos), 23, 108-10
Theseus, 19, 86, 143-4, 183
Thetis, 182
Thiakon Point (Andros), 101
Thouridha Point (Andros), 101
Thucydides, 46, 201-2
Tiberius, Emperor, 39, 248
Tighani (Samos), 213, 214-15, 216
Tinos, 104-7, 116, 170
Tombazes brothers, 92, 93
Toy, Sidney, 242
Tozer, Rev., 265-6
Trabaccola (ship), 97
Trackonderi (boat), 100

Trade routes, 17, 20, 22, 28, 90-91, 92, 121
Tragonesi islet, 119
Trebuki Bay (Skyros), 183-4
Trees, 61, 84, 118, 173, 192, 232, 254
Troezen, 80, 84, 85-6
Troy, 189, 205
Trypanis (poet), 255
Tsikudia (wine), 261
Turkey, Turks, 29, 69, 70, 71, 75, 88, 89, 91-2, 111, 142, 187, 202, 216, 219, 239, 240, 261. *See also* Ottoman Empire
Turkish delight, 113
Turlo Bay (Mykonos), 115, 117

Ulysses, 27, 46-7, 50-51, 56, 61, 182
Underwater fishing, 66, 95, 193, 251

Vakkhos Point (Naxos), 143
Varkala (boat), 100
Vathi (Samos), 213, 216
Vathi, Port (Amorgos), 156, 158
Vathi, Port (Ithaca), 46, 48-9, 51
Vathi, Port (Pholegandros), 155
Vegetation, 26, 29-30, 36-7, 58-9, 88-9, 173, 180, 197-8, 245-6, 254-5
Venetian Empire, 25, 27-8, 29-30, 54, 60, 71, 75, 89, 90, 100, 142, 144-5, 187, 256, 261
Venus de Milo, 136, 137
Vidhi, 85
Vineyards, 117, 132, 165
Vlikho Bay (Levkas), 46
Vlychos (Hydra), 95
Volcanoes, 60-1, 136, 160-1, 187, 189, 252
Volonakis, Michael, 251
Volos, 173, 174, 181
Vorias (wind), 117
Vouni (Sikinos), 154
Vourkari (Zea), 107-8
Vromolimni (Methana), 81

Water, 29, 30, 78 89, 150, 166-7

287

Index

Water-mills, 57
Weaving, 119-20, 163
White Mountains (Crete), 264
Wigram, W. A., 266
Wilhelm II, Kaiser, 36
Windmills, 151-2
Winds, 17-18, 20-2, 96, 98, 99, 101-2,
   107, 115, 117, 137, 138, 152, 174,
   179, 254, 256-7, 267
Wines, 30, 41, 42, 44, 63, 72, 79, 80,
   108, 113, 117, 136, 139, 146, 163,
   168, 192, 199, 206, 217, 245, 261

Xenophon, 233

Xerxes, 64, 65-6, 142, 174-5
Yachting, 38, 82, 120, 197, 203, 213,
   214, 267
Yavales islets, 251
Yera Bay, 197, 198, 203
Yerakari (Zante), 63

Zalonga cliffs, 45
Zante, 25, 59-63
Zara, 27-8
Zea, 107-8
Zea Channel, 98
Zeus, 16, 72, 121, 187, 252, 265
Zia, Mount (Naxos), 138, 147

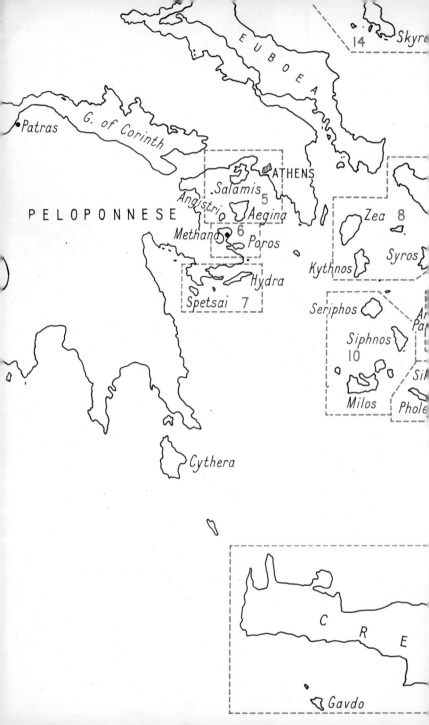